The Robe of God

Reconciliation, the Believers Church Essential

Myron S. Augsburger

With a Foreword by
Richard J. Mouw

Herald
Press

Scottdale, Pennsylvania
Waterloo, Ontario

Library of Congress Cataloging-in-Publication Data
Augsburger, Myron S.
  The robe of God : reconciliation, the believers church essential /
  Myron S. Augsburger. p. cm.
  Includes bibliographical references and index.
  ISBN 0-8361-9136-6 (alk. paper)
  1. Reconciliation—Religious aspects—Anabaptists. I. Title.
  BX4931.2.A94 2000
  234'.5—dc21

                                                            00-033453

The paper used in this publication is recycled and meets the minimum requirements
of American National Standard for Information Sciences—Permanence of Paper for
Printed Library materials, ANSI Z39.48-1984.

Scripture is used by permission, with all rights reserved, and unless otherwise noted,
is from the *New Revised Standard Version Bible*, copyright 1989 by the Division of
Christian Education of the National Council of the Churches of Christ in the USA.
KJV, *King James Version of the Holy Bible*, adapted somewhat to modern English.
NEB, from *The New English Bible*, © The Delegates of the Oxford Univ. Press and
the Syndics of the Cambridge Univ. Press 1961, 1970. NIV, from *Holy Bible, New
International Version* ®, copyright © 1973, 1978, 1984 by International Bible Society,
Zondervan Publishing House. Phillips, from *The New Testament in Modern English,*
© Macmillan, 1947-57, © J. B. Phillips, 1958.

THE ROBE OF GOD
Copyright © 2000 by Herald Press, Scottdale, Pa. 15683
  Published simultaneously in Canada by Herald Press,
  Waterloo, Ont. N2L 6H7. All rights reserved
Library of Congress Catalog Card Number: 00-033453
International Standard Book Number: 0-8361-9136-6
Printed in the United States of America
Photos on cover and page 2: "God's Robe of Love," a sculpture by
  Esther K. Augsburger

09 08 07 06 05 04 03 02 01 00 10 9 8 7 6 5 4 3 2 1

To order or request information, please call 1-800-759-4447 (individuals);
1-800-245-7894 (trade). Website: www.mph.org

"Deeply rooted in biblical theology and the rich traditions of Anabaptism, Myron Augsburger has written a fascinating book on reconciliation that speaks to all Christians everywhere. In a fractured culture marked by deep rifts, here is a message of hope and good news based on the New Testament gospel—God in Christ reconciling the world to himself."
—*Timothy F. George, Dean, Beeson Divinity School,*
  Samford University, Birmingham, Alabama

"The crowning work of a master evangelist, theologian, and pastor! In *The Robe of God*, Augsburger offers a mature manifesto of Christian faith informed by a lifetime of study and ministry. Rich in story and ideas, the book reflects the author's trademark combination of evangelical spirit, Anabaptist convictions, and ecumenical reach. There is much here to inspire the spiritual reflections of the thoughtful reader and the strategic planning of the church leader."
—*George R. Brunk III, Professor of New Testament,*
  Eastern Mennonite Seminary, Harrisonburg, Virginia

"For many years, Myron Augsburger has been the leading Anabaptist voice in the evangelical community. With *The Robe of God*, he once again shows us why. His message that the grace of God in Christ both reconciles us with God and frees us to live in fellowship with each other is central to the gospel. Augsburger's emphasis on reconciliation is at the heart of a biblical spirituality that results in an ethic of Christian discipleship. I am blessed to have Myron as a friend and brother, and I highly commend this book as the latest of his many gifts to the church."
—*Jim Wallis, Editor-in-Chief of* Sojourners, *published at*
  Washington, D.C.; and Author of Faith Works: Lessons
  from the Life of an Activist Preacher

The Father said, "Bring the best robe and put it on him."

—*Luke 15:22*

To the Washington community fellowship,
a multidenominational congregation on Capitol Hill,
affiliated with the Mennonite Church and
seeking together in life to glorify Christ—
the congregation that encouraged me in writing this book,
to extend the emphasis of my preaching

Contents

Foreword

WE ARE LIVING in a time of "posts": post-Christian, postmodern, post-Enlightenment, post-denominational. I'm not always clear about what people mean when they toss these labels around, but I am clear about this: we definitely are not in a post-ecclesiological era. Much attention is being given these days to how the church conducts its worshiping life and its missional outreach. Yet the attention to these matters is not always linked to careful theological reflection. With the significant changes taking place in the larger culture, and the far-reaching experiments being conducted within the Christian community, it has never been more urgent that we think clearly about the nature and mission of the church.

In these pages Myron Augsburger provides us some much-needed ecclesiological explorations. His discussion is bold, probing, and insightful. And the theology is solid, while at the same time sensitive to contemporary challenges. This book is an important tract for our times.

Two decades ago Myron and I engaged in a public debate at a church in Lancaster County, Pennsylvania, on the subject of Christian peacemaking. As we conferred together prior to the event, he reminded me that our Anabaptist and Calvinist ancestors in the sixteenth century often engaged in intensely acrimonious public disputations. "Let's do it differently than they did," he proposed. "Before we get into our differences, let's each of us begin by telling what it is about the other group's perspective that we find attractive." That's what we did, and it was a wonderful dialogue. The spirit of that evening left a permanent imprint on me.

I thought about Myron's proposal again as I read this book. These pages vibrate with that same kind of ecumenical graciousness. He is willing to mine various ecclesiological traditions for whatever wealth they have to offer: Lutheran, Reformed, Roman Catholic. (He even has a few kind words—not too many, mind you!—to say about the "state churches" of the past.) Myron not only makes the case for the centrality of reconciliation for our understanding of the church; he also shows us how to set forth a point of view *as* a reconciler.

In all of this, though, he is clearly writing as someone firmly committed to the believers church movement. As Myron develops this perspective, there are some core emphases that will reassure readers who want to preserve an evangelical faith: the believers church as a community of people who have a vital personal relationship with Jesus Christ, a relationship that in turn is made possible only by the substitutionary atoning work completed on the cross. But he is not content only to reassure. He insists that the divine Savior who shed his blood at Calvary is also the one in whom true humanness is restored, as well as the sovereign Lord who calls us to walk the costly path of radical discipleship.

I spend most of my time these days in that part of the Christian world where there is much talk about "seeker-sensitive worship." While I am pleased and encouraged that this topic is high on the agenda, I also wonder—sometimes I even worry more than a little—about how the important emphasis on the evangelistic dimensions of worship is to be related to patterns of growth in discipleship.

How can a church that welcomes seekers into its fellowship also be a community where believers grow into a mature knowledge of the full authority of the One who exercises lordship over all of creation? I learned much about how to answer this question from Myron Augsburger's exploration of ways the believers church tradition can be recontextualized for the exciting times in which we are living.

I hope that many others will be challenged and instructed by the important lessons taught in these pages.

—*Richard J. Mouw, President*
Fuller Theological Seminary
Pasadena, California

Preface

MY PRIMARY REASON for writing this work is the failure of much Christian thought and commitment to focus on our actual relationship with God and with each other. Faith is often reduced to exercises of piety, doctrinal affirmations, or claiming things from Jesus Christ, rather than living in solidarity with Christ and in fellowship with his people.

I have been blessed with many opportunities to preach across North America and in various countries. After years of teaching and serving as president of Eastern Mennonite College and Seminary, I moved to Washington, D.C. My wife and I planted a thriving congregation on Capitol Hill. The members of this fellowship have encouraged me to put into print the emphases that have grown out of my years of study, teaching, preaching, and experience.

In this book, I proclaim the gospel of reconciliation even further than I can by speaking one place at a time. This also preserves the record of evangelical and Anabaptist themes I have identified and developed, and the perspective I call *Christological Realism*. I present the gospel of reconciliation. I trust that God will work through these chapters in ways beyond my imagination, so that many more people will be reconciled to God, to fellow human beings, and to all that God is doing in the world.

One's life is shaped by influences, choices, and convictions, and these influences are special gifts of grace. I am especially grateful to Esther, my wife of fifty years, who shares so deeply with me, has encouraged me in writing this volume, and has done me a service of careful editing.

I also express my gratitude to various mentors in the fellowship of the church and in academic settings where I have studied. I am indebted to so many people for contributions to my life during my activity in educational, evangelistic, pastoral, ecumenical, and international roles. These involvements have served to broaden my life beyond the cultural ethnicity of my background.

Finally, I offer this book so that the audience can weigh its gospel message. As Paul said, "Test everything; hold fast to what is good" (1 Thess. 5:21). The subject of this book is not simply a matter of individual interpretation. I welcome dialogue and discernment on all these themes centered on *reconciliation, the believers church essential.*

—Myron S. Augsburger

Introduction

MUCH CHRISTIAN THOUGHT and commitment have failed to focus on our actual relationship with God. Too often, faith that should be centered on Christ is reduced to exercises of piety, doctrinal affirmations, or claiming things from Jesus Christ rather than living in solidarity with him. People speak of a "new birth" or "justification by faith" as an experience. Then they often fail to stress reconciliation with Christ as the Lord with whom we daily walk in faith, and reconciliation with other people, the social dimension.

Some others may reduce the emphasis on discipleship, following Christ, to extracting values from Jesus—such as peace, justice, and social responsibility—and then fail to emphasize solidarity with the redeeming Lord and life with a community of love.

Reconciliation is more than a concept, a doctrine. It points to a relational faith, a belonging in love. God's amazing grace is shown as he calls us and accepts us into a relationship with himself. In this reconciling act, God comes to us and calls us to join in covenant with him and his people. (My use of masculine pronouns for God makes my statements more relational and personal and does not imply gender; God is beyond gender.)

I believe that the marvelous grace of God in reconciliation is the heart of the gospel, the center of Christian faith. A theology that recognizes reconciliation as the core of faith focuses on meanings of the Incarnation, the cross, the resurrection, the church, and the gospel bringing peace on earth. God, through his involvement in history and ultimately in Christ, has acted to reconcile the world to himself (2 Cor. 5:19). All Christians believe this in general, yet too few stress that reconciliation is central to our faith. Salvation is first reconciliation between us and God; at the same time it is reconciliation between us and what God is doing in our neighbors and in our world. In the gospel, reconciliation surely has vertical and horizontal dimensions (Volf; see Bibliography).

Spiritual renewal in the church calls for a clearer understanding of the primacy of grace, divine reconciling grace, God's grace! Grace is the extension of God's kindness and graciousness toward us. God in love invites us into fellowship with himself. God takes the initiative and moves first. In grace, God calls us and welcomes us into his family. God's grace draws us into a new covenant relationship and enables us to live as children of God.

This new relationship is one of solidarity with Jesus, gathered as his disciples. With this identity, we now discipline ourselves in the grace of God to live as he lived (1 John 2:6), to love as he loved (3:23; 4:7). Living *sola gratia*, by grace alone, is not just an idea or a confession to recite; grace is an actual transforming activity of the Holy Spirit. That is what is so amazing about grace: God is sharing himself with us and making the new creation. With its penetrating and inspiring message, Philip Yancey's book *What's So Amazing About Grace?* supplies a needed corrective. Above all, he defines grace as a "gift that costs everything for the giver and nothing for the recipient" (Yancey: 25).

As we move into the twenty-first century, it is important to reaffirm the core of our faith. I agree with Bonhoeffer that "Jesus Christ alone is the certainty of faith" (1951). In Christ, who is the Incarnation of God, we are given information about God, but that's not all. We are also given invitation, the call of grace to reconciliation, to end our rebellion against God. Thus we are a people of hope, believing that the kingdom of Christ is continually breaking into time and culture, moving us in God's purpose toward the ultimate expression of the kingdom. Our hope in Christ's return rests on believing that reconciliation is God's work to unite all things in Christ Jesus (Eph. 1:10; Col. 1:20).

I maintain that reconciliation is the central experience and doc-

trine of the Christian faith. Thus British theologian and pastor James Denney asserts: "Just because the experience of reconciliation is the central and fundamental experience of the Christian religion, the doctrine of reconciliation is not so much one doctrine as the inspiration and focus of all" (6). We in the Christian church need to rediscover this truth in experience, and move reconciliation to the front and center in our living and in our proclaiming.

Our theology is influenced by the perspective we bring to the task. Yet theology must be tested for faithfulness to the Scriptures and relevance to the context in which we experience redemption. I am writing with a perspective from the Third or Radical Wing of the sixteenth-century Reformation. In so doing, I want to relate the thought of this movement to the larger theological community. As to context, I wish to do theology in relation to the global community striding into the new millennium. This book is also intended to help guide us, in the free-church movement, as we project our faith into the future.

Several concerns of the Radical Reformation have been adopted by other denominations and historians who once regarded Anabaptists as heretics. We who are Anabaptists rejoice that the Holy Spirit has brought to the fore in other Protestant groups, as well as through Vatican II, certain convictions similar to those we have long held. In turn, we recognize how much we have been enriched by the insights and challenges of other groups. Yet these are also fractious and fragmented times, when differences are magnified. I believe that fragmentation in the body of Christ has resulted, in part, from an inadequate theology of reconciliation.

An emphasis on reconciliation with God, in grace, expresses the evangelical conviction of a new life in Christ, of life in solidarity with the Prince of Peace and in a community of love. Reconciliation is God's action in grace. God moves first and calls us to respond. Salvation is not our work of coming to God; it is God coming to us and awakening our response. The work of grace in reconciliation is the precondition for the doctrine of justification by faith and for a biblical emphasis on discipleship of Christ.

Reconciliation thus supplies the basis for the Reformation doctrine of justification by faith—which is a marvelous doctrine, but it would be empty without the reconciling work of Christ. Furthermore, reconciliation also provides the basis for all meaningful exercises in spirituality, for pursuits and practices of piety, for the dynamic of a new life in the Spirit, and for ethical behavior in a pluralist society.

The ethic of freedom in the new life in Christ is an expression of a right relationship with God. But we need to understand this righteousness primarily as a "rightened" relationship with God—"rightened" by grace. As Markus Barth writes,

> Grace means solid covenant, truthfulness, and special concern for a man in need of help. In being true to his covenant and promise, God is true to himself. . . . Even in his judging, his judicial concern is ultimately "setting things right" in a judicious way. . . . God's righteousness is "God's way of righting wrong" (Rom. 1:17, NEB). (1971:42)

In a special note on God's righteousness, Isaiah says, "He has clothed me with the garments of salvation, / He has covered me with the robe of righteousness" (61:10). God's robe of righteousness is the symbol of belonging, the identity of being in the family of God. In Jesus' story of the prodigal son, when the son returns, the father says, "Bring the best robe and put it on him" (Luke 15:22, NIV). "The best robe" is a symbol of full restoration into the family of God. These texts provide the title for this book: *The Robe of God.*

My thesis in this book is that experiencing reconciliation is basic to the enjoyment of transforming grace.

Communicating primitive ideas is difficult. It is much more difficult to communicate about God, grace, reconciliation, and redemption. Hence, we must work at our theology with humility. The words we use are necessarily inadequate, and thus we run the risk of losing the majesty and grandeur of God. Nevertheless, speak of God we must, in the faith that dares to affirm the infinite One in all his glory and majesty, the God of glory and of grace. This God is our God, the God and Father of our Lord Jesus Christ.

The theologies of the Reformation have supplied the basic perspectives for Western religious thinking. But these systems of thought are hardly perfect or static; they need to be interpreted for our times and culture. Melanchthon interpreted Luther. Bullinger and then Calvin built on Zwingli. Likewise, in the Anabaptist or free-church movement, there has been a continuous stream of interpreters and reinterpreters.

One of my professors, Harold S. Bender, recognized the particularly unique manifestation of the Spirit amid the evident polygenesis of the Anabaptist movement. From these groups has developed what we now identify as the evangelical or peaceful wing of *The Radical Reformation*, so labeled by George Williams.

Through the centuries, this continuum has enjoyed developments of theology and life through God's work, as have other groups in their own ways. There have been changing manifestations of faith and renewal in the church. The Baptists, with believers church roots, arose in England by the 1620s. The seventeenth-century German Pietistic movement emerged, and so did the eighteenth-century Wesleyan movement. John Wesley was a friend of the Mennonite preacher Jeme Deknatel of Amsterdam.

The believers church stressed personal conversion to Christ. We see that same emphasis also in the Great Awakenings in America and other revival movements, including the later Pentecostal movement. Now it continues to flourish in free-church expressions of the two-thirds world.

Alongside black theology, liberation theology, and feminist theology, we interpret the faith for the next century, hoping that people will take Anabaptist theology seriously. The laboratory of history has tested the work of the Reformers and has enabled Christian thinkers to continue the task of relating our understanding of God to the culture and times in which we live.

My theology begins with *Christological Realism* and is founded on a biblicism focused by the revelation of God in Jesus the Christ. This realism takes seriously the kingdom of God as Jesus announced it, the life and teachings of the *earthly Jesus,* and the present role of the risen Christ. Primarily in this context of reconciliation, such a realism focuses on Christ and his life, the cross and redemption, and resurrection and ascension.

Christological Realism sees the sovereignty of God in a way that acknowledges human freedom and responsibility without determinism. It celebrates God's sovereign movement as the acts of God and not as a projection of human desires. It recognizes, with joy, that God is the one who has moved to us in Jesus, and that in his grace we are accepted by God.

This realism sees the church as a voluntary and visible fellowship of the redeemed that is free in society to operate under the mandate of Christ. We live as a new community in grace and love because we are reconciled. Such a realism sets ethics in a christological context of freedom. Its foundation is the person and behavior of Christ, who has demonstrated living in the will of God. It regards the Bible as God's authoritative Word when understood through Christ. This realism rejects a flat-book view of Scripture that overlooks God's unfolding revelation, lest we reduce Christ to a rescuing role rather than seeing him as sovereign Lord of our faith and our lives.

Christological Realism respects the sovereign presence of the Holy Spirit as the promised gift of Christ, as the God of glory and of grace acting within, among, and through us. It holds to a separation of church and state that emphasizes the special calling of the church in the kingdom of Christ. We dare to affirm that there is one Lord, and we refuse to render to Caesar the loyalty that belongs to God. We see the victory of Christ, of good over evil, not by God exercising coercive power but through the demonstration of God's superior goodness in holiness, justice, mercy, and peace (Rom. 1:4, 16; 11:23; 1 Cor. 1:17-18, 24; Acts 1:8).

With the increased awareness of religious pluralism and the claim that all roads lead to the top of the mountain, to salvation, we must understand what is meant by the singularity of Jesus Christ. To confess that there is "no other name" is actually good news (Acts 4:12). It is the announcement that God can be known fully in Jesus Christ. Jesus is the one in whom "God was pleased to have all his fullness dwell" (Col. 1:19). That is good news: God has made himself known to humanity and has brought an end to humanity's vain search for ultimate reality.

Soli Deo gloria. To God alone be the glory for his gracious work of reconciliation through Christ.

1

Reconciliation, the Biblical Essential

Therefore, since we are justified by faith, we have peace with God through our Lord Jesus Christ, through whom we have obtained access to this grace in which we stand; and we boast in our hope of sharing the glory of God. And not only that, but we also boast in our sufferings, knowing that suffering produces endurance, and endurance produces character, and character produces hope, and hope does not disappoint us, because God's love has been poured into our hearts through the Holy Spirit that has been given to us.

For while we were still weak, at the right time Christ died for the ungodly. Indeed, rarely will anyone die for a righteous person—though perhaps for a good person someone might actually dare to die. But God proves his love for us in that while we still were sinners Christ died for us. Much more surely then, now that we have been justified by his blood, will we be saved through him from the wrath of God. For if while we were enemies, we were reconciled to God through the death of his Son, much more surely, having been reconciled, will we be saved by his life. But more than that, we even boast in God through our Lord Jesus Christ, through whom we have now received reconciliation. (Rom. 5:1-11)

WHAT A FANTASTIC MESSAGE; reconciling grace! How amazing! How liberating! In this reconciliation, we become "a new creation" (2 Cor. 5:17). This is the marvel of the message of Christ. He calls us into a new life in grace, a life in relation with God, so that we live by love and know its freedom. This is the message of the Scriptures, the authoritative Word that continues to guide and check our thinking. It is a call to stand in faith.

In a class setting, my friend the Bishop John Kivuva of the Anglican Church of Kenya shared a striking story from Ethiopia. The Marxists had arrested a Christian brother. In the interrogation, a soldier ordered the man, "Give me your Bible so I can search it."

"You do not search the Bible," the Christian responded. "The Bible searches you."

We shall keep in mind the searching dynamic of Scripture as we work through these themes of reconciliation (cf. Heb. 4:12-13).

The message of grace comes through so well in Jesus' story of the prodigal son, a timeless cross-cultural story of the Gospel (Luke 15:11-32). *The waiting father* is the dramatic center of the story.

When the prodigal son finally comes to his senses, he decides to return to his father. The waiting father does an unexpected thing in his culture: he gets up and runs to meet his son. The father running to welcome the son is the most amazing element portrayed in the story. The father calls for the best robe in his closet and wraps it around his son. With this amazing act, the father shows that he cares more about his son than about what the son has done. Above all, the father clothes his son with the robe of belonging, "the robe of righteousness" or of right relation with himself, enfolding the son in his love (cf. Isa. 61:10; Baruch 5:2; Rev. 19:8).

Our response cannot be other than gratitude and praise for God's grace. Theology is doxology! It is the praise of our minds, of our best thinking. But our work in this discipline is to be an exercise of worship. Our words about God can only be in praise of God, for theology is never master; it is always servant. We cannot speak of God adequately, and yet speak of God we must, in faith.

We dare to speak in praise through a faith that honors God, even while our limited understanding and our sinfulness limit our ability to speak correctly. Through God's grace we are his people, members of his family, redeemed by his work in Christ. We are being transformed by the work of his Spirit. We belong to God even while we seek to understand the mystery of his majesty.

Nevertheless, this freedom to praise God is costly as believers face unfreedom in our world. A little-known reformer of this century, Alexander Men, was a remarkable priest in the Russian Orthodox Church. We learned about him while working with one of his disciples, Vladimir Illushenko of the Russian Orthodox Church, a professor in Moscow. My wife, Esther, and her colleague Tim Bentch had convened a conference for Christians in art, primarily for Russian artists; there we met Illushenko, who told us about Men.

Alexander Men was something of a Martin Luther in the Russian Orthodox Church, calling for a renewal of faith in personal commitment and solidarity with Christ. He dealt extensively with intellectual problems confronting Christians. Men spoke to the significance of Russian experience in this century, the advent of Communism, and the collapse of religion. He articulated a clear vision for the future of the Christian church. Men called upon Christians to take up their personal responsibility in the struggle between good and evil. Since he was considered a threat to the system in his witness to freedom, religious and political leaders opposed him.

One cold morning in 1990, while Men was walking through a wooded area to a speaking engagement, several assassins attacked him with an ax, struck him in the head, and seriously wounded him. The murderers fled, and Men dragged himself to the nearest station, but died before the bleeding could be stopped. People think his assassination was by collaboration between religious leaders and the KGB (State Security Committee). The death of this man shows the price one witness paid for freedom in Christ.

As sinners, we have been enemies of God, but this estrangement is overcome by God's act of reconciliation in Christ (Rom. 5:9). Through reconciliation we experience God's call upon our lives. In the psychological depths of response and repentance, we find ourselves giving up self-centeredness to become God-centered. This kind of surrender does not come easily. But such a surrender to God is made possible by God's wonderful, accepting, and empowering grace.

Reconciliation is, in my understanding of biblical teaching, the central aspect of God's overarching covenant of grace. It spans both Testaments as the unifying theme and finds its full expression in Christ. As I study history, I see reconciliation as a central motif in the sixteenth-century experiential faith of the Anabaptists. This actual covenant relation includes awareness that such a participation in reconciliation initiates the "obedience of faith," showing solidarity with Jesus (Rom. 1:5; 16:26).

Each of us and all humanity have been estranged from God in sin and need to be reconciled to God and to neighbors. One of the great discoveries we make in life is our need for forgiveness and redemption. As Albrecht Ritschl writes, "Reconciliation of those who were formerly engaged in active contradiction of God brings with it a growing understanding of our need and God's loving action."

Because of his liberal theology, Ritschl's stimulating discussion has not received the attention it deserves in some circles. He helps us see that reconciliation opens up the more comprehensive range of forgiveness; reconciliation bears fruit in mutual fellowship between God and humanity.

The early church did not really have a well-defined understanding of reconciliation. Even after the Reformation, reconciliation was eclipsed by concern for how one with a guilty conscience could find forgiveness. Theologians paid little attention to how we can live in a reconciled relation with God. They saw grace more as dealing with guilt than as changing relationships.

Christianity had various forms in the sixteenth century: sacramental, theological, and existential; among them, only the Radical Reformation emphasized actually living out reconciled and reconciling relationships. The Magisterial (state-church) Reformers stressed justification by faith more than reconciliation in grace. Yet there could be no justification without the preceding act of God in reconciliation.

James Denney agrees that the ancient church never developed a defined doctrine of reconciliation:

> The Church has never had in the same sense (as of the Trinity and the Incarnation) a dogma of reconciliation. There is nothing in the history of Christian thought on this subject analogous to the definition of "homoousion" at Nicaea. It was not until after the Reformation, when dogma in the old sense had become impossible, that the various branches of the Church began to frame explicit official statements about the way in which Christ reconciled men to God, and especially about the meaning of His sufferings and death. (Denney: 27-28)

The sixteenth-century Reformation stressed redemption and reconciliation, though not in a uniform way. The Magisterial Reformers focused more on justification; the Radical Reformers (Anabaptists) focused more on the relational aspects of being "in Christ." The in-Christ approach to interpretation calls us from a legalistic stance some see in the Old Testament (OT) to the relational stance highlighted in the New Testament (NT).

In developing a relational understanding of salvation, we may try to distinguish between emphasizing the *objective concept* of justification or the *subjective experience* of a transformed life. Nevertheless, it is my conviction that reconciliation, understood more broadly than justification, holds together both concept and experience, belief and walk.

Luther came to salvation chiefly through the insight of justification by faith. The Anabaptists came to salvation chiefly by the conviction of reconciliation in Christ as an actual experiential happening. Nevertheless, Luther was also involved in a personal faith relation, and the believers church also understood and affirmed justification by faith as a part of the salvation relationship. Thus Luther wrote,

> Faith is a divine work in us which changes us and makes us to be born anew of God. It kills the old Adam and makes us altogether different [persons], in heart and spirit and mind and power. . . .
> It is impossible for it not to be doing good works incessantly.
> ("Preface," *Commentary on Romans*, via Finger, 2:169)

The Anabaptists did, however, place a more prominent emphasis on the new birth or regeneration and on the new life of discipleship actualized in grace by this relationship. Though they did not develop a system of theology, they did have a clear understanding of salvation through grace. They did not articulate a theology of reconciliation as such; yet their emphasis on *assurance of salvation* is essentially assurance of being reconciled with God in and through Jesus Christ. We see a good example of this in the lengthy letters between Jerome Segers and his wife, Lijsken Dircks, imprisoned in Antwerp, and martyred in 1551 (van Braght: 504-522).

The reconciling acts of God in Jesus the Christ are expressed in the

Incarnation, and especially in the atonement and the resurrection. "All this is from God, who reconciled us to himself through Christ" (2 Cor. 5:18). The principal subject of Christian theology comprises the saving act of God in his Son: Jesus Christ actualizes God's self-disclosure and accomplishes God's redemptive work. Even as we study the Incarnation in the Jesus of history, we are seeking the knowledge of God that the Spirit brings to us from, in, and through the Son of Man, Jesus of Nazareth. God, as Paul says, acted in Christ to reconcile us to himself.

Theologians have found it too easy to distinguish between the *Jesus of history* on one side and *the Christ of experience* on the other. This may be due to a lack of emphasis on the resurrection of "this same Jesus" as the Lord we serve (Acts 1:11, KJV). Yet Jesus' followers have produced the Gospels primarily from their relationship with the Christ of experience, from their firsthand experience with the resurrected Jesus. They present the Jesus of history, who demonstrated the concrete form of the divine reality. They also proclaim this Jesus as sovereign Lord at God's right hand.

The Spirit now gives universal scope to "this Jesus" (Acts 1:8, 11). When we see "this same Jesus" as the Christ of experience in the biblical context, we recognize that the work of the Spirit is not tied to one period but is relevant in any specific time (Acts 2:36, KJV). Paul speaks of this Jesus, the historical Jesus, who died and rose again: "He is our peace," both with God and with our neighbors. He broke down the wall between groups and made one new humanity out of Jew and Gentile, after abolishing the enmity between the two created by the law (Eph. 2:14-15).

William Pannell of Fuller Seminary, in a chapel sermon at Eastern Mennonite College (now University), once defined our personal faith as "that attitude which allows God to be himself in us." The Christ of God is our peace; he is our love.

The Holy Spirit makes the historical Christ present with his reconciling power. According to James Denney,

> There is certainly no reconciliation but through the historical Christ; there is no other Christ of whom we know anything whatsoever. But the historical Christ does not belong to the past. The living Spirit of God makes Him present and eternal. It is not from

Palestine, nor from the first century of the Christian era, but here and now that his reconciling power is felt. (9)

Reconciliation is a continuing dynamic of divine grace, transforming people and social structures by creating a new community of the reconciled.

God in grace, in his graciousness, has moved to us in Christ, to reconcile us to himself. We are a people called to "belong to Jesus Christ" (Rom. 1:6). Hence, we are to walk with him in life as his disciples. We are called to make his kingdom visible in society by our lives, our faith, and our spirit. Belonging to Jesus, we as believers are described in the NT as "his body" in the world (Col. 1:24). Just as one's body gives visibility to one's personality, so we make Jesus visible to society. Amid our network of denominations, we seek the essential mission of the church; the Bible answers that the church's mission is to be a presence for Christ, agents of reconciliation (2 Cor. 5:19).

In both Covenants, God's disclosure is his gracious purpose of reconciliation. One of the early and profound statements of this truth is found in God's words to Moses:

> I have remembered my covenant. Say therefore to the Israelites, "I am the Lord, and I will free you from the burdens of the Egyptians and deliver you from slavery to them. I will redeem you with an outstretched arm and with mighty acts of judgment. I will take you as my people, and I will be your God. You shall know that I am the Lord your God, who has freed you from the burdens of the Egyptians. I will bring you into the land that I swore to give to Abraham, Isaac, and Jacob; I will give it to you for a possession. I am the Lord." (Exod. 6:5-8)

Throughout the OT, this message occurs frequently, especially in the message of the prophets. God works out his covenant of mercy, calling God's erring people to repentance and reconciliation. This is especially clear in Isaiah, a prophetic book that may be called the Romans of the OT.

The NT message centers in Jesus' mission: "The Son of Man came not to be served but to serve, and to give his life a ransom for many" (Matt. 20:28). Paul says this mission is accomplished through divine activity: "In Christ, God was reconciling the world to himself" (2 Cor.

5:19). According to Leon Morris (1988:173), Paul's words on reconciliation in Romans 3 may make up the most important single paragraph ever written:

> But now, apart from law, the righteousness of God has been disclosed, and is attested by the law and the prophets, the righteousness of God through faith in Jesus Christ for all who believe. For there is no distinction, since all have sinned and fall short of the glory of God; they are now justified by his grace as a gift, through the redemption that is in Christ Jesus, whom God put forward as a sacrifice of atonement by his blood, effective through faith. He did this to show his righteousness, because in his divine forbearance he had passed over the sins previously committed; it was to prove at the present time that he himself is righteous and that he justifies the one who has faith in Jesus. (Rom. 3:21-26)

In this classic statement, Paul says that justification is related directly with the righteousness of God. Righteousness as "rightness" basically means a right-relatedness with God in faith and action. God provides this relationship in grace known through Jesus Christ. This right-relatedness is our reconciliation with God. Such a relationship is shown in both our worship and in our walk.

Reconciliation is more than a symbol or a dogma; it is a reality that has come through God's love demonstrated concretely in Jesus' death on the cross, as James Denney says:

> Love proved itself in the Passion of Jesus to be the final reality, and no truth which takes possession of the heart of man can ever have power to subdue and reconcile like this. If we wish to experience or preach reconciliation, which depends upon such love, we must not lose the revelation of it by reducing it to a symbol, like the cross, or to a dogma, like that of Satisfaction; we must keep before ourselves and others the concrete facts in which the reality first came home to humanity. Christ crucified must be "evidently set forth"—placarded (Gal. 3:1) before men's eyes. (18)

The theme of reconciliation as the covenant of grace encompasses both Testaments. In this truth of reconciliation as the gracious activity of God, we have the expression of God's forgiving and transforming grace, as stressed by John R. W. Stott (1995:108-137). Joachim Jeremias affirms that "justification is forgiveness, nothing but forgiveness" (via Stott, 1995:110). Stott and Jeremias, however, seem to represent forgiveness as a pronouncement of release and thus fail to emphasize that forgiveness is only and always experienced in relationship. Forgiveness is always a dynamic of reconciliation (see chap. 5, below). It is the extension of grace that costs the giver but is free to the recipient.

Thus also Ralph P. Martin says, "Reconciliation really matters because it touches human lives and produces the effect of a changed human character." Martin builds this idea on an exegesis of Colossians 1:21-22: Paul's presentation "does not pass lightly over the moral demands whether of God's nature or of man's response to his offer" (via Banks: 114-115). This new relationship with Christ the Reconciler creates a new life for the reconciled. In this covenant relationship, we live by the bond of love.

The Christian message is that our Sovereign God has elevated Jesus of Nazareth to the supreme position, on God's right hand. Jesus the Christ is now Lord of all. He is head of the church. In his kingdom of the Spirit, he is now sovereign Lord over all principalities and powers. Christ has defeated the demonic by his cross and resurrection. Though evil continues through time, it is defeated, unmasked, exposed for what it is: parasite, perversion, and subversion. Its defeat serves God's purpose in challenging people to choose between God's will and the way of evil.

The "warrior God" of the OT defeated the gods of the nations. In doing so, God exposed and destroyed the idols of the time, often by overcoming the nations in battle. Thus God rescued his people and gave them a clear choice (e.g., Exod. 19:3-8; Josh. 24; Isa. 40).

This same victory comes now through the "warrior Christ," who defeats the idolatrous gods of our times, creating for us both a clear decision and a call to discipleship. He has been at warfare with the demonic, with the Baal of evil, and he defeated evil ultimately at the cross, triumphing over rulers and powers (Col. 2:14-15). Thus Paul writes, "Our warfare is not against flesh and blood, but against the authorities, against the powers of this dark world and against the spiritual forces of evil in the heavenly realms" (Eph. 6:12). In the midst of this spiritual warfare, we stand in the victory of Christ.

We need to examine how Christians deal with evil. Many have tried to gain a victory for the cause of Christ by using political power, and at times even using arms and the military. On the other hand, disciples of Christ are called to have a radically different spirit of grace and peace. This stands in contrast to those whose idea of religion is much like that of Islam and/or Judaism, which both sometimes appear to act as religions of violence.

Jesus spoiled principalities and powers: he unmasked them in his victory over them, exposing their true nature so we wouldn't place our faith in their power or patterns (Col. 2:15). Jesus calls his disciples to love rather than violence, to service rather than domination (Matt. 20:25-28). While his rule is beyond time, it keeps breaking into time, calling us to live by the reign of God.

In 1987 Esther and I were in Pune, India, serving at the Union Biblical Seminary. I taught courses in theology. The administration commissioned Esther to build a sculpture at the center of the new campus. She made several models, and they chose a semiabstract presentation of Jesus washing Peter's feet. The two figures were more than life-size; the one of Peter sitting before the kneeling figure of Jesus was nine feet tall. They were made of concrete. The final coat had Italian marble chips added to the white cement to make it appear like a marble sculpture.

One day while Esther was working, a busload of soldiers drove onto the campus. Most of them were Christians and were interested in visiting the school. An officer, a Sikh who had less interest in the school program, came and watched Esther at work. After some time he asked what this work represented. The seminary students told him that it was a sculpture of Jesus washing his disciple's feet.

He objected: "You Christians say that Jesus was God, and God would never have washed a man's feet."

A student said, "Mrs. Augsburger, you'll need to answer that."

So she explained: "We believe God came as a human being among us. His style was one of service, and he did wash the disciples' feet to model for us what it means to be forgiving and loving to one another. He actually gave his life for us."

The officer stood in silence, thinking, then shook his head in amazement and walked off across the grounds.

Jesus' kingdom is what Donald Kraybill has called *The Upside-Down Kingdom,* with a radically different lifestyle. This spirit and demonstration of the rule of God can change the world. God's reign is in process: the kingdom has about it what theologians have called "the already" and "the not yet." We live by the rule of God, in which we share the aspects of that which is "already." Yet we look for its full expression in the future, ultimately at Christ's return.

The kingdom of God is served by a network of people spread around the world who consciously seek to live by the rule of God. God's people form the one movement that is free, transcultural, and transnational; in self-giving love, they incorporate representatives from all races and countries and count them as equals. In this day of the global community, it is important to recognize the movement of the Holy Spirit in calling people to Christ beyond and even in spite of different systems of thought.

At the Mennonite World Conference that we attended in Calcutta on January 6-12, 1997, nearly 5,000 Mennonite Christians gathered from 65 countries of the world. They had cultural and racial diversity, but were united by the spirit of kingdom love and oneness in Christ, which we could truly sense. An Indian gentleman, Bishop Shant Kunjam, wrote the following theme song, and it became a catalyst of love among us:

> Hear what the Spirit is saying to the churches,
> To God's people,
> May we hear what you've heard,
> Our brother, our sister,
> May we follow, obey what we've heard.
> Hear what the Spirit is saying to the churches,
> To God's people, to the churches, to God's people. . . .

Through this conference in the Eastern world, we of the West were called to think with them in their understanding of the Scripture and of faith. This was a good experience for those of us from the West, where the church has tended to view Christianity primarily from Catholic, Reformation, Protestant, and Anabaptist traditions. Protestant thought has focused primarily on Luther and Calvin and the following traditions. Most people have a limited understanding of the Third Wing of the Reformation, a position which basically is a theology of reconciliation.

Various Evangelicals have arrived at certain beliefs and doctrines earlier held by the believers church. Yet Evangelicals and the heirs of the Anabaptists have been reluctant to dialogue on essentials regarding discipleship and following Christ, kingdom priorities for all of life, and the way of peace and justice in social problems. This reluctance may be because many Christians assume that a people cannot really live by nonviolence or pacifism in a violent world. Yet in India and in many countries of the world, the people need an emphasis on living out Christ's unconditional love.

Every theology is written from a particular perspective. Hence, it is best for a theologian to admit a bias and then practice fairness and understanding in making comparisons and differentiating one's views alongside other thought systems. This is what Arthur Holmes, professor of philosophy at Wheaton College, meant in saying that theology is "perspectival." We can clarify the character and strengths of a system of beliefs without disparaging another's understanding of God.

Many theological perspectives have enriched me as I have ministered ecumenically and internationally. I have been challenged by Catholic, Protestant, Evangelical, and mainline denominations alike. Yet we are enriched when we understand and are committed to a particular system of theology. Then it is possible to interface one's theology with that of others, for mutual benefit.

We can do theological thinking together in a contemporary and contextual manner, without negating the additional rich heritages of the broader Christian community. This is possible because we have the security of Presence, the special gift of the immediacy of the Holy Spirit. Through the Spirit's work in the hermeneutical or interpretive community, we together can discern the will of God. Together we can interpret God's written Word, drawing from the history of the Christian community. We can work with each other in implementing God's will for the common life.

As we do such joint interpretation together in any culture, we need prayerful alertness to discern when things in a culture tend to idolatry. This discernment enables any group to move beyond ethnicity and truly become a people of God in a given society.

To contextualize the gospel, we need an in-depth understanding of our culture, and of that culture's impact in shaping the expressions of our faith. As we do this in a given church group or denomination, we must face the issue of how we read the Bible in an authentic manner for a given situation. In the modern context, it is not easy to interpret the Reformation continuum, with its lasting values. A lot of change has taken place in the last half millennium. Among the various denominations, we must also recognize certain perspectives from a scientific worldview that have been brought to our biblicism and actually create differences among us.

Amid the pluralism of our society, the differences call for real dialogue, not just casual conversation; we need to discuss and test ideas and concepts, and to clarify essential meanings that shape our lives. When we view something theologically, we look at it in contrast and comparison with our contemporary culture. But this is not a simple exercise; not everyone around us comes from the same cultural background. Some are living in the past, some are living in future hope, and some seem to live for the present, without any historical reference. This situation challenges us to seek honesty and authenticity.

Reconstructionist historians of the sixteenth-century Anabaptist movement are emphasizing the polygenesis of the movement: there was not just one source; in numerous settings, this spiritual quest came to expression. Though a variety of groups made up the source and matrix for this heritage, I believe some contemporary historians give to "marginal" characters more credence than they merit. After all, the Spirit's work had led many to come to a new faith. I think we must take more seriously the witness of the Holy Spirit in and through history. The Spirit has called and guided us in various movements toward a "unity of the faith" (Eph. 4:13).

The new generation of theologians needs to be more conscious of the work of the Spirit in our history and development. Discernment takes time. There is abundant evidence of the Spirit's guidance in clarifying the essentials of Christian faith. Through the quality of *the redeemed community*, the Spirit has shown us many creative aspects of faith that are biblical and blessed of God. This has happened in the Anabaptist continuum and among other groups. The Lord continues to be at work among us for his purposes.

In *Thinking the Faith,* Douglas John Hall wants theologians to build their theology in and against their cultural setting:

> The attempt to comprehend one's culture—to grasp at some depth its aspirations, its priorities, its anxieties; to discern the dominant ideational motifs of its history; to distinguish its real from its rhetorical mores—all this belongs to the theological task as such. (75)

This is not easy and implies risk, yet doing theology in context is a must. If we don't figure out God's perspective on the world *now,* we have little or nothing to say about the future. Hall says, "When this dialogical quality is lacking at the level of the church's doctrinal reflection, no amount of practicality and concreteness at the level of 'applied Christianity' will make up for the lack" (76).

Ego labels must be discarded if we are to share in reconciling love. We also need to share insights with others rather than close them off by defensiveness and refusal to dialogue.

During a public meeting in South Africa, a young man challenged Samuel Hines, the outstanding pastor of Third Street Church of God in Washington, D.C., about his emphasis on love and nonviolence as the best way to change society. The youth stood up in the audience and shouted, "Your position is too soft!"

Vicky Hines reports that her husband responded to the young man in a straightforward manner, meeting him on his own terms rather than being judgmental: "As a revolutionary you say, 'There is a problem, and I am going out to solve it, and if you get in my way, I'll kill you.' Is my interpretation of your position correct?"

"Yes," the youth responded.

"I too am a revolutionary," said Hines, "but one who is a reconciler. I say, 'There is a problem, and I am going out to solve it, and if you get in my way, I'll lay down my life for you!' Now which one is soft?" This nondefensive response met the young man where he was and gave him an alternative to ponder.

We need to rethink our way of displaying the gospel so that we do not alter its content. Our society is extremely polarized between Republican and Democrat, right and left, conservative and liberal, the powerful and the powerless, rich and poor, white and those of color. The Christian community must find a way to free itself from these labels and their implications, and to relate with one another in Christ's reconciling love. This calls us to confess the kingdom of Christ as our highest loyalty, and Christ and his will as our one imperial mandate.

In seeking freedom from divisions stimulated by these labels, I propose that the church is a "third race" or "new race," as it was known in the early centuries (Ep. to Diognetus 1). The term *third race* was first used as an insult and then became an insight. The "church of God" (1 Cor. 10:32) is neither Jew nor Greek but God's people (Acts 18:10; 2 Cor. 6:16), God's "holy nation" (Exod. 19:6; 1 Pet. 2:9). In the church, two formerly hostile groups are joined into one body (Eph. 2:11-22; 1 Cor. 12:13).

We need to discover what this Third Way of living means as we follow the priorities of the kingdom of God and share in his message and ministry of reconciliation (2 Cor. 5:18-19). This new way offers us as disciples of Christ a stance of freedom and of selectivity as we walk among and select from either side.

Obedience itself is a way of knowing (John 7:17), as the sixteenth-century Anabaptist Hans Denck says, "No one may truly know Christ unless one follows him in life, and no one may follow Christ without first knowing him" (in Klaassen: 87, adapted). Dietrich Bonhoeffer agrees: "Only he who obeys truly believes, . . . and only he who believes truly obeys" (1951:60).

Doing theology is not simply a function centered in the thinker who deals with the concept of God as a theory or position held, thus making God into a "thing," "it," or "object." Instead, theology is thinking in relationship. As Buber says, we must distinguish between an "I-It" relation and an "I-Thou" relation; when we come to God, we are coming to the THOU of the universe!

Theology is our attempt to give guidance in how we come to God and speak of our experience of relating to God. This involves the whole of our human personality; we relate to God as to a personal Being, in a love that opens our total life to God. This love includes the heart or affection, the soul or ambition, the mind or attitude and thought, and our strength or activity and praxis in life. To love our neighbor as ourself, we must open our life to God in love, open our life to all that God is doing and would do in our neighbor (Matt. 22:37-38). This life of love gives us a different ethic, calling us to be global citizens, actualizing the fellowship of the kingdom across all class, racial, cultural, and national lines.

In thinking of the histories of Christian thought, we need to recognize that each has enriched the other by dialoguing together. Early leaders in the Anabaptist movement did not have the privileges we have to read Luther extensively, or Calvin's *Institutes of the Christian Religion*, or John Wesley, or theological works that have characterized the half millennium since Luther. As we read these and many other writers, we dialogue with the larger community of faith.

Though there are deep differences among the writers, there is also a mutuality in seeking to better understand Christ and his grace. In Catholicism, we see a sacramental form of Christianity, and also a movement for a more personal experience with the Lord. In Lutheranism, the sacramentalism is tied more to the preached Word, yet the experience of salvation is often related to a theology of forensic, arguable justification, slighting our need for a relational faith in the Justifier. This has frequently stimulated calls among Lutherans for renewal in personal relationship with Christ.

The system of Reformed or Calvinist theology tends to become legalistic in its attitude toward God's sovereignly predestined roles; yet it also includes a strong emphasis on knowing and experiencing the will of God in life. Some streams focus heavily on a theology of creation and divine purpose, calling us to rethink a theology of redemption and transformation, relating a theology of creation and a theology of God's reign.

The believers church movement began with a focus on a theology of reconciling grace, in a personal relationship with the risen Christ. This meant experiencing the new birth and the inner baptism with the Holy Spirit, that enables us to live this new life in discipleship. The diversity in this grassroots movement does not wipe out the "core" elements of faith that gave it a unique character. This Anabaptist faith has a Reformation theology that includes the following:

• Accepting *sola scriptura* as an expression of *sola gratia*. This means that God moves first, taking the initiative in offering us grace; God has disclosed himself, as explained in Scripture.

• Accepting *sola gratia* and *sola fide;* our experience of God's forgiving and transforming grace calls forth faith in a discipleship of solidarity with Christ.

• Accepting the universal priesthood of believers, each having direct access to God through Christ, and also that each is a priest to serve the neighbor.

• Accepting that all of life is holy and this shapes the common life. We are stewards of God's gifts of life, and refuse to invade the space or violate the rights of any other person or group.

To live in grace is to live in Christ and have the total of one's life oriented around him rather than around oneself. This is not a primitivism, trying to reproduce the precise form of the first-century church. Instead, each of us should seek the primary experience of a relationship with the risen Christ. The book of Acts is not primarily a presentation of (vague) mystical experiences but a declaration that this risen Christ is continuing his work through the Holy Spirit.

We might coin the word *primalism* to label this quest for the primary experience of solidarity with Christ, of a life filled with the Holy Spirit. Thus we regard the church as a community of the reborn. People come to Christ in the personal experience of relationship with him, "born from above" and living in and by the Spirit (John 3:3-8). The life of faith is far more than a doctrinal concept. It is relationship at the highest level. One of Charles Wesley's hymns gives our hearts' praise as reconciled people: "Thou, O Christ, art all I want, more than all in Thee I find."

Such a relational faith will help the believing community pass on to following generations the meanings of faith and still respect personal voluntary commitment. Authentic faith avoids legalisms of ethnicity or theology; it shows its reality in a spirituality of discipleship: life in the Spirit, a life of solidarity with Jesus.

Discipleship as a life in fellowship with the risen Christ is not a humanistic understanding of a Christian lifestyle. It is not achieved by following the model of the historical Jesus without the Spirit. True discipleship presupposes the regenerating and transforming power of the Spirit of Christ. As J. Lawrence Burkholder has pointed out, Mennonites have typically failed to understand and therefore appreciate Paul's doctrine of justification by faith. . . . We have reacted so rigorously to "cheap grace" that we have juxtaposed discipleship and grace as if they were antithetical . . . [and] generally resisted mystical interpretations of faith, including the Christ-mysticism of the apostle Paul. We have emphasized the historical Jesus without seeking to understand the more philosophical developments of Paul and his followers which led to concepts such as the Logos Christ of Ephesians and Colossians. . . . Without denying mystical faith, we have left its implications for piety and theology to other traditions. (1994)

Burkholder calls us to think more dialectically, to interface Paul and the Gospels or other writings. We need to do this because of the richness of Paul's theology, and because of the complexity and the ambiguity of life itself. A clearer focus on reconciliation will provide a bridge for relating these perspectives of faith: the historical, and the personal or experiential.

Much Protestant theology brings Jesus onto the scene chiefly as our Savior from sin, since our fallenness is the basic human problem of our rebellion in self-centeredness. This stream of thought moves on from redemption to emphasize Christ's second coming. It fails to give a serious and careful treatment of the present role of the risen Christ. At God's right hand, Christ rules as Lord in our lives by the sovereign presence of his Spirit *today* (Acts 2:33-36). By this presence, Christ both transforms and enables life in the will of God.

Protestant theology also tends to move from creation to the Fall to redemption to the second coming of Christ. It says too little about the present role of the church under the headship of the exalted Christ (Col. 1:18), and of our call to walk in the Spirit as members of his kingdom *now*.

Central to a theology of reconciliation is the recognition that Jesus is our Savior. But he is our Savior by being our Lord and calling us to focus all of life in relation to him (Rom. 10:9-11). From this point of view, Ritschl comments, "We may count on it that the justification which is successfully dispensed by God finds its manifestation and response in definite functions of the person reconciled." It is impossible for us to be in an actual reconciled relationship with God without thereby experiencing a change in our life.

I believe that a theology of the Third Way is a call for us to walk with Jesus in life; from his life and in his lordship, we find the meanings of the kingdom rule. This Third Way is not a middle-of-the-road position, but one that enables us to chose aspects from different positions, whether right, left, or center. We make our selections with a freedom to best express the priority of the kingdom of Christ over any and all party systems or ideologies.

A theology of reconciliation is a theology of freedom; we refuse to put the kingdom in a box or to reduce the significance of the universal movement of the kingdom of Christ by labels that create barriers. Each of us needs to join in the quest to know Christ better (Phil. 3:10). In this knowledge of Jesus, we enjoy and become a part of his mission.

Many Evangelical writers have displayed a limited understanding of a theology of reconciliation as emphasized in Anabaptist thought. Thus in *The Evangelical Essential,* Philip Janowsky attacks those who emphasize the teachings of the earthly Jesus. He sees this as an identification with law rather than with "justification by faith," and argues that we should minimize the teachings of the "earthly Jesus." Then we can see Paul as God's chosen voice to interpret justification by faith as the value of Jesus' redemptive work, he asserts (chap. 3).

Anabaptists do not minimize the place of Paul among other NT writers; he is the Holy Spirit's agent in interpreting the gospel. Yet we must protest Janowsky's low view of Christology. Paul's emphasis on justification is relational rather than a pronouncement that is only forensic, a legal argument. According to Janowsky, God simply pronounces us just without change on our part. We respond that as Paul relates justification to the righteousness of God, he actually emphasizes reconciling grace.

With a high view of the atonement, we see the cross as the central aspect of Jesus' work as Reconciler. The cross is the reconciling demonstration of his work. It is not to be separated from the significance of the Incarnation as Jesus' full disclosure of the will of God, nor from the resurrection as his triumph, verifying that he is the Son of God (Rom. 1:4). Paul's great affirmation is our assurance: "Therefore, since we are justified by faith, we have peace with God through our Lord Jesus Christ, through whom we have obtained access to this grace in which we stand. We boast in our hope of sharing the glory of God" (Rom. 5:1-2).

In Jesus Christ our Lord, we are reconciled to God, and this is through the same Jesus who lived and taught the will of God among us. As Paul says, "If while we were enemies we were reconciled to God through the death of his Son, much more surely, having been reconciled, we will be saved by his life. But more than that, we even boast in God through our Lord Jesus Christ, through whom we have now received reconciliation" (Rom. 5:10-11).

Some Evangelical systems of interpretation fail to recognize Jesus as the One whose coming was not "to destroy the law or the prophets, but to fulfill" them, to "fill full" the meaning of the law. Jesus calls us to a righteousness that exceeds that of the scribes and Pharisees (Matt. 5:17-20), a righteousness of right-relatedness.

The prophet Isaiah declares, "He has covered me with the robe of righteousness" (61:10). When I read that, after preaching on righteousness as relational, I asked myself whether the picture in Isaiah is somehow different. Then I thought about the prodigal son. The father's act of clothing the son with his robe shows that the son belongs to the family; it is a declaration of relationship.

Brevard S. Childs says the law is fulfilled in the sense of "effect," not in abolishing or dispensing with the law. "The law is actualized by the radical claim of discipleship as a following in the way of righteousness demanded by the law" (72-73). This life of discipleship is a relationship, not as the pursuit of a moral code; it is right living from a right relationship.

Too often theologians fail to emphasize how justification by faith means that one enters an actual right relationship with God in Christ. Reconciliation through our Lord Jesus Christ is not to relate so much to a function of his work but to Jesus himself, to the whole Jesus, who has made atonement through his blood and reconciled us to walk with him in life. Righteousness is a quality of active living, as demonstrated by Christ and made possible by him.

On this matter, Paul identifies his goal: "That I may gain Christ and be found in him, not having a righteousness of my own that comes from the law, but one that comes through faith in Christ, the righteousness from God based on faith" (Phil. 3:8-9). The righteousness by faith in Christ is a right-relatedness with God in and through the grace of Jesus Christ. In him, we do not simply have a "Go-between" to connect us to God, but the One in whom we meet God and are reconciled with God.

We begin with reconciliation as the first premise of salvation rather than with the doctrine of justification by faith. This reconciliation actually serves to give substance to justification by faith and to sanctification in grace. Reconciliation holds the two in a dynamic relationship not generally reflected in Protestantism.

Some Christians fear they may be emphasizing "works" if they stress discipleship. Dietrich Bonhoeffer speaks to this by comparing "cheap grace" and "costly grace" (1951). Costly grace requires our total commitment to being identified with Christ. Similarly, Gordon Kaufman points out that the phrase "justification by faith" suggests in itself that justification is not simply a forensic act in heaven; it includes the believer's act of faith (450).

In international conversation today, we dialogue with people from various religions and denominations. Each of us must recognize the perspective from which we come to theological conversation. Our understanding of truth must be more than the historical conditioning each of us has received in our theological systems of thought; we must discern the meaning of God's Word in the context in which we find ourselves.

This is a day of pluralism in society, of postenlightenment, modernism, postmodernism, and global involvement, with a global community. These and other factors have led to a paradigm shift that calls us to engage the times responsibly, seeking to better express the truth "as truth is in Jesus" (Eph. 4:21).

No one system of theology has answers to all of the issues, nor has any one denomination captured the kingdom of God. We need to hear each other and do so in a common quest to discern where and how the Holy Spirit is working. Christ Jesus is sovereign Lord and continues to be creatively active in his work in an ever-changing world. In the body of Christ, we must encourage each other to process things together as we think with the Spirit of God, and then to articulate a gospel consistent with Christ and his word. We must make this clear for the minds of people who describe their situation as a Christian culture though obedience to God is absent.

As believers, our life is based on solidarity with Jesus, on following him in discipleship. This is a life of walking with Jesus in the way. We understand his word not in merely conceptual patterns or abstract principles; we practice his word and learn by doing (Matt. 7:21). We know Christ by walking with him. Such knowing is only genuine through his transforming grace. This initiates a life of regeneration from the heart, with an ongoing sanctification. In faith, we share in both God's intention and God's action.

Our knowledge of God is authentic as we find him in Christ, "for in him all the fullness of God was pleased to dwell" (Col. 1:19; 2:9). With *Christological Realism* as the essential center of faith, we find a hermeneutical stance from which we can consistently interpret Scripture. We take the whole Jesus as the expression of the word and will of God. We refuse to divide the historic Jesus from the present risen Christ.

Thus we hold the teachings of the "earthly Jesus" in direct relationship with the character of our fellowship with the risen Christ, and this in spite of the views of the "Jesus Seminar." In Christ, we will participate together in a discipleship of joy. This is the dynamic of our union with our risen Lord.

2

The Centrality of Christ in Reconciliation

He has rescued us from the power of darkness and transferred us into the kingdom of his beloved Son, in whom we have redemption, the forgiveness of sins.

He is the image of the invisible God, the firstborn of all creation; for in him all things in heaven and on earth were created, things visible and invisible, whether thrones or dominions or rulers or powers—all things have been created through him and for him. He himself is before all things, and in him all things hold together. He is the head of the body, the church; he is the beginning, the firstborn from the dead, so that he might come to have first place in everything. For in him all the fullness of God was pleased to dwell, and through him God was pleased to reconcile to himself all things, whether on earth or in heaven, by making peace through the blood of his cross.

And you who were once estranged and hostile in mind, doing evil deeds, he has now reconciled in his fleshly body through death, so as to present you holy and blameless and irreproachable before him—provided that you continue securely established and steadfast in the faith, without shifting from the hope promised by the gospel. (Col. 1:13-23)

THE BOOK *I Dared to Call Him Father* gives the amazing account of how Madam Bilquis Sheikh of Pakistan came to Christ from her Muslim faith. She experienced happenings she felt were supernatural and then pondered many questions. Sheikh had read the Koran for some days, with its sharp words against people of any other faith. As she started reading a Bible, new convictions began to grow within her, especially from a passage she read in Romans. Then a special fragrance in her garden, followed by several vivid dreams, began to open new questions.

Her first dream was of Jesus, and of John the Baptist, who especially was a stranger to her. Her curiosity led her to call at Mitchells' mission home. The husband was away, but his wife responded to her questions, identifying John the Baptist as the one who baptized Jesus. This word *baptize* caught her attention. The two of them knelt on the floor, and Mrs. Mitchell prayed that the Holy Spirit would convince Sheikh of who Jesus is. Step by step, she came to an awareness of the possibility of knowing God in Jesus.

Sheikh's grandson was in the hospital at Rawlpindi, where a nun responded to her questions about God: "Just begin by calling him Father." She began to call out, "Oh Father, my Father, . . . Father God." There on her knees, the peace of God and the fragrance she had met as a Presence in her garden filled her life. She reached over, picked up the Bible, and prayerfully asked God, "Which book?" The answer came: "In which book do you meet me as your Father?"

Her wonderful reconciliation with God led her through intense suffering and rejection. Yet God surrounded her with his love and care and brought her to a freedom in which she could share her faith pilgrimage in this remarkable story.

Christology is the truth that reconciliation doesn't happen at a distance. This is true in experiences between individuals and even more so in our relation with God. God is not aloof. God took the initiative and came to us in Christ: "The Word became flesh and lived [dwelled] among us" (John 1:14). God continues to take the initiative in calling us in his grace. The work of the Spirit is God's continuing presence, God's gracious action of meeting us where we are and calling us to himself.

The Incarnation is God stepping across the gulf and identifying with us. The Greeks, especially the Gnostics, could not accept the Incarnation. People who are Greek oriented in their thinking still have difficulty accepting this truth. Yet on hearing the gospel, we know there is nothing so stupendous as the grace of God: God takes it upon himself to come to us in love. Though this great covenant of grace covers the entire sweep of the Scriptures, it is expressed supremely and personally in Jesus Christ. He is the Reconciler who has come to us, identified with us, forgiven us, and accepted us. In a reconciled relationship, we as believers now live in solidarity with Christ; we are his disciples, walking with him.

God is the awesome, holy Other, the transcendent One, the God of glory and of grace. As Moses found at the burning bush, God is the great I Am, the burning Presence that does not consume but transforms. This God has become concrete in Jesus of Nazareth as Emmanuel, God with us (Matt. 1:23). Yet Jesus said it was necessary for him to go away. His departure made possible the coming of the Spirit. It also makes clear that we do not now localize God, as was true in Jesus' earthly ministry. Through the Spirit, God has universal scope and action (John 16:5-15).

In the coming of the Spirit, God is imminent, but God is also universal. The God who is Spirit is expressed in three *persona*, in what has been called a community of love, a community of *perechoresis*, mutual interrelatedness. This Threeness is a necessary aspect of how God discloses himself to us in all of his majesty. God is One, yet he is revealed to us as Creator, Redeemer, and Sanctifier, the One God known as Father, Son, and Holy Spirit.

We know this truth in and through Jesus Christ, who made the Father known to us. He said, "All things have been committed to me by my Father. No one knows the Son except the Father, and no one knows the Father except the Son and those to whom the Son chooses to reveal him" (Matt. 11:27).

During the twentieth century, various theologians, beginning with Karl Barth, have turned again to Christology as the central aspect of Christian theology. We find this move among such European voices as Moltmann and Pannenberg and also such Latin American theologians as Jon Sobrino and Samuel Escobar. Barth reacted to and sought to correct a liberal Christology; the Latin American theologians see Christ inaugurating his kingdom and are correcting a privatized pietistic Christology.

In Evangelicalism, we find some of the clearer statements in Carl F. H. Henry's theological works in which he presents the classical position of Calvin and Hodge (in Althaus; cf. Calvin, *Institutes*, 129-41; Hodge, *Systematic Theology*, 1:483-521).

Within my tradition, the Anabaptist fellowship, John Howard Yoder has made a signal contribution with his work *The Politics of Jesus*. I have also found significance in C. Norman Kraus's book *Jesus Christ Our Lord*, though some wondered if his emphasis on the humanity of Jesus may minimize divine aspects of Jesus Christ as Son of God. Kraus has graciously heard these concerns and dealt with them in a more recent work, *God Our Savior*, which I highly recommend. Thomas Finger's *Christian Theology* is an outstanding work, giving us a brief but helpful discussion on Christology.

The impact of these and other writers on our denominational thought patterns serves to call us to think *about* Christ and to attempt to think *with* Christ.

My emphasis on the authentic Jesus Christ is not just of the mystical Christ of salvation. I am confronting contemporary Christianity with a call to take a fresh look at the Jesus of the NT, a Jesus of salvation but also of social involvement. Jesus calls us to reconciliation, as the Savior of our souls but also as the one who mediates a new relation between us and our erstwhile enemies.

Yes, Jesus saves us; yet in this saving relationship, he expects discipleship. He asks from us a spirit of obedience to the Father, the same life-shaping spirit of obedience Jesus manifested in loving us even while we were his enemies. We are saved for a reason, to be in relationship, to belong. This is reconciliation, and this is what makes Jesus unique. As Yoder says, we must see

> faith as discipleship, not only a subjectivity. The element of debate in the presentation may make it seem that the "other" or "traditional" elements in each case—Jesus as sacrifice, God as creator, faith as subjectivity—is being rejected. It should therefore be restated that . . . such a disjunction is not intended. We are rather defending the NT against the exclusion of the "messianic" element. This disjunction must be laid to the account of the traditional view, not ours. It is those other views that say that because Jesus is seen as sacrifice he may not be seen as King, or because he is seen as Word made flesh he cannot be seen as normative man. (1972:232)

In our day of pluralism, we face the danger of compromising the uniqueness of the Incarnation by seeing Jesus as one way to God among many others. Some argue that there are many paths to the top of the mountain, to bliss, whether Hindu, Buddhist, Islam, Shinto, or whatever. In this view, Jesus becomes another holy man, a great teacher, but one among many teachers of God.

Some Christian theologians have accepted conclusions from pluralism to the degree of moving from a christological center to a theocentric position; they assume that we can come to an understanding of God through many religious leaders. They include Jesus as one of these teachers without recognizing that in Jesus Christ, God has come to us and made himself known uniquely and supremely (Col. 1:15-19). Yet a biblicism that takes the disclosure of God in Christ as the ultimate word will hold Christology at the center of God's message to humanity (see Calvin Shenk).

We cannot overlook the reality of God's self-disclosure in people's lives. God keeps revealing himself to us. But the knowledge we gain, the light we experience, is partial. Apart from Christ, human perception falters badly; even with Christ, we confess that we now "know only in part" but later "will know fully" (1 Cor. 13:12). John's prologue says, "The true light, which enlightens everyone, was coming into the world" (John 1:9). This light, shining in varying degrees, has found its full focus in Jesus Christ. He is the light of God, the light of the world (9:5). As the light keeps shining in the darkness, it beckons us to move toward its source.

If people simply sit and contemplate the light they are experiencing, they fail to move toward God himself; as the Scripture says, "God is light" (1 John 1:5). God's redemptive, reconciling grace is never simply the blessing of light in contemplative minds; instead, it is a light that calls us to follow, to fellowship with him. John writes, "If we walk in the light as he himself is in the light, we have fellowship with one another, and the blood of Jesus his Son cleanses us from all sin" (1 John 1:7).

In history, God has kept moving humanity further—beyond the elementary stages of perception of his disclosure, beyond the limited rays of light that broke into the human arena—to the full expression of God's glory in Jesus Christ. In our world, the light keeps breaking into human consciousness as a dim though beckoning glimmer, calling us always to move to Christ, the source of the light. As we do so, we discover that the Creator God is the one "who has shone in our hearts to give the light of the knowledge of the glory of God in the face of Jesus Christ" (2 Cor. 4:6).

When we share in witness dialogue amid the religious pluralism of our day, we should not argue that our religion, as religion, is better than other religions. Instead, we need to show how the light in any religion needs to be brought into focus through and in the person of Jesus Christ. Religion, when an end in itself, will block the way to an authentic faith that brings one to humbly surrender to God. Even in the Christian religion, some who profess faith in Christ are still living in drastically limited light and need to discover how the light of God is focused in Christ. In this discovery, they can keep moving toward the source of true light and enjoy a greater and more authentic fellowship with God.

A biblical understanding of Christology will help us as Christians in our witness. We do not need to enter into an argument on the relative merits of our religion in comparison to theirs; we need only to show how Christ is the completion and complement for all religions. Christ calls us to know the God who is Creator, Redeemer, and Sovereign Lord. Such was Paul's message at Athens as he called the philosophers to faith in Christ (Acts 17:22-33).

This is not a universalism saying that God must save everyone if he is a God of grace and love. Though God opens his grace to everyone, his love does not coerce anyone. It is our responsibility to respond to the true light. However, we do affirm that God's grace is his universal concern: "God so loved the world that he gave his only Son, so that everyone who believes in him may not perish but have eternal life" (John 3:16). God does not want any to perish (2 Pet. 3:9). We are ambassadors for Christ, agents of reconciliation who carry the message and the mission of reconciliation. It is our mission to bring the light into focus for people by presenting the gospel of the person of Christ (2 Cor. 5:18-20).

As an artist, my wife, Esther, has been involved in convening area conferences for Christians in art. For this purpose, we have traveled in India, other parts of Asia, and Eastern Europe, including a conference of Russian artists. A group of Romanian artists came to such a conference at Mittersill, Austria, and then created a Christian fellowship that attracted more and more artists. Several years later, Esther convened such a meeting in Budapest, attended by a large contingent of Romanian artists, especially from Cluj.

The Romanians brought along Livia, the curator of the National Art Gallery in Cluj, though she was not a Christian. For the first part of the conference, Livia was on the fringes, critical, and even somewhat obnoxious. However, Esther kept relating to her and recruited her to help prepare the exhibit each conference arranged for the public to see, at the end of their assembly.

Late at night, while walking back from this work to their lodging, Livia suddenly said to Esther, "I am so wicked, . . . I can't come to God. My husband and I are having a terrible time. I'm so wicked, I just can't come to God."

Esther simply said, "Livia, you don't have to come to God. God has already come to you. All you need to do is to say yes to Jesus."

Livia looked at her in some surprise: "Do you mean that?"

"Yes," Esther said, "all you need to do is just say yes to Jesus."

The next day they participated with the group in hosting the exhibit. The following morning as Esther was leading the closing session, she felt led to open the meeting for others to speak: "Some of you may like to share what has happened to you in this conference."

Before she could finish the statement, Livia was out of her seat and hurrying to the front. "I just want to tell you all that I'm saying yes to Jesus."

The crowd was joyful in response and quite supportive.

What followed was further evidence of a changed life. She went back to Cluj, began attending the local Baptist church, was baptized, and became involved with such fine spirit that her husband was supportive of her in the change. A year later Esther and I taught for a week at the seminary in Osijek, Croatia, and at the conclusion we made a trip to Romania. On Sunday morning I preached in the Baptist church. Sitting in front of the pulpit with radiant attention was Livia, responding to the word and sharing in the worship of Christ. Jesus is building his church!

When I speak of Christology, I do not separate the theological interpretation of Christ from the significance of the earthly, historical Jesus, his being and relevance. The story of Jesus is the basis for our understanding of the divine self-disclosure in this person, Jesus of Nazareth. The Jesus who announced the gospel of the kingdom is now the King of kings, the sovereign Lord of that kingdom. Stanley Hauerwas speaks of this kingdom proclamation in his book on ethics, *The Peaceable Kingdom:*

> There is a deep difficulty with the strategy that attempts to avoid dealing with Jesus as he is portrayed in the Gospels. Christologies which emphasize the cosmic and ontological Christ tend to make Jesus' earthly life almost incidental to what is assumed to be a more profound theological point. In particular the eschatological aspects of Jesus' message are downplayed. Yet there is widespread agreement that one of the most significant discoveries of recent scholarship is that Jesus' teaching was not first of all focused on his own status but on the proclamation of the kingdom of God. Jesus, it seems, did not direct attention to himself, but through his teachings, healings, and miracles tried to indicate the nature and immediacy of God's kingdom. (73)

James Denny's statements help us to see how the Incarnation supports Jesus' work of reconciling humanity to God:

> If we keep our minds close to the facts, what we really mean by the Incarnation is that the life which Jesus lived in the flesh—that moral and spiritual life in the concrete fulness and wealth which the evangelists display—was divine. . . . He united the human nature to the divine; and in principle the atonement or the reconciliation of humanity to God was accomplished. (36-37)
> This is to say, uniting with humanity He, as divine, repaired the breach between us and God, a union verified in unconditional love at or by the cross, and in this sense "the Incarnation and atonement, or the Incarnation and the work of reconciling humanity to God, were all one. (184).

Systematic theology divides the discussion of Christology into two main phases: the person of Christ, and the work of Christ. Discussion of his person usually focuses on the matter of his deity, his relation to the Trinity, with more limited discussion of his earthly life and work. But if we take the Incarnation seriously, we must give both the human and the divine aspects of Jesus the Christ our most honest and careful attention. Furthermore, just as we must look carefully at his life and work, so we must look just as carefully at his death and resurrection. Christological Realism is the recognition that the historic Jesus, confirmed by his resurrection as the Son of God, is now the reigning Christ (Rom. 1:4).

The ancient Apostles' Creed says that Jesus Christ is seated "on the right hand of God the Father Almighty; from thence he shall come to judge the living and the dead." Thus the creed assures us that our risen Lord will come from this sovereign position, "from thence," and that he is the ultimate authority for all the living, not just for believers. Hence, we must take Jesus as seriously and with the same realism the disciples showed in their walk with him, a walk that extended beyond his resurrection and ascension. We now serve Jesus Christ as our sovereign Lord; we share his kingdom, which is to be completed at his return. This is our faith: "this same Jesus" who lived among us, who taught us, is the Jesus we worship and follow as our Lord (Acts 1:11, KJV; 2:36).

We recognize the ultimate disclosure of God in Jesus Christ. In accepting Jesus, we accept the whole person, his Incarnation, his Godness and his humanness, his life as the Teacher of righteousness, his atonement, his resurrection, and his exaltation as sovereign Lord. Some theologians omit an emphasis on the Teacher of righteousness and move immediately to the cross. In the Scriptures we first know Jesus in his earthly ministry; only through his life and teachings are we then able to relate to the risen Jesus. The Christ shared in the Acts and in the Epistles is the Jesus who lived and taught in Galilee and Judea.

As reported earlier, some have argued that those who take the teachings of the historic Jesus seriously as a basis for the understanding of the Christian life, are thereby missing out on the great doctrine of justification by faith. The doctrine of justification, it is claimed, is found in Paul and not in the historical Jesus. In response, I must affirm that one cannot read the Gospels without finding that Jesus is the Reconciler, that he has come to reconcile us to the Father, "to give his life a ransom for many" (Matt. 20:28).

Reconciliation is the precondition for any doctrine of justification by faith. We thus must move beyond any interpretation of justification by faith that is limited by tending to overlook a biblical emphasis on reconciliation. One can well speak of justification by God's faithfulness. This is a covenant of faith-relationship and faith-identity. By this relationship, we have solidarity with the risen Christ, an awareness of the meaning of Paul's frequently used phrase "in Christ." This solidarity with Jesus is not merely a mystical feeling; it is an understanding of Jesus gained from the Gospels and confirmed by our conscious identification with him as his disciples.

There is no way we can know the historic Jesus except through the Scriptures, especially in the four Gospels. Our knowledge of Jesus depends on the record that has been passed along to us by his disciples. One kind of knowing occurs only when the other person speaks to us, when we relate to that person rather than thinking of the other as we think of an object. Such an "I-Thou" knowing happens as we hear Jesus speak in the Scripture.

Lesslie Newbigin, in his work *Christ Our Eternal Contemporary*, makes a special distinction between knowing things as a scientist and knowing people in relationship; both have elements that are at the same time destructive and creative. There is the element of commitment in which one takes an imaginative leap forward, as Einstein did when other scientists did not believe the frontier could be breached (10).

Knowing Christ calls for an awareness of commitment; we dare to reach out to him as risen Lord. Scripture presents to us the living Savior, and we can now take the "leap of faith" that opens our lives to his work. Knowing Jesus is not like knowing some historical figure who lived and died as an example; it is to know Jesus as our contemporary, our resurrected Lord. As we know him in relationship, we will be transformed in his grace.

In such a faith-relationship, as people in grace "called to belong to Jesus," we identify with him in the whole of our lives: our minds, emotions, wills, and actions. This identity, this union with Christ, is with the risen Christ at God's right hand, our sovereign Lord. Paul appeals to our solidarity with Christ: "If you have been raised with Christ, seek the things that are above" (Col. 3:1). In *The Schleitheim*

Confession of February 24, 1527, the first "Protestant" Synod, the gathered Anabaptists agreed that baptism is for "all those who desire to walk in the resurrection of Jesus Christ" (art. 1) We walk in the victory and the fellowship of the risen Christ, knowing him now as our risen Lord. We cannot go back and live on the other side of the empty tomb.

For over forty years, Newbigin served in the Church of South India as a missionary and bishop; he shares insights that few of us have dealt with in the same way in our culture. In preaching Jesus, his death, and resurrection, Newbigen gives us an apt illustration:

> There is a way of preaching Jesus, a very familiar way which somehow stops short of that fact. Many of you will have often seen a picture which used to be very prominent in the coffee shops in the bazaar—a picture with three figures on it, in one corner The Buddha under a tree, in another corner Jesus on the cross, and in the middle Gandhi. Many of you must have seen that picture. It would present a conception of Jesus which is exceedingly common and which is, if I may say so, very easy to put across, a conception of Jesus as one of the great holy men of history, one of the masters, one of the great souls. That way of preaching Jesus is popular and easy because it makes and calls for no radical commitment. It leaves the world as it was. It leaves you as you are. But if Jesus is the One who died and rose again, then the matter is quite different; the picture is quite different. You have to tear that picture up; it does not fit. (1968:4)

The early creeds give us significant interpretations of the foundational aspects of Christian faith. But they are shaped by the issues of the times and are not in themselves a full statement of theology for our day. For example, the Apostles' Creed moves directly from the birth of Jesus to his suffering "under Pontius Pilate." When the creed was being formed, the church needed to meet a particular social challenge to its understanding of Jesus; the creed was its unifying answer. But that statement ignores the significance of Jesus' life as the expression of God in humanness, showing the will of God.

In the creed after the phrase "born of the virgin Mary," I would add something like this: "lived and taught the will of God" (Mark 3:35; Matt. 28:20). This strikes me as a better approach than some liberation theologians interpreting the phrase "suffered under Pontius Pilate" more as a reference to the powerless suffering at the hands of the powerful than as meaning atonement for our sins.

The Nicene Creed (325) is the statement of the church in the fourth century in answering the question "Who is this Jesus?" The answer stands in Christian history and theology: Jesus is "very God of very God, and very man of very man." The church struggled to put in words what it knew in faith, that Christ was "of the same substance with the Father."

Then came the need, partly satisfied by the councils of Constantinople (381) and Chalcedon (451), to interpret the relation of the Spirit in the triune God and especially to answer the question of how we can think of Jesus as having two natures, divine and human, in one person. The answer used the positive power of negative affirmations: these two natures are in the one person without confusion, separation, distinction, or alteration.

The Incarnation, in all its mystery, remains central to God's revelation. The fullness of God's self-disclosure is in his coming to humanity in Jesus of Nazareth. In his life we understand the person and love of God; only in Christ can we grasp the meaning of God's suffering love. In his life we understand the will of God, through his deeds and words; thereby we have a basis for both faith and ethics in our reflection on the will of God for our lives as disciples. Jesus demonstrated how one lives out the righteousness of the law by living in the Spirit, in a lifestyle that is not a legalism but is the free expression of obedience in the Spirit.

Later Paul says that God sent his Son "so that the just requirement of the law might be fulfilled in us, who walk not according to the flesh but according to the Spirit" (Rom. 8:3-4). Supremely, the incarnate Christ Jesus is the same Jesus Christ who is resurrected and is at God's right hand today (8:34).

Evangelicals have held what is called a "high view of Scripture," with firm belief in its full inspiration; a true evangelical faith also holds a high view of the Incarnation: the eternal Word actually became flesh and dwelt among us (John 1:14). Some evangelicals appear to have a limited view of the incarnate Christ, emphasizing his deity but failing to see in his humanness the full and very Word of

God. In his life as a person, Jesus the Christ stands in the stream of history as the one in whom God actually has engaged humanness, and at the same time as the one in whom "the whole fullness of deity dwells bodily" (Col. 2:9; 1:19).

We would have a truncated gospel if we failed to present the whole Jesus, if we separated the divine and human natures of Jesus, if we emphasized the divine work of redemption and neglected the redemptive aspects of our Lord in his true humanity. The Incarnation shows us that humanness and sinfulness are not synonymous. Sinfulness is a perversion of humanness. God could become human without being sinful (Heb. 4:15).

In reconciling humanity with God, Christ redeems us with a work that restores true humanness. In Christ we are new creatures, sharing both a new fellowship with God and finding in our experience a new order of restored humanness, a new creation (Gal. 6:15; 2 Cor. 5:17). In Jesus we are called to live godly lives (2 Tim. 3:12; Titus 2:12). Ethics for the Christian grows out of this new character, in being "new creatures," reconciled to the very "ground of our being," becoming what God intended in our creation.

A wholistic understanding of Christology implies much. In affirming Jesus Christ as the one ultimate Word, the Logos of God, we do not thereby minimize the "Word of God written" with its authority, full inspiration, and infallible rule for faith and life. With Barth in his christological theology, we must give priority to the person of Jesus Christ as the divine disclosure. But I have some difference with Barth because I cannot minimize the authority of the written Word as a concrete form of revelation. In this very Word, inspired by the Holy Spirit, we have the revelation of Jesus Christ.

Nevertheless, in a somewhat different way, Barth does declare the authority of Scripture. He says that in any area of research, we go back to the original sources, as near to the founding events as we can get. So we do the same in Christianity, with the Gospels being the closest we can get to the Christ event; hence, they are authority. I like this point from Barth.

The Incarnation is the one absolute expression of what God is like and also of what true humanity is like. Jesus is our one infallible demonstration of true person, divine and human. He shows the will of God lived out in the human arena. Jesus' life is the example of how one who does the will of God should live: saying "no" to sin, guided by the fullness of the Spirit, following the way of love even to death, accepting the cost of love in the way of the cross, and living in faithfulness to God. Jesus is our Master, and as such he is our Mentor (1 Pet. 2:21).

In Jesus we have the full knowledge of God. The writer of Hebrews says, "God, who at different times and in fragmentary ways has spoken in the past to our fathers by the prophets, in little snatches here and there, has in these last days [last, meaning the final disclosure] spoken unto us by his Son" (Heb. 1:1-2, author's trans.). In Jesus we therefore have the true knowledge of God. As Karl Barth said of the Incarnation, "Either Jesus Christ was actually God, or we don't have a full revelation yet." Our knowledge of God is not primarily in natural theology, in philosophical theology, or in existential experience, but in Jesus Christ of Nazareth.

God is not known primarily in subjective experience but in the objective reality of the incarnate Christ. Both are aspects of believing faith, but the subjective is dependent upon the objective reality. Our experience is always to be tested by the message of the Word shared in the interpreting community.

The Jewish theologian Martin Buber made a great contribution in theology by calling us to have an I-Thou relationship with God. He also tells us to recognize that we come to the Thou awareness through or after we have a consciousness of the "It" as actual Reality. This is what an evangelical theologian Francis Schaeffer has expressed as *The God Who Is There.*

When we meet God as person and open ourselves intimately to him in love, there is an experiential relationship. We find a subjective dimension of surrender and of inner peace in our solidarity with him. But God is known in a covenant of faith that recognizes God in his Word and as a Reality beyond our subjective experience.

The new covenant calls us to walk with Jesus in life, acknowledge his lordship in life, and converse with him over his Word. The experience of God may be in "a sound of sheer silence," as we wait for his word to us (1 Kings 19:12). But we are not left only with subjective aspects of relationship; in Christ we see the One who revealed the person of God in both a concrete and a universal expression. In Jesus as the Christ, we have both the concrete (Jesus) and the universal (the resurrected Christ). Jesus said, "The one who has seen me has seen the Father" (John 14:9).

In opening our lives to Christ, we experience the grace of God, and by this grace we rest in his acceptance. This is our assurance of salvation: we are reconciled to God in Jesus Christ.

We understand God as we are introduced to him in Jesus. "For God so loved the world that he gave his only Son, so that everyone who believes in him may not perish but may have eternal life" (John 3:16). In this golden text of the Bible, we have the declaration of a God of love, a God who interacts with the world in his Son. In Christ, God comes to us and says, "Your problem is now my problem." He shares this problem even to death.

In Christ, we understand God as a loving, self-giving, forgiving, accepting, redeeming, transforming, sharing, and present God; a God of compassion, mercy, and justice; a God of grace who takes the initiative and comes to us in reconciliation. God is gracious and participates in our lives in an accepting way, without manipulating us. His grace calls us, and we are free to say yes or no to God.

This God, the Father of our Lord Jesus Christ, is both transcendent and imminent; he comes to us in the presence of the Holy Spirit and lives within us. He is our gracious companion, hearing and answering our prayers, moving in our lives step by step as we invite him. Since God doesn't coerce our response of faith, our prayers give him the freedom to work with us.

Christological Realism recognizes in Jesus the Logos, the Word of God, the full expression of God in humanity. The Incarnation means that this man Jesus was truly God—or we don't have a full disclosure of God in humanness. It also means that this man Jesus was truly man—or we don't have an authentic identification with or disclosure of genuine humanity. Evangelical Christians hold some form of this statement in their theology of the Incarnation.

Jesus lived among us in authentic humanness as an expression of the person and the will of God. From the life of the man Jesus of Nazareth, we can therefore learn the most clear understanding of God's will. Similarly, as we consider the meaning of Jesus' death, we can see this same divine-human relationship at work. For us, the cross has become an authentic saving experience in which God has overcome the rebellion of humanity in Jesus; at the same time, the man Jesus was bearing humanity's rebellion, our sin, bearing it to God and bearing it for God. This mystery can only be grasped when we see God being involved at the deepest level of redemptive substitution: God in Jesus substituted himself in forgiveness; Christ "himself bore our sins in his body on the cross" (1 Pet. 2:24).

As we speak of God's existence and of God's reconciling work, the Christian faith recognizes the fact of mystery in every aspect of our relation with God. Some seek proof for the existence of God, without recognizing that a stance of proof is superior to what is being proved. If we could prove God, we would in the very act no longer have God. We can only bow in humility before the majesty and mystery of God—including the majesty and mystery of the Incarnation and of God's presence in and with Jesus at the cross.

Central to NT Christology is the reality of the resurrection of Jesus Christ. This is the essential heart of the gospel: if Christ is not risen, then God has not verified the work that makes it possible for us to be his children. Without a resurrection, there would not be the creative work of God that involves the body as well as the soul in the transforming work of God.

The resurrection means far more than Jesus being alive and well in another world. Scripture declares that God raised him from the dead. This resurrection and his many appearances took place in this world. The risen Jesus declared, "A spirit does not have flesh and bones as you see that I have" (Luke 24:39). Those who saw him found the risen Jesus to have form and substance: at first they took him for some other human till he made himself known to them.

Jesus' resurrection means that he was/is who he said he was (Rom. 1:4). He has defeated death and evil and broken their dominion, even though their activity continues. Jesus' atoning sacrifice is acceptable to God, who raised him. The resurrection gives his life continuing meaning. He is head of a new community of God's people; he is Lord, and all history is interpreted through him. As Lord, he gives the promised Holy Spirit and imparts resurrection power to his disciples.

Jesus works through his communities of grace to confront society and governments with the reality of his kingdom. He will come again to complete history and the purpose of God. We may do Christology from above (starting with our understanding of his deity) or from below (starting with the earthly Jesus of Nazareth). Either way, from the perspective of the resurrection, we come to him as the One whom God declared to be his Son "by resurrection from the dead" (Rom. 1:4).

Leslie Newbigin has said, "The resurrection fits no other worldview but that of the victory of the transcendent and yet immanent God" (lectures, Coalition of Christian Colleges and Universities, Washington, D.C., 1992). With God, even death's finality is not final. The resurrection means that Jesus' victory over evil extends into our lives. As countless Christians have proved, we can draw upon the power of the resurrection. Further, the resurrection means that we have a security in our faith; it is anchored in Jesus' position as sovereign Lord. The resurrection also confirms the ministry of the incarnate Christ.

In a significant way, the resurrection means the extension of Jesus' life and teachings into the present. This is an important aspect of the resurrection of Jesus that is not given adequate emphasis in much theological reflection. The NT emphasizes that it is "this same Jesus" who is alive and has ascended to God's right hand (Acts 1:11, KJV; 2:33-36). This is the same Jesus who modeled the will of God in his life, and the same Jesus who in God's will through his death showed God's self-giving love. This is the same Jesus who taught all people the will of God as he explained the new life (John 3), abiding in him (John 15), the behavior expected of disciples (Matthew 5-7), and so much more.

The authority of Jesus' word and teaching is certified by his resurrection. There is no part of the teaching of Jesus that can be ignored by disciples of Christ; as we think of Jesus as the master Teacher, we must recognize that *this same Jesus* is our Lord and continues to guide us by his unchanging word.

Christological Realism draws a direct relationship between the Incarnation and Jesus' use of Scripture. It is pivotal that Jesus perceived himself as Word: he took upon himself the authority to say, "It was said, . . . but I say unto you" (Matt. 5:21-48), or again, "The Son of Man is Lord of the Sabbath" (12:8). Thus we look at the new covenant as the answer to the old covenant, and we interpret the Old through the New even though the Old is preparation to understand the New. Theologians call this "progress of doctrine" or "progressive revelation."

Christological Realism rejects a flat-book view of the Bible. It recognizes in Scripture an unfolding revelation: God continued to disclose more and more about himself through salvation history as presented in Scripture, until he said it better in Jesus Christ.

This hermeneutic is not a simple elevation of the NT above the Old, nor is it in any way a rejection of the OT. Instead, we recognize the covenant of grace that encompasses OT and NT; through all of Scripture, we see the disclosure of a reconciling God now known more fully in Jesus Christ. The OT and NT testify to this "grace upon grace" that we have received (John 1:16-18).

Among sixteenth-century Anabaptists was a clear emphasis that the OT message related to the NT message as *promise* to *fulfillment*. If we miss the progress in Scripture, we miss the purpose of God's full self-disclosure in Christ. A literalistic "flat-book" view tends to elevate the words of God above the disclosure of God; instead, we need to count the words as communication of God himself. In the inspired words, we meet God; in his unfolding revelation, we now test each word against the person to whom it points—God.

Such a Christology affects our interpretation of Scripture: hermeneutics is one of the more unique contributions of Anabaptist thought to Christian theology. This perspective produces a different approach to issues of Christian thought and life: questions of justice and human freedom, slavery, taking part in war, the church as a community of the Spirit and not merely an institution, the role of leadership in the church, equity for roles of women, service rather than power as Christian responsibility, the present reality of the kingdom of God, and more. Willard Swartley describes this interpretative approach in *Slavery, Sabbath, War and Women.*

On the matter of power, as John H. Yoder says, Christians should not seek to run society from the top down, as has been the pattern since Constantine. Instead, we are called as disciples to work at reconciliation in roles of service and proclamation that confront people with the higher will of God. It is the role of the state to establish and maintain social order. The church's task is to offer society the means of redemption (1998:65ff.).

In contrast, Calvinist Lester DeKoster fails to understand the Anabaptist view of the separate roles of church and state and sees the position as a threat to the state: "The lawful use of force, in war, as well as in other ways, is the only alternative a society has to submersion in violence. . . . The Anabaptists were apprehended as seditious. At issue then, and now, is always the continuation of that order essential to social survival" (via *Kingdom, Cross, and Community*, ed. J. R. Burkholder, 155).

The christological view of hermeneutics means that with utmost seriousness we count Jesus as Lord of the Scripture. Jesus states his position clearly: "It was said, . . . but I say unto you" (Matt. 5). The writer of Hebrews put it precisely: "God spoke to us in the past by the prophets in little snatches here and there, but has in these last days spoken to us by his Son" (Heb. 1:1-3, trans. author). Jesus is *the* Word of God, the Logos, the One in whom we have the full knowledge of God's redemptive plan.

The good news we have to share is not an argument over the supremacy of the Bible against the books of other religions, though we believe that the Scripture is a unique disclosure of God. Instead, the good news is the message of the person of Christ, of his redemptive and reconciling work, and of his kingdom of grace. But what other book presents such a Reconciler?

The Scripture is not a message about a religion we hold; instead, it shares a conviction that God has laid hold of us. While religions reach "groping hands" to find God, the message of the Bible is the other way around: God has taken the initiative and reached out to us. Those who respond to his call through the Scripture escape from moral corruption and thus become "participants of the divine nature" (2 Pet. 1:4). God counts them as part of the very body of Christ (1 Cor. 12:27).

Thus we are reconciled to God in Christ, a people in grace. By God's grace to us, we have been enabled to turn from rebellion and enmity, and turn to fellowship with God. We have turned to walk with God in life, and thereby walk with him in a mission. God has acted to reconcile us to himself, and now gives to us the message and the ministry of reconciliation. We share the reality of the kingdom as "righteousness and peace and joy in the Holy Spirit" (Rom. 14:17).

We worship by singing our joy: "Hallelujah! what a Savior!" (P. P. Bliss). We witness by sharing this supreme good news with others. I have been a Christian for fifty-five years; in my personal testimony, Jesus is my Savior today, and he is saving me now from being what I would be without him.

3

Sovereignty as God's Self-Determination

Blessed be the God and Father of our Lord Jesus Christ, who has blessed us in Christ with every spiritual blessing in the heavenly places, just as he chose us in Christ before the foundation of the world to be holy and blameless before him in love. He destined us for adoption as his children through Jesus Christ, according to the good pleasure of his will, to the praise of his glorious grace that he freely bestowed on us in the Beloved. In him we have redemption through his blood, the forgiveness of our trespasses, according to the riches of his grace that he lavished on us. With all wisdom and insight he has made known to us the mystery of his will, according to his good pleasure that he set forth in Christ, as a plan for the fullness of time, to gather up all things in him, things in heaven and things on earth. In Christ we have also obtained an inheritance, having been destined according to the purpose of him who accomplishes all things according to his counsel and will. (Eph. 1:3-11)

IN THE LATE 1970s, I was strolling down a sidewalk in Philadelphia, toward an interview; I had been invited to consider an administrative position in a school of higher education. As I walked, I was talking with God and asking for his guidance in this matter. Suddenly I noticed some deep footprints in the sidewalk before me. Someone had stepped in the soft concrete when this sidewalk was being poured, and the prints were now fixed in the hard cement. I stopped and looked at them.

The footprints had been made by someone with rather small feet. I could not tell if that person was a woman or a man, young or old. But on one point I had no doubt: someone had stepped there. I looked up toward heaven and said, "God, there is a lot I don't know about you. There is mystery even while I come to you and claim you as my God. But of one thing I am sure: you have walked in my life, and today you are here."

I went on to the interview with the assurance of God's leading. The interview was positive, and the search committee recommended that the board appoint me. The appointment did not take place. Because I differed with several board members over my convictions on the priorities and pattern of peace, I felt led of God to withdraw. Twenty years later, it seems strange that a major decision was made on this point of difference, but I am sure that God's sovereign steps were there, and I followed them.

Some have said of our times that the world is experiencing the absence of God. Secular minds are wondering how Christians can believe in a sovereign God if this God is not using his sovereign power to correct the human predicament. Neither of these statements display an understanding of how a God of reconciling grace is at work in the world. Both of these positions, I believe, arise from an inadequate interpretation of divine sovereignty. If we interpret from authoritarian and deterministic assumptions, we will fail to answer the questions being raised.

In our work in the inner city, Washington, D.C., for fourteen years, I have found that many people misinterpret God's sovereignty as though it means "whatever will be, will be," or "if it is your time, you can't change it." This is a practical fatalism. We need to understand God's sovereignty as being more personal and less philosophical.

Such views are similar to a prominent cultural pattern I found in India, one that militates against planning and expediting work. The people of India have a common sense of fatalism; it leads them to accept the circumstances of life as inevitable, as a part of their karma. Hence, they may not adequately seize opportunities for industry and other economic achievement. Meanwhile, they believe in a multiplicity of gods, some 33 million, and lack belief in a personal God who is sovereign.

In our society, many who believe there is a personal God have some sense of his sovereign purpose, and they pursue life more aggressively. On the other hand, many of us here in the West miss opportunities of faith. We fail to walk with God in his power. Like the third man in the parable of the talents, we bury our possibilities and never take up God's challenge to live in his grace.

A story from El Salvador illustrates the perception of this God of grace. Some peasants were telling their visiting priest about their horrible suffering from those in power: rape, killings, and torture.

The priest listened to the group for a while and then cried out in empathy, "Where was God to let this happen?"

The peasants looked at him with surprise: "What kind of God are you talking about when you ask, 'Where was God?' The God we know has been right here, suffering with us!"

Recently our son, John, asked me to explain the difference between faith and superstition.

I tried to answer: "Faith is basically response to evidence based on factuality; superstition is built on interpretation of phenomena that, if taken as evidence, lack a factual base. Yet faith reaches beyond proof; if everything we believe can be proved, then we would have proved facts and need no faith. So faith means taking the evidence with a seriousness that projects its meaning for life."

He responded as a professional counselor. "I have a definition to suggest: Superstition is based on fear, and faith is based on hope."

"Yours is the better answer," I replied.

Paul writes to the Romans about the relation between faith and hope: "In this hope we were saved. But hope that is seen is no hope at all. Who hopes for what he already has? But if we hope for what we do not yet have, we wait for it patiently" (Rom. 8:24-25). Our hope is in God as revealed in Scripture, a God of sovereign grace.

For too long we have spent too much energy in debates between Calvinism and Arminianism, the Reformed and the Wesleyan, the Reformed and Lutheran and Anabaptist. Instead, we need to think together on how to present the majesty of God's sovereignty and the wonder of God's grace to a secular, fatalistic, and hopeless society. We need to find a biblical way to express God's sovereignty, a way that will make this wonderful truth more accessible to our society. I am not here intending to critique process theology or the more recent presentation of "The Openness of God." However, I am offering an interpretation that grows out of my own Anabaptist beliefs.

I prefer what I call a "Semi-Augustinian" view. With Augustine of Hippo, I take seriously human depravity and the primacy of divine grace. Yet I emphasize human freedom as our ability to respond to grace. This is an important balance for a society shaped by the subjectivism of experience, by the self-in-triumph movement, or by the therapeutic movement. Here is the basic concern of a Semi-Augustinian position:

By God's grace we are reconciled to God; God moves to us when we can in no way move to him; God himself makes "purification for sins" (Heb. 1:3). As a consequence of God's work of grace, God calls us to move next in response, to open ourselves to him, to join covenant in a reconciled walk with him.

Just as we cannot ask intelligent questions unless we first have some knowledge of the issue, so we cannot even ask good questions about God unless and until God gives us some answers. God's gracious movement to us makes possible our response-movement. This view holds together the sovereign action of God's reconciling grace on one hand, and human responsibility for the response and obedience of faith on the other hand.

Some do not count the sovereignty of God as a prominent theme; I appeal for us all to renew our understanding of the awesome holiness and transcendence of a sovereign God. The technological achievements of our time seem to have so elevated humanity that we exalt ourselves and minimize God. But in a world of material and technological achievements, we are still a broken society with broken relationships, ethnic rivalries, racial tensions, and violence. We are unable to make and live by covenant. We are guilty of perversions that elevate the sensual and practically exclude the spiritual—in the sense of what comes from God's Spirit.

For Christians to confront such a world, we need to redefine our beliefs and enrich our worship by acknowledging and restating the sovereignty of God. He is the "God of grace and God of glory," and in worship we bow before this God of glory, humbly recognizing the majesty of our transcendent God.

In the Reformation movement of the sixteenth century, the Anabaptists had a position before the Calvinist-Arminian controversy erupted over determinism and the sovereignty of God. The Anabaptists could not fit their understanding with either Arminianism or Calvinism. The position I am presenting here is not a view that was fully worked out in the sixteenth century; yet it appears to have been the working basis for this movement in its history. The early Anabaptist leaders were conditioned by Erasmian humanism, which emphasized human responsibility and freedom; nevertheless, this was set in the context of the sovereignty of God and salvation by grace.

The early educated Anabaptist leaders, for the most part, didn't live more than several years of the Reformation before being killed for their faith. Thus our findings are based mostly on records of disputations between them and various groups; we glean theological premises often by inferring them from their arguments. One remarkable series was the Frankenthal Disputations of 1571, with seventy sessions. The authorities allowed some Anabaptists freedom from prison to attend on the condition that while released they would not convert or baptize anyone.

There are several exceptions to the early martyrdom of Anabaptist leaders: Pilgram Marpeck (of South Germany and Austria) and Menno Simons (of the Netherlands) each served as a leader for a little more than twenty-five years.

Michael Sattler was an early voice in the Anabaptist movement and an influential leader. In 1527 he was burned at the stake at Rottenburg, on the Neckar River in South Germany. Sattler affirmed that "faith in Jesus Christ reconciles us with the Father and gives us access to him" (Yoder, 1973:22). He commented about God's sovereignty: "So good is God with his elect, that in all things he disposes for good out of his fatherly will" (93). Sattler believed that God in sovereignty calls whom he wills, "that according to his election, God places his seed in the heart of the elect, whereby they are brought to yieldedness and to the fear of God which moves the spirit of the children of God" (95-96).

Sattler stated the biblical affirmation of redemption through "the precious blood of Christ, through which alone we are washed, which alone is to be praised, through which alone we are redeemed for life, for resurrection and for the kingdom of God, through which we recognize the sovereign goodness and grace of God" (94-95).

As we relate with a postmodern society, we in Christian theology must review our approach in discussing the sovereignty of God. Through the centuries, belief in the sovereignty of God has been held as a basic tenet of Christian theology within the community of faith, from Paul to Augustine, Aquinas, Luther, Calvin, Grebel, Sattler, and on to Wesley and the present. Outside of the community of faith, reference to the sovereignty of God is often taken as a determinism. Our society sees a natural catastrophe as an "act of God" and judges God accordingly. If God is sovereign, society asks, why doesn't he correct the problems of disease and oppression, poverty, and violence?

I well remember my major professor, John Leith, stating in class at Union Theological Seminary (Va.), "God made this old world precarious so that we wouldn't find our security here." Accidents happen and catastrophes occur. Leith said this as an outstanding Calvinist scholar who believes deeply in the sovereignty of God. I am indebted to him for his exacting thought and for his respect for me in coming from another tradition. As we dialogued, we sought for clear and careful thought. Most of us need a renewal of faith in the sovereign activity of God in our world. History doesn't contain its own fulfillment; God will bring it to its completion.

Rather than thinking of God's sovereignty deterministically, we do better to think in personal terms: God is self-determined. God told Moses, "I WILL BE WHAT I WILL BE" (Exod. 3:14, NRSV note). Thus God acts from himself, from his own character, rather than in response to what we cause to happen in relation to God.

We can draw a parallel: Sovereignty in God is like self-determination in a person. God's actions are not capricious. They are consistent with his very self. Since God is a God of love, he does not violate or manipulate people, but is patient and long-suffering (2 Pet. 3:9). God respects human freedom to say yes or no to him.

There is some similarity in this to the position of those theologians who have written *The Openness of God* (Pinnock, ed.). The position I am advocating emphasizes human responsibility. I am not proposing that God himself is in a process of change.

What, then, of the power of evil in the world? In various ways, both God and Satan confront us. Yet we are not dealing with two Gods; Satan is at an inferior level and is not a second god, though some serve him as a god (2 Cor. 4:4). Further, Satan has been defeated by Christ in the cross and resurrection; he has no power in our life except what we give him (1 John 5:18). We should be careful not to give Satan too much attention. Our focus is on the Christ who has redeemed us.

Even here, as suggested by Abelard, the various forms of the ransom theory of the atonement place too much emphasis on the devil rather than on reconciliation with God. Evil itself is a parasite, living off the good. Evil self-destructs, even though it is constantly present as a perversion of the good.

If we could withdraw everything good, then evil left alone with itself is hell. God cannot prevent evil without violating the very love that respects human freedom for decision. Yet through the existence of evil, a sovereign God is speaking to the world. God is always breaking into human experience with the good; thus by contrast and effect, God is always exposing evil as it self-destructs. For the world to see, God exposes the nature of evil by placing in contrast his own expression of the good. God makes himself known in holiness, love, mercy, justice, and grace. This stands in direct contrast to all that is evil. It is also in contrast to the social problems of one-on-one violence, racial bigotry, genocide, and war.

To understand divine sovereignty, we must recognize God as God. He is sovereign. But this should not exclude recognition of human responsibility and accountability. God's sovereignty does not negate human choice or human responsibility for the consequences of those choices. A careful study of Jesus' life and work reflects not a deterministic view of sovereignty, but a personal and relational understanding of God. Jesus walked with the Father and sought his will. He drew on divine power, but never in ways that violated human personality; instead, he restored human personality.

Jesus' unusual miracles in relation to nature, turning water into wine, walking on the sea, healing the lame and blind, and raising the dead—these all were witnesses to Jesus being the great Creator among us. They showed that his creative power is self-determined and is the express nature of God. He did not use the sovereign power of God for selfish goals, for his own glory, but rather as a power that he appropriated to fulfill the work of God and to glorify the Father (John 5:30-47).

God moves to us in grace, calls us, and elects us in Christ to share eternal life. He extends his work of grace in our lives, thereby empowering us to do God's will and thereby show his sovereignty. God elects us to covenant, to a reconciled relationship in which we participate with him in his work. There is no power of evil that can prevent God from coming through to us when we offer even the smallest openness to him. "He will not break a bruised reed or quench a smoldering wick" (Matt. 12:20).

God's sovereign grace moves to us as light moves into the world; wherever there is the smallest crack or opening, the light moves through and enables all to see who will to see. God's choice to claim us for himself is a function of sovereign grace that calls forth faith in our minds and hearts. God's activity in our lives by the Holy Spirit is to make his sovereign power and presence personal and immediate.

From their theological systems, some judge that if a people are not Calvinists, they must therefore be Arminian. They believe that if a people cannot accept their idea that Christ died for a limited number of the elect, then they must be universalists who believe that his death saves all. I prefer a Third Way that avoids contrasting positions of what appears to be a determinism on one side, and unqualified freedom of the will on the other. Even before the Calvinist-Arminian controversy, the sixteenth-century Anabaptists stressed the primacy of God's grace and yet emphasized human freedom as a provision of God's sovereign grace.

This Semi-Augustinian position adopts from Augustine the strong emphasis on the primacy of grace; yet it also holds strongly to human responsibility, rather than seeing human response as completely determined by God, as Augustine appears to do. Semi-Augustinianism sees God's grace as primary: God moves first, and we can only move after and because God has moved. But because God has moved to us, and in us, we can and must respond by a decision that is personally made and owned.

This position is based on the above interpretation of God's sovereignty: God is sovereign and self-determined. God acts by his purpose and does not function by reacting to the choices or the preferences of humans. God functions from his own Being, from who God is, and from what he decides. God is not acting on the basis of what happens to him but on the basis of who God is in himself.

This very attribute makes possible God's patience. His act of extending to us freedom to respond to his self-determined actions is an essential aspect of God's sovereign love. God will not manipulate or violate a human personality but relates instead in calling and convicting. God's very sovereignty as self-determination means that he is not threatened by the decisions we make in the freedom God grants to us. Yet God's sovereignty provides a firm basis for our faith. God is to be trusted; he is eternally faithful. Our salvation is based on this faithfulness.

We should not take God's sovereign presence and activity in our lives as an authoritarian determinism but as the extension of God's authoritative purpose. God's overall purpose for the world will be carried through whether each of us identifies with it or not. Prayer is our recognition that since God does not violate personality, he is free to move in proportion to the way in which we recognize and honor him.

Here is one aspect of what it means to pray in the name of Jesus: We pray according to the will of God as well as in the merits of God's grace. Praying in Jesus' name is prayer that identifies both our creatureliness and his identification with the realm of the creature in self-giving love. Such prayer "moves the hand of God" because it gives God the freedom to move without violating us. Without our prayers, God would restrain his movement consistent with his love. He does not coerce or manipulate us.

A remarkable example of how prayer can affect God and his decisions is found in the account of Moses' vigorous prayer of intercession. It shows that "the Lord changed his mind about the disaster that he planned to bring on his people" (Exod. 32:11-14).

Augustine's *City of God* confronts us with the sovereign purpose of God in history: a God of grace takes the initiative and moves to and within us. Since Augustine believed that history is "going somewhere," he has been called the father of the linear view of history. Similarly, his *Confessions* confront us with the in-depth experiences of God's grace at work to liberate and restore a person. Here we meet Augustine as "the father of the psychology of Christian experience."

No other literature in Greek or Roman history compares with Augustine's thought. For over a millennium and a half, his theology has shaped the Christian church, Catholic and Protestant, by its emphatic emphasis on the primacy of God's grace. This stress is strongly affirmed by an Anabaptist theology clearly taking the grace of God to be the one ground on which we can come to God for salvation. God has moved to us in grace; now it is our move.

On this issue of freedom in our response, we Anabaptists are set apart from other Reformers: we affirm human freedom of choice rather than removing choice by a particular emphasis on God's sovereign grace. We do not see our response as in some way having human merit, but rather as enabled by God's effective grace moving to us. Our response is itself not a credit to us but is enabled by God's unfathomable and solicitous call of grace.

By speaking of God's sovereignty as his self-determination, we answer the question of those who seek to avoid their responsibility by saying "Leave it to God," for God is not a servant to humanity. This understanding of sovereignty places responsibility with us for our predicaments, the tragedies of human hostility and violence. Even the so-called acts of God in earthquakes and storms may sometimes result from our mismanagement of the earth and its resources.

The gospel gives an answer to the question of God's sovereignty as self-determination: the message of God's self-giving love. God has not withdrawn from the world. He is not, as the deists say, the Creator who simply set up natural laws and then withdrew to let the world take its own course and be determined by natural law and human actions. Nor can we say, as some death-of-God theologians, that we are experiencing the absence of God. On the contrary, God is acting and does act effectively where he is acknowledged, worshiped, and invited into the human situation.

By our faith-act, God is "released" to do what God has been wanting to do but waits until our response permits God's moving without violating his own integrity. God is just, and he does not contradict himself. Neither can we say that humanity has matured and now doesn't need to depend on God.

Some have tended to read Bonhoeffer this way: "Modern man has come of age and is able to cope with life without recourse to God" (1967). True, with our modern science we now explain many things that in previous years were simply attributed to God. We watch the satellite reports of movements of clouds and know when it will rain; this has often displaced our praying for rain. On the other hand, modern people may see the advancements of science as having removed the human tendency to turn to God for everything we need, using God as our "cosmic bellhop." Instead, we are called to turn to God because of who God is, because he is God and worthy of our loving obedience, which is our worship.

God is sovereign, the continuing Creator who through the Son sustains the world "by his powerful word" (Heb. 1:3). Jesus said, "My Father is still working, and I also am working" (John 5:17). The sovereign Lord God acts in creation, even allowing or arranging changes in nature to achieve his purpose; yet God primarily brings things to pass that will serve his long-range purposes for humanity. He acts much like a parent doing things for children far beyond their understanding or temporary choice, yet doing them for the good of the children. Their response is their own responsibility; likewise, we bear responsibility for our response to the actions of God and the resultant effects in our lives.

To live in a world where God is sovereign gives us security. It provides us with a basis for faith and enables us to accept God's promises that he will act for coming generations in the same "steadfast mercy" he showed for past generations. His sovereignty provides us with a basis for prayer; in prayer we seek the will of God and invite God to affect our lives.

God's grace (graciousness) is the extension of his unlimited love. God offers total self-giving love even at great cost, as demonstrated in the crucifixion of Jesus. God's love is an accepting, embracing, forgiving, and transforming work within our lives. Grace is God opening himself intimately to us and sharing our lives to the depth of saying, "Your problem is now my problem!" The more deeply we grasp this, the more ardently we sing, "Amazing grace! how sweet the sound, that saved a wretch like me!" (John Newton). God is Savior: my Savior because he saved me in the past, but also because he saves me now from being what I would be without him.

As noted, my wife and I had the privilege of being God's servants in planting a church on Capitol Hill, Washington, D.C., in 1981. Our fourteen years in the inner city brought us enriching and meaningful experiences. We had a chance to test everything we believed and had shared for fifteen years in educational work, and for the fifteen before that in pastoral and evangelistic ministries.

As we look back, we see God's sovereignty in the call to this role over against some other good opportunities for Christian work that were open to us. We see God's sovereignty in the timing. At that time people, unknown to us, were praying for a church in D.C. that would more adequately balance the evangelical and the social aspects of the gospel. During six months, several empty church buildings on Capitol Hill were sold; we were able to secure one.

Above all, God's sovereignty was evident in the development of the congregation. We structured our affiliation and identity with our Mennonite denomination but retained an open polity that allowed us to grow as a multidenominational congregation. God's sovereignty has been clearly visible as the Holy Spirit guided us in the creation of a membership covenant that enabled unity with diversity; we had an evangelical ecumenicity that went beyond many other ecumenical programs.

In our congregation, people could join by taking this covenant and be Mennonite or Presbyterian or Baptist or Free Church or Episcopal or whatever—each together affirming the same covenant. Our covenant also allowed more freedom of racial or cultural distinctions and tastes. We had an exciting and dedicated congregation, accepting the challenge that we shared freely from our diversity while expressing our oneness in calling.

In many ways, with the complex nature of our development, we were "with Christ in the school of prayer," for he taught us step by step as we walked softly before him. Under God's sovereignty we recognized the importance of prayer. It became for us communion with God, the means for us to discern God's will and identify with God's purpose. Further, we found that prayer moves the hand of God: as we pray, we give God the moral freedom to do things in our lives that in God's sovereign self-determining love he would not have done arbitrarily in violation of our personhoods.

God's love doesn't violate people; until we open ourselves to God, he waits to move in with personal changes. This does not obstruct God's sovereign work in convicting and calling us, or in arranging circumstances to move us toward reconsidering a course of action. God often shows his grace in and through the lives of others to motivate us to right decisions. But God's work toward and upon us is still limited by his respect for our personal response. God acts fully only when we invite him to work within us.

In many ways, we saw God work answers to prayer in the life of the congregation: clarification of our covenant of membership, study and development of our orders of worship, extension of community in small covenant groups, disciplines of the congregation in accountability, polity and calling of elders and of deacons, equitable calling of women and men to leadership roles, formation of a pastoral team, cooperation as a team, equitable involvement of people of various races in the fellowship, development of neighborhood ministries, involvement of members in an intercessory group, and more.

It is difficult to select illustrations, for the total life of the congregation was dependent upon the work of the Holy Spirit and under the sovereign grace of our Lord.

We experienced God's sovereign grace when Esther and I shared in a special service of anointing with oil for healing. Her brother Paul Kniss, with his wife, also an Esther, had been in mission work in Bihar, India, for forty-three years. On furlough several years ago, she developed arteritis, inflammation of the arteries in her head, a life-threatening condition. The doctors put her on a heavy dosage of prednisone that corrected the inflammation but caused her bones to become soft.

Back in India during the next two years, she suffered six compression fractures in her spine and was practically immobilized. The doctor told them that she would need to leave for the States. With great difficulty they flew home. In the next weeks she suffered two more fractures. After prayer and careful consideration, they called for an anointing service and shared their plan for this service with family and missionary friends. The result was four prayer meetings in different states at the same hour as we gathered for the anointing service with them in Harrisonburg, Virginia.

We proceeded with fear and trembling, feeling humbled in our request to God. We meditated on James 5:13-18 and administered the anointing oil in the name of the Father, Son, and Holy Spirit. To the glory of our sovereign God, he touched her body, and she began immediate progress. This was in the late fall; before the year-end, she was walking two miles a day. She made several trips to other States, and by the end of the next year, the two of them flew back to India for three months to complete their service and farewells.

Today Esther Kniss is doing remarkably well and has spent several months of service each winter in India. As we see her walking, even working in the garden, we can only praise God. I write this with some hesitancy, concerned that we see only the glory of a sovereign God in his healing grace.

Other implications of this interpretation of sovereignty impact our understanding as we study the Scripture. One illustration concerns how we interpret Romans 9–11, where Paul speaks of God's purpose as it relates to Israel. Most commentators see these chapters as a parenthesis in the epistle, as a deviation from Paul's main presentation of a theology of Christian experience. In his commentary on *Romans*, John R. W. Stott quotes many who see these chapters inserting another topic; they claim that one can smoothly move from chapter eight to chapter twelve. On the other hand, I maintain that these three chapters (Rom. 9–11) make up a unit that can well be entitled "Reconciliation."

With this premise, let us look at the different sections of Romans as salvation (chaps. 1–3), justification (4–5), sanctification (6–8), reconciliation (9–11), and consecration (12–16). Chapter 9 emphasizes the place of election in reconciliation: we are reconciled by God's grace, not by an ethnic tradition. Chapter 10 stresses the place of faith in Christ in reconciliation, showing that faith has always been the way into God's righteousness or right-relatedness. Chapter 11 highlights the place of Israel in reconciliation: God spoke through Israel as an avenue for "the reconciliation of the world" (11:15). This message of grace shows that in this manner "all Israel will be saved" (11:26; cf. Acts 15:15-18).

The emphasis of these three chapters is on the equity of grace in reconciliation. This illustrates how a theology of reconciliation influences hermeneutics.

A penetrating treatise of Paul's same argument appears in Ephesians 2:11-22. Paul explains Christ's purpose to "create in himself one new humanity in place of the two," making Jew and Gentile into "one new humanity." God does this to "reconcile both groups to God in one body through the cross," "thus making peace" (2:15-16). This is one of the most explicit passages supporting a theology of reconciliation and grounding reconciliation in the cross. In the cross, God has reconciled us to himself and to each other, and in so doing he has created a new kind of humanity with his gift of salvation.

As Paul says in Romans, "There is no distinction between Jew and Greek; the same Lord is Lord of all and is generous to all who call on him. For, 'Everyone who calls on the name of the Lord shall be saved'" (10:12-13).

A conviction of God's sovereignty does not mean that we can excuse ourselves from responsibility before God and our fellows. Instead, this means that as we walk with God, our actions are determined by our relationship with God. We share in his purpose and his work, and we do so with the conviction that "the one who began a good work among you will bring it to completion by the day of Jesus Christ" (Phil. 1:6). In thinking of God's sovereignty and self-determination, we recognize that the actions of his providence at work among us are determined by his holiness and love. In response, we can only join in praise with the words of Paul:

> O the depth of the riches and wisdom and knowledge of God!
> How unsearchable are his judgments and how inscrutable his
> ways!
> "For who has known the mind of the Lord?
> Or who has been his counselor?"
> "Or who has given a gift to him, to receive a gift in return?"
> For from him and through him and to him are all things.
> To him be the glory forever. Amen. (Rom. 11:33-36)

4

The Inbreaking
of the Kingdom

*Pilate entered the headquarters again, summoned Jesus,
and asked him, "Are you the King of the Jews?" . . . Jesus
answered, "My kingdom is not from this world. If my
kingdom were from this world, my followers would be
fighting to keep me from being handed over to the [Jewish
leaders]. But as it is, my kingdom is not from here." Pilate
asked him, "So you are a king?" Jesus answered, "You say
that I am a king. For this I was born, and for this I came into
the world, to testify to the truth. Everyone who belongs to
the truth listens to my voice." (John 18:33, 36-37)*

*After his suffering [Jesus] presented himself alive to [the
apostles] by many convincing proofs, appearing to them
during forty days and speaking about the kingdom of God.
(Acts 1:3)*

*Now I [Paul] know that none of you, among whom I have
gone about proclaiming the kingdom, will ever see my face
again. Therefore I declare to you this day that I am not
responsible for the blood of any of you, for I did not shrink
from declaring to you the whole purpose of God. (Acts
20:25-27)*

*[God] has rescued us from the power of darkness and
transferred us into the kingdom of his beloved Son, in whom
we have redemption, the forgiveness of sins. (Col. 1:13-14)*

ALL THROUGH HISTORY, God's acts engaging humanity in grace have been to create a people for himself. His reconciling work is a common thread in OT Israel and the NT church, the Judeo-Christian community. People of faith are serving the kingdom, this new order in which God rules. We believe God has made us into the greatest social reality in the world. Our directive is in Jesus' words: "Give therefore to the emperor [only] the things that are the emperor's, and to God the things that are God's" (Matt. 22:21). If we are clear about giving to God the things that are God's, there will be little problem about giving to Caesar (or any human government) those things that are Caesar's.

When we see reconciliation in the context of the kingdom of God, we are moved beyond a private piety to a sense of social responsibility. Spiritual experience, arising from our relationship with Christ in the Spirit, is both personal and social: we personally become disciples of Christ, and as such we share in the corporate body of disciples. In this kingdom relationship, we become aware of the social dimensions of the gospel, of the call to justice, equity, peace, and service in relation to others.

Reconciliation calls us to love our neighbors as ourselves, to seek the best for others, to move across all racial barriers, to assist the powerless and lift the fallen, to serve others in the love of Christ, and to share with them the meaning of life in Christ. When we seek justice for others, we extend the love of God in action. Justice is the action of love, the effort to correct problems in loving concern. The new humanity that the Spirit is creating includes the marginalized, the powerless, the suffering (Mark 2:15-17; Matt. 11:19).

During a three-month teaching stint in India, we learned a story that illustrates how membership in the kingdom of God leads to an altogether different lifestyle. Esther and I spent a wonderful semester teaching at Union Biblical Seminary, Pune, India. While there, she built a large sculpture of Jesus washing Peter's feet, and it became the visual center of the campus. One weekend we were invited to Madras to serve at the St. George Cathedral. After the morning service, we met the people and then were walking across the grounds with Bishop Azariah. Suddenly he stopped.

The bishop pointed across Cathedral Road to a rather large group of people, poor people, beggars, and lepers. He called our attention to a man with his young son, standing at the edge of the group: "You must meet that man; but let me first tell you his story."

This man was a shoe cobbler who sat on the sidewalk each day in the hot sun, repairing shoes. On a good day he might make as much as twenty-five rupees, seventy cents in U.S. money. One day someone left a baby girl at their doorstep; he and his wife took her in and raised her with their three children.

When the girl became a teenager, she left to find her mother, but returned pregnant. They took her back and cared for her. When the baby was born, they paid the hospital bill from their meager savings. He took her to his church, where she was baptized and the baby was christened. Later his wife died, and the young woman took the baby and left. Now he stood there with his youngest son by his side, a boy who was blind, and cared for him alone; he had sent the two older children away to a boarding school.

Bishop Azariah said, "One day I went to the staff here at the cathedral and said, 'Every day our friend sits on the sidewalk in the hot sun, at his work. Let's take up an offering for him, to build a platform to get him up off the sidewalk, and to put a shade over his head.' So we raised several hundred rupees, and I walked across the street to make the presentation.

"I said, 'My friend, we see you sitting here each day on the hot sidewalk under the sun's heat. Your friends here at the cathedral have taken up an offering to give you so you can build a platform, get up off the sidewalk, and put a shade over your head. Here are two hundred rupees to pay for it.' The man looked at me and said, 'Thank you, but no thanks.' Gesturing to the people near him, he explained, 'Just as soon as you lift me one foot above the sidewalk, my friends will no longer come and sit alongside me and talk.'"

I looked at the bishop and responded, "That is a louder sermon than the one I preached this morning." In the Western world, we are so caught up in status and success that we fail to give our association with others the significant place it deserves. Hence, we fail to be agents of reconciliation.

To be reconciled to God means that we have joined his family; God is our Father, and we are part of his movement. God is our one imperial Authority, the eternal King; his rule is extended into "time" and made a reality for us through our faith response. As we pray, "Thy kingdom come, Thy will be done on earth as it is in heaven," we participate in the reality of his rule, his kingdom now; we do this even though God's reign is to be completed and fulfilled with the return of Christ. For a world crumbling in anarchy, this is indeed good news: God is building his kingdom now, in each generation and from all peoples and cultures. Together we can live in the hope of a *telos* or culmination of God's redemptive mission.

We should take more seriously the words of Jesus: "Strive first for the kingdom of God and his righteousness" (Matt. 6:33). In doing so, we recognize that the kingdom of God is founded upon a covenant with Christ in a spirit of loyalty; it is not a nationalistic or institutional structure (Luke 17:20-21). Jesus announced the good news of the kingdom (Luke 8: l; 12:31-32; 16:16).

Paul went about preaching the gospel of the kingdom (Acts 20:25; 28:23, 31). He tells the church in Rome, "The kingdom of God is not food and drink but righteousness and peace and joy in the Holy Spirit" (Rom. 14:17). This order of life makes concrete the activity of God's kingdom in history. To the Colossians, Paul writes that God "has rescued us from the power of darkness and transferred us into the kingdom of his beloved Son"—a *present* experience (Col. 1:13).

We find a new awareness of the place of the kingdom in theology as we develop an evangelicalism with a sound theological position, not limited by the narrowness of Fundamentalism or washed out by the secularity of Liberalism. As John Howard Yoder has observed in *The Politics of Jesus*, much evangelical exegesis is raising the same theological and ethical issues also pondered by those who are reexamining Anabaptism.

To handle the question of authority in theology, we turn back to the Scriptures; here the Spirit confronts us with the person and claims of Christ. Christ is the one who announced the kingdom and who brings the reality of the kingdom into the world. We, his people, are harbingers of the new order inaugurated by Christ; his redemptive work makes possible a rule of God in our lives by his Spirit.

There is a basic dualism in the world: with Paul, we see the contrasts between the kingdom of the human "flesh" or self and the kingdom of the Spirit, the kingdom of light and the kingdom of darkness, the kingdom of good and the kingdom of evil, the kingdom of Christ and the kingdom of Belial, the kingdom of God and the kingdom of Satan (2 Cor. 6:14-18). The OT consistently presents God's rule as the primary frame of reference. Over against God's reign was the worship of idols, leading to demeaning and dehumanizing religious practices. In numerous settings, the OT shows the "Warrior God" overcoming the idols of Baal, of Ashtaroth, and so on, calling Israel to an understanding that God is One, and that there is no other (Deut. 6:4; Isa. 45:5-6).

In the NT, Jesus becomes this expression of the "Warrior God" overcoming the demonic. He triumphed over evil through the power of his life and the humility of his death, and he continues to empower his disciples in our triumphant battle. Our warfare is not carnal, but we have "divine power to destroy strongholds" (2 Cor. 10:4). Therefore, Paul says, "Put on the whole armor of God, so that you may be able to stand against the wiles of the devil. For our struggle is not against enemies of blood and flesh" (Eph. 6:11-12). Ours is a warfare of spirit, not of the flesh. "The word of God," using persuasion, is our sword rather than bayonets, guns, and bombs (Eph. 6:17; Heb. 4:12; Rev. 1:16).

Jesus was accused of being a tool of Satan. In response to his critics, he contrasted his reconciling and healing work with the evil work of Beelzebub, the prince of demons. Then he pointed out, "If it is by the finger/Spirit of God that I cast out the demons, then the kingdom of God has come to you" (Luke 11:20‖Matt. 12:28). At Calvary, Jesus defeated the enemy and overcame the demonic. Now we see Satan for what he is—not another deity in the world, but a defeated usurper who vents his hostility toward God through those who do evil.

God is unaltered as he continues to accomplish his redemption through the new life in Christ. His saving gospel is in contrast to the perversions of evil around us. Jesus "unmasked the powers" to show their weakness and perversion (Col. 2:15), and thereby has called us to live in this awareness, in freedom, not in fear.

Jude, a brother of Jesus, does not claim that sibling status as a credential in starting his epistle: "Jude, a servant of Jesus Christ and brother of James." Five times in this brief epistle, Jude refers to Jesus

Christ as Master and Lord. James likewise begins by referring to the Lord Jesus Christ, though he too was a sibling of Jesus. These men became heralds of the kingdom of the Messiah, convinced by the resurrection of Jesus from the dead. Jesus was their lead brother in a new family or kingdom.

John the Baptist came announcing the inbreaking of the kingdom of God and above all the presence of the King, Jesus the Christ. The nature of Jesus' kingship has raised basic questions for John, but Jesus points to his own works as demonstrating the rule of God. John asks, "Are you the one who is to come, or are we to wait for another?" (Luke 7:20). Jesus simply speaks to the character and quality of his kingdom ministry in serving the deepest human needs: "Go and tell John what you have seen and heard: the blind receive their sight, the lame walk, the lepers are cleansed, the deaf hear, the dead are raised, the poor have good news brought to them. And blessed is anyone who takes no offense at me" (7:22-23).

Jesus came announcing the gospel of the kingdom, the good news of the rule of God. His announcement and his life showed that the rule of God was ultimately important, not the rule of Rome, or the rule of the Sanhedrin. So today, there is one imperial mandate, that of our Sovereign Lord, and not that of the kingdoms of the earth. God's kingdom has priority, as Jesus says, "Strive first for the kingdom of God and his righteousness" (Matt. 6:33). When we are reconciled to God, we are reconciled to his cause and live by the rule of God. As followers of Christ, we are expressions of the inbreaking of his kingdom, in life with Jesus. Jesus is giving us a kingdom that cannot be shaken (Heb. 12:28).

Jesus came announcing "the good news of the kingdom" (Mark 1:14), but not only that. The synoptic Gospels each report on Jesus sending out the Twelve to proclaim this same good news of the kingdom (Matt. 10; Mark 6:6-13; Luke 9:1-6). Luke also tells of Jesus sending out the Seventy (Luke 10). In his preaching, Jesus emphasized the message of the prophets on justice to all and special compassion for the poor. He brought healing for the sick and the freedom of fairness for the marginalized.

In his inaugural address at Nazareth, Jesus quotes Isaiah: "The Spirit of the Lord is upon me, because he has anointed me to bring good news to the poor. He has sent me to proclaim release to the captives and recovery of sight to the blind, to let the oppressed go free, and to proclaim the year of the Lord's favor" (Luke 4:18-19). In the Sermon on the Mount, Jesus begins his ministry by proclaiming the gospel to the poor, especially in the Beatitudes. He makes a manifesto of the kingdom that includes all peoples (Matt. 5–7). We who share in his kingdom will continue his vision of love, equity, justice, and peace as our spiritual and social mission.

Jesus makes a striking statement of his vision for the future: "This good news of the kingdom will be proclaimed throughout the world, as a testimony to all the nations; and then the end will come" (Matt. 24:14). This calls us who believe in the return of Christ to be engaged in proclaiming the rule of God, a kingdom breaking in now but yet to come in its fullness. We refuse to be sidetracked into thinking of the kingdom in some organizational or structural form. Instead, we proclaim the kingdom as the rule of God, the ministry of the Spirit among us to actualize the rule of Christ (Luke 17:20-21).

Jesus says, "If I drive out demons by the finger of God, then the kingdom of God has come to you" (Luke 11:20, NIV). "I confer on you a kingdom, just as my Father conferred one on me" (22:29, NIV). This is a present reality, the gift of being a part of the people of God in a wicked and destructive world here and now.

In his ministry, Jesus is beginning to accomplish "God's futuristic purpose," as explained by Hauerwas:

> To begin to understand Jesus' announcement of the kingdom, we must first rid ourselves of the notion that the world we experience will exist indefinitely. We must learn to see the world as Israel had learned to understand it; that is, eschatologically, that is God's futuristic purpose. Though it sounds powerful and intimidating, in fact it is quite simple, for to view the world eschatologically is to see it in terms of a story, with a beginning, a continuing drama, and an end. . . . It is against this background that Jesus' announcement of the kingdom must be seen, for he came to announce an end that, while not yet final, nonetheless provided a necessary perspective for our continuing life in the world. (1983:82)

Let's look at Jesus' nighttime conversation with Nicodemus (John 3). When people refer to being "born again" (3:3, KJV) or "born from above" (NRSV), they often mean only an inner experience. Yet Jesus says we are "born" into his kingdom; in our new life, we come under the rule of God (3:3). Through God's Spirit, this new birth brings inner regeneration. It introduces us to a new and living relation with God, a quickening of new life in which we have a new Lord, a new heart or motive, a new purpose, a new identity.

Above all, there is a change from being self-centered to becoming God-centered. This new center or heart in one's life marks an onto-logical change (a change in the essence of one's person), a change from *eros* (self-satisfying love) to *agapē* (self-giving love). This change recreates in us the nature of true humanness. The new birth is the be-ginning of a life with God. It introduces us to the quality of being that God intended in the creation of humanity. We become members of a new communion, reconciled to God and to all others in God's family.

This kingdom is a spirit of life rather than an organizational enti-ty. The reality of the kingdom now becomes a key factor in deter-mining our behavior. Jesus tells Pilate, "My kingdom is not from this world. If my kingdom were from this world, my followers would be fighting to keep me from being handed over to the Jews. But as it is, my kingdom is not from here" (John 18:36). Jesus calls us to behav-ior marked by peacemaking and self-giving love rather than by vio-lence and self-defense.

This is a unique call for us to live as members of the kingdom of heaven, and thus to live a life of separation unto God in this world. A life of separation to God is thereby different from the world's pat-tern, with its "warring madness," even though we are still living in the world. We are "in the world" but not "of the world" (John 17:11-16, KJV).

Jesus lived a life in which everything he did pleased the Father (John 8:28-29); he manifested the kingdom through his life and min-istry. He asks us to love our neighbor as ourselves, and to love and forgive our enemies. This is the way of life by which he has lived; he fully intends for us to follow the same way. It is a life of nonviolence, with a spirit that does not try to get even. This is the only life of true freedom and joy.

Our local paper covered the arrest of a local neurosurgeon who was stalking a professor at a medical school. He thought the professor had delayed his admission to the school. Through the years, his bitterness ate at his spirit until, with a plot to kill the professor, he landed in jail and ruined his own life. There is no freedom in resentment, hatred, and violence. When we practice the teachings of Jesus, we have freedom to live in relationship with others, a freedom with mutual benefit. The kingdom introduces us to a new community of discipleship; in it we learn to relinquish our own self-interests and live for the good of the larger community.

The biblical good news of the kingdom, the gospel of Jesus Christ, brings people to eternal life. One of my associates and vice presidents at the Coalition of Christian Colleges and Universities, Karen Longman, spent a summer teaching English in Mongolia in 1992. She helped a woman read the Gospel of John and come to Christ directly from reading the Scriptures. This woman had no understanding of the teachings of Luther, Calvin, the Anabaptists, the Wesleys, nor the Pentecostals. The word of Scripture was effective. In reading about Jesus, she met the Master, the One who is King of kings and Lord of lords, our Savior, our Reconciler.

As we follow the first Christians through the book of Acts, the message is the gospel of the kingdom. Jesus, as risen Lord, met with the disciples over a forty-day period (a lengthy seminar) and spoke with them about the *kingdom of God* (Acts 1:1-8). Later Philip, one of the early evangelists, went to Samaria and "preached the good news of the kingdom of God and the name of Jesus Christ" (Acts 8:12, NIV).

Paul says that at Ephesus and in the surrounding areas, he preached the *gospel of the kingdom* (Acts 20:25). Paul writes of the kingdom in his epistles. He reminds the Colossians that God has transferred them from the power of darkness into the *kingdom of his beloved Son* (Col. 1:13). Paul also asks the Thessalonians to "lead a life worthy of God, who calls you into *his own kingdom* and glory" (1 Thess. 2:12).

When Paul finally reaches Rome, for two years he has his own rented house and is teaching those who come to him: "From morning until evening he explained the matter to them, testifying to the *kingdom of God* and trying to convince them about Jesus both from the law of Moses and from the prophets" (Acts 28:23). Acts ends on a positive note: Paul is "proclaiming *the kingdom of God* and teaching about the Lord Jesus Christ with all boldness and without hindrance" (28:31).

Augustine, the leading theologian and philosophical mind of the church in the fourth century, wrote of the two kingdoms in his treatise on *The City of God Against the Pagans*. He has creatively influenced Christian theology for 1,500 years. In the Middle Ages, the leading theologian was Thomas Aquinas, whose philosophical theology shaped the church in its quest to be an expression of the rule of God in society. However, Aquinas submerged the doctrine of grace under the doctrine and authority of the church.

It took a work of God in and through Martin Luther to bring the truth of God's grace to the fore again, as stated in the doctrine of justification by faith. Both Martin Luther and John Calvin emphasized the primacy of God's grace in calling and election, as God's act of creating a people for himself. At the same time, the strongly evangelical group of the Reformation, the Anabaptists, believed that the meaning of grace is not only forgiving grace in justification but is also transforming grace in reconciliation. They became witnesses to the kingdom that Christ is creating.

Anabaptists were evangelists to the populace in the Reformation period. Through their witness, thousands of people began walking with Christ. The Anabaptists taught a radical separation for those receiving the reign of God; this kingdom or rule is to be shown in the lives of those who are disciples of Jesus Christ. They emphasized what Paul calls the "obedience of faith" (Rom. 1:5), which others sometimes viewed as a righteousness of works. The Anabaptists stressed reconciliation with God in Christ, a teaching slighted by the Magisterial Reformation.

Some Reformers emphasized justification "by faith alone" and seemed to minimize Paul's words of a "faith working through love" (Gal. 5:6), as valued in the Radical Reformation. The Anabaptists had a strong stress on justification by faith and the assurance of salvation for the believer. This they held because they understood that God's work of divine grace acts to bring reconciliation. They had a clear conviction of God's faithfulness.

Robert Friedmann, a modern Austrian Jew converted to the faith of Christ, has written a fine chapter on "The Doctrine of the Two Worlds: Kingdom Theology" (36ff.). He identifies this emphasis on the kingdom as the heart of the "implicit theology of Anabaptism." Friedmann presents the biblical basis of their thought, with a special interest in the four Gospels and Jesus' teachings on the kingdom as formative for Anabaptist theology. I agree that the Anabaptists believed in the reality of God's kingdom in the present. They believed that even though they might die and not get to see its fulfillment, the kingdom would ultimately triumph.

The Schleitheim Confession (1527) shows that the Anabaptists held the present aspects of the kingdom or rule of God as a way of life: "Now there is nothing else in the world and all creation than good or evil, believing and unbelieving, darkness and light, the world and those who are [come] out of the world, God's temple and idols, Christ and Belial, and none will have part with the other" (art. 4).

Believers with this stance always live at the edge of civilization and are never captive to it. The Renaissance, the Enlightenment, and the scientific revolution—all that makes up our Western civilization—cannot be equated with the kingdom of God.

Our calling, as followers of Jesus, is to "strive first for the kingdom of God and his righteousness" (Matt. 6:33). One practical implication of this truth is that the Christian community, with all of its diversity, needs to join in the common cause of God's kingdom rather than spending so much time sparring with each other. Jesus says, "By this everyone will know that you are my disciples, if you have love for one another" (John 13:35).

In their book, *Resident Aliens*, Hauerwas and Willimon of Duke University call us to recognize that our highest loyalty is faithfulness to the kingdom of Christ and not to the orders of society. Believers have their identity as a personal and inner unity with Christ, yet their identity is also public; it is personal but never private. To know Christ is to know him as Lord of one's total life, living in the reality of his rule now, walking in the light of his ultimate goal, the purpose and fulfillment of history.

As Hauerwas and Willimon say,

There is no way to remove the eschatology of Christian ethics. We have learned that Jesus' teaching was not first focused on his own status but on the proclamation of the in-breaking of the kingdom of God, which brought an end to other kingdoms. His teaching, miracles, and healings indicate the nature and the presence of the kingdom. The Sermon on the Mount begins as an announcement of something that God has done to change the history of the world. In the Sermon we see the end of history, an ending made most explicit and visible in the crucifixion and resurrection of Jesus. Therefore, as Christians we do not begin our ethics with anxious, self-serving questions of what we ought to do as individuals to make history come out right, because in Christ, God has already made history come out right. The Sermon on the Mount is the inaugural manifesto of how the world looks now that God in Christ has taken matters in hand. And essential to the way that God has taken matters in hand is an invitation to all people to become citizens of a new kingdom, a messianic community where the world God is creating takes visible, practical form. (87)

In each period and culture, the church is to serve and express the larger meaning of the rule of God. As communities of the redeemed, we are heralds of the kingdom, a people who now live by its priorities. We affirm the lordship of Christ and his rule over and in his people. This kingdom is not, as Rauschenbush said, "Society organized according to the will of God." Instead, it is God's people living by the will of God, to accomplish his purposes. This is a new community within the larger society. We, the people of faith, are his church, a people who live under Christ's headship and are members of God's kingdom.

The understanding of the kingdom is diverse in Christian thought. Dispensational theology postpones the kingdom for the future millennium; Christ's thousand-year reign is counted as future (Rev. 20:4). In classical premillenialism, the fullness of the kingdom lies in the future millennium; yet there is recognition that we already live in the *eschaton* (last time), now sharing the reality of the future as we put hope in God's intention to complete what he has begun. In the amillennial position, the kingdom is present in the activity of Christ in the church, with no thought of a future millennium.

While early Anabaptists believed strongly in the present aspect of the kingdom, they also believed in a future *telos* (culmination) that will fully display the reign of Christ. In their writings, it is not clear whether they see this as happening on earth or as a celebration of Christ's victory when we are introduced into heaven.

I have developed the concept of a victory celebration that I call "transmillennialism," believing that there will be an actual reign of Christ, a celebration of his victory (1 Cor. 15:24). But this will be a spiritual rather than a material happening. It will be our celebration of the victory of Christ and our introduction into heaven. Just as Jesus' resurrection actually happened but was in nature beyond being solely material, so the *telos* or millennium may well be an actual happening but beyond the realm of the material.

The reign of Christ in the culmination of the kingdom may be the declaration of his victory before the hosts of heaven and the legions of hell (1 Pet. 3:19); that victory is not necessarily confined to this earth. The millennium as our Lord's victory and future reign may be taken as our orientation into heaven and the eternal order.

When we speak of the kingdom of God, we recognize that God expects us to understand and accept his sovereignty and the place he has given Jesus as Lord. Jesus came preaching the good news of the kingdom, and God has granted him a kingdom. In *The Politics of Jesus*, John H. Yoder presents us with the basic issue of Jesus' claim to be the one sovereign Lord. We cannot recognize his sovereignty without at the same time placing all other loyalties at a secondary level. As disciples of Christ, our lifestyle follows the teachings of Jesus, our guide for living; *this same Jesus* is now risen and exalted, and guiding us by his Spirit.

The phrase, "this same Jesus" is the bridge between the historical Jesus and the risen Christ (Acts 1:11, KJV; 2:33-36). It means that the teachings of the "earthly Jesus" are extended for all time by his resurrection and exaltation. As John Stott says in *Christian Counter Culture*, Jesus calls us to be a distinct people in society, people who live in the way of Christ.

We are to accept responsibility to be "resident aliens" in society, taking seriously Paul's words that we are "a colony of heaven" here on earth (Phil. 3:20). Paul also writes to the Romans, "Do not be conformed to this world," or as Phillips translates, "Don't let the world around you squeeze you into its own mold" (Rom. 12:2). Nonconformity to the orders of this age provides us with the freedom to be a people of God. Consider again the affirmation of Jesus to Pilate: "My kingdom is not from this world. If my kingdom were from this world, my followers would be fighting to keep me from being handed over to the Jews. But as it is, my kingdom is not from here" (John 18:36).

Nevertheless, many expressions of the religious community reflect the secular orders around us; we fail to be salt and light in society. In the film *Sargent York*, the commanding officer confronts York with Jesus' words that his kingdom is not from this world, or his servants would fight. York, the conscientious objector, replies, "That's just the point." Jesus' kingdom is other than our nationalism. We can and should be loyal to the nation to which we belong without surrendering to a nationalism that supersedes Christ's kingdom and justifies fighting.

In the early 1980s, I was serving as a pastor in Washington, D.C., and met with a group of church leaders for a New Year's retreat. In the group were Frank Gabelein, Carl F. H. Henry, Richard Halverson, and Ronald Sider. It was also near the time of the twenty-fifth anniversary for the magazine *Christianity Today*. In the conversation one participant asked Carl Henry whether there are any especially positive changes that he has witnessed in the evangelical church during this twenty-five years.

He immediately responded, "Oh yes, twenty-five years ago we weren't saying much about discipleship, and we weren't teaching about the reality and presence of the kingdom. A very important change is that today we are teaching discipleship, and we are speaking of the 'already' and the 'not yet' of the kingdom."

In late 1526 Michael Sattler, the South German Anabaptist leader, left the security of Strasbourg because he could not accept the union of church and state. In his letter to Martin Bucer, he made a special point of God's calling for Christians to separate themselves from the orders of the state, in fidelity to the one imperial mandate we have from our Lord. The church is the one body that is not bound by political lines, a body that can network around the world with peoples of all races, cultures, and nationalities.

Contemporary evangelicalism has become so closely identified with political agendas that we may lose our ability to evangelize. Our dalliance with political power may be our Achilles' heel in relation to the global mission to which we are called. If the gospel is identified with Americanism or any other nationality or ethnicity, it is heard as something other than and less than the "gospel of the kingdom of God" (Mark 1:14; Acts 20:25; 28:23, 31).

In the parable of the sower, Jesus teaches on the kingdom (Matt. 13:1-23). Jesus no doubt sees himself as the sower. He is a realist, knowing the different ways in which he will be heard. His point is that one keeps on sowing the seed, knowing that not all will grow and produce fruit. The parable emphasizes that we are responsible for how we hear of the truth and respond to it.

In his interpretation to the disciples, Jesus describes the hearers as types of soil: some people think only in safe and comfortable ways: "Love your enemy sounds good but won't work." Some think superficially, never challenging the assumptions that we live with; or they try to live on the emotional high of a special experience. Some think only through the grid of self-interests, of getting ahead, a lust for things, putting money first. Some few think openly, interfacing truth with the basic issues of our lives, understanding that in a secular age we should act on and by the gospel.

When we affirm the kingdom as God's rule, we take a faith-stance that God is at work in our midst, and that we are a people reconciled both to God and to one another. As a result, we take upon ourselves the responsibility to hear God in his Word, his Spirit, and his community, and to walk by his leading. We need to keep our identity and purpose in mind: "You are a chosen race, a royal priesthood, a holy nation, God's own people, in order that you may proclaim the mighty acts of him who called you out of darkness into his marvelous light" (1 Pet. 2:9).

In terms of the kingdom and reconciliation, we need to recognize that the kingdom of God is global, transcultural, transracial, transnational, crossing all lines and boundaries. The gospel of Christ and his kingdom is a universal message, calling people to walk with God in any and every culture. God keeps extending his kingdom in the world, giving or bringing the kingdom to us. Meanwhile, we the members of his kingdom work as agents of reconciliation, being a bridge between peoples and our Lord. We love them, pray with them, and share with them the good news of the kingdom of God in which they too can share. This is our privilege and our mission.

By way of summary, the kingdom is being expressed wherever the resurrected Christ rules. Second, the kingdom is the central aspect of God's plan for history, the reconciliation of all peoples into his purposeful community. Third, the kingdom is experienced as we undergo the transforming work of the Holy Spirit. As disciples of Christ, we should follow Paul's encouragement to "lead a life worthy of God, who calls [us] into his own kingdom and glory" (1 Thess. 2:12). We are called to live in fellowship with God and to walk in the will of God.

In the OT the presence of God led Israel as a pillar of fire by night and a pillar of cloud by day, giving visibility to the rule of God in life (Exod. 40:34-38). In the story, when the cloud lifted and moved, the people of Israel broke camp and moved; when it stopped, the people of Israel stopped. Day or night, the presence of God was evident in this pillar.

Since the Christ event and Pentecost (Acts 2), God's presence is now within us by the Holy Spirit. When we live by the rule of God, we live in the Spirit, to be led by the Spirit, to be surrendered to his sovereign will. Such a transformed people of God becomes the visible sign of God's rule, his kingdom present, even as we anticipate the "not yet" of its coming fulfillment.

5

Forgiveness in Relationship

*For to this you have been called, because Christ also suffered
for you, leaving you an example, so that you should follow
in his steps.*

*"He committed no sin, and no deceit was found in his
mouth."*

*When he was abused, he did not return abuse; when he
suffered, he did not threaten; but he entrusted himself to the
one who judges justly. He himself bore our sins in his body
on the cross, so that, free from sins, we might live for
righteousness; by his wounds you have been healed. For you
were going astray like sheep, but now you have returned to
the shepherd and guardian of your souls. (1 Pet. 2:21-25)*

IN 1974 it was my privilege to take part in the Lausanne Congress
on Evangelism, serving on the planning committee and with a work-
shop on higher education. By sharing with many wonderful Christians, I received far more than I contributed. One story I shall never
forget is that of Festo Kivengere of Uganda. On a Sunday afternoon in
the sports arena, he followed several other speakers, one a Christian
man from India, formerly a Hindu; and another a Japanese evangelist, formerly a Buddhist. Festo shared his heart-wrenching account
of social and political difficulty and the pain and cost of forgiveness.

On a traumatic occasion, Festo stood with Archbishop Janani Lu-
wum before Idi Amin. Then on February 19, 1977, the archbishop
was assassinated; Festo and his wife fled from Uganda. During the
night, they traveled through the mountains into a neighboring coun-

try, then flew to England. He told of how the Ugandan government of Idi Amin would not release the body of the archbishop for a funeral service. But thousands of believers gathered around an empty grave, celebrated the archbiship's faith, and affirmed their own faith in the resurrection.

For several days, Festo went to All Souls Anglican Church to meditate and pray. He wrestled at length with his bitterness toward Idi Amin. Finally he was able to ask God to forgive him of his bitterness of spirit. Then he asked God to enable him to forgive Idi Amin for killing his friend and for destroying the lives of so many believers in Uganda. As he came through the darkness to the light of Christ, he shared his victory in a little booklet, *I Love Idi Amin*. This is a dramatic testimony on the cost and freedom of forgiveness.

There is a cross in reconciliation. In fact, there is no reconciliation without the cross, for there is a cross in forgiveness. There is sacrifice in forgiveness, a sacrifice of self-substitution. The sacrifice of the cross is Jesus' self-substitution. Paul writes, "Christ our passover is sacrificed for us" (1 Cor. 5:7, KJV). There is no way for those estranged to come together unless a price is paid in the healing of that estrangement. At least one person must suffer for the reconciliation. This is grace: the giver pays the cost, and the other receives freely.

A theology of the cross is central to the Christian faith. Yet we need to set the cross in the context of God's continuing work. The cross laid bare what was in the heart of God from the dawn of creation: God's self-giving love. This quality and action of divine love extends through all time. We must ask about the meaning of the cross today, both in reconciliation with God and in reconciliation between peoples. Our global village has deep problems of alienation and estrangement in its ethnic and social fiber. It is critically important for us to receive and extend forgiveness through the suffering love of reconciliation.

Each of us must begin with ourselves. We must face honestly our sins that estrange us from God and from one another. Leon Morris has said, "Every man must have a mercy-seat, a place of propitiation" (via David Allan Hubbard, in Banks). This is the message of the cross, of God's mercy extending forgiveness, and of the reality of grace as we receive forgiveness. Reconciliation recognizes both the cost to God as he extends forgiveness, and what it costs us in honesty and humility as we receive forgiveness. Forgiveness is the most costly of all transactions and the most liberating. Forgiveness is at the heart of reconciliation.

A theology of reconciliation means an actual right-relatedness with God in and through Jesus Christ. Markus Barth says, "God is righteous and he makes righteous" (Rom. 3:26; 1964:88). This new relationship gives us assurance of salvation and results in the newness of life characteristic of a people in covenant with Christ. Such a right-relatedness goes beyond the rites of religion in a sacramental exercise, and beyond a creedal or theological confessionalism that is primarily a conceptual awareness.

A biblical emphasis on reconciliation focuses on a faith-relation with the risen Christ. He alone is our Savior. Christ alone is our Mediator, the one who mediates between us and God in representing us who are accepted in him (1 Tim. 2:5). In his mediation, he is fully identified with our humanness and fully identified with God; he mediates the divine to us as he gives us his Spirit. He mediates grace as he extends to us the full meaning of the finished atonement and our claim of being his inheritance now (Heb. 4:14-16; Eph. 1:18). God has given us to Christ (John 17:9).

It is important for us, children of God who believe deeply in "justification by faith," to note the context of this doctrine in Romans 5. We need to grasp the relationship between justification and reconciliation. Paul writes,

> Therefore, since we are *justified by faith*, we have peace with God through our Lord Jesus Christ, through whom we have obtained access to this grace in which we stand; and we boast in our hope of sharing the glory of God. (Rom. 5:1-2)
>
> If while we were enemies, we were *reconciled* to God through the death of his Son, much more surely, having been *reconciled*, will we be saved by his life. But more than that, we even boast in God through our Lord Jesus Christ, through whom we have now received *reconciliation*. (Rom. 5:10-11)

Similarly, Paul tells the Ephesian community that God chose us in Christ before the foundation of the world to become members of his family. We are to experience forgiveness through his blood and have a transforming relationship, so that we may be "holy and blameless before [God] in love" (Eph. 1:4-8). Forgiveness, in contrast to the emphasis of other world religions, is one of the more unique elements in Christian faith. Only in Christianity do we have a personal God who acts in grace to forgive and reconcile erring people to himself.

Uniquely, God takes the initiative; we do not make atonement to him, but God makes the atonement for us. God acts to reconcile us. God pays the price, the innocent suffering for the guilty. This is the nature and cost of forgiveness, the innocent One resolving God's wrath on the sin of another, bearing in himself the cost of that sin, and extending release to the other. This is grace at a cost to the Giver but not to the recipient.

All Christian theologies teach forgiveness as a unique aspect of Christianity, with a personal God forgiving in grace. Yet one does not often find forgiveness presented as a central interpretation of the atonement. Markus Barth writes, "What Paul calls justification, redemption or reconciliation is the same powerful event that is described as 'forgiveness' in other NT books" (1971:85). Paul explains this in his sermon at Pisidian Antioch: "Through this man forgiveness of sins is proclaimed to you; by this Jesus everyone who believes is set free from all those sins from which you could not be freed by the law of Moses" (Acts 13:38-39).

According to T. H. Hughes, "in the NT the basic idea of the Atonement is that of reconciliation" (312). Vincent Taylor agrees: "The best NT word to describe the purpose of the Atonement is Reconciliation" (146).

Albrecht Ritschl also shares this insight: "Nevertheless, the conception of reconciliation has a wider range and greater definition than justification or pardon, namely, that the person who is pardoned actually enters upon the relationship which is established" (78). This is the freedom and joy of the experience or relationship of salvation. The more comprehensive aspect of forgiveness is reconciliation, the completion of a reciprocal harmony with "the removal of contradiction to God" (79). Forgiveness is grace effectively bringing about mutual fellowship between God and humanity.

James Oliver Buswell is another theologian who recognizes the centrality of forgiveness in the atonement. He fails to systematically interpret the atonement from this premise. Yet he does make an important statement that expresses the truth in a nutshell:

> The scriptural doctrine of the substitutionary atonement should be conceived of in terms of the forgiving act by which the party sinned against voluntarily accepts the direct consequences of the sin and chooses to bear these consequences in the place of the party who commits the sin. It is my contention that in every case of genuine forgiveness (not mere politeness) the offended party bears the direct evil consequence of the sin committed against him. (2:104)

This view corresponds to my thesis, that the offended one resolves his own indignation about the sin of the offending one, and corrects the relationship in healing love. As Buswell says, "In the course of justice, it is impossible that a third party, not concerned in the sin, could bear the punishment in the place of the sinner" (2:105-106). God himself was in Christ, reconciling the world to himself (2 Cor. 5:19). God has acted in Christ, giving himself for us, in a suffering love.

Leon Morris deals with this in a careful biblical study on reconciliation: God as the offended one acts to reconcile those who are his enemies, doing so in a love that carries in itself God's wrath on sin (1955:186f.). The good news of the gospel is that through the cross, God has acted out of his own initiative to overcome our hostility and thereby remove the enmity (Eph. 2:14-15).

In *An Ethic for Enemies*, Donald Shriver draws on a modern Jewish secular political philosopher, Hannah Arendt, who believed that forgiveness is learned in a community. She saw this as "basic to the ethical teachings of Jesus," and she "credited him and his imitators in the early Christian movement with the 'discovery' of the indispensable role of forgiveness in processes of social change" (34-35). Shriver comments,

> Even if Jesus was not the "discoverer" of the place of forgiveness in human affairs, it came into new prominence in his teachings, and it acquired very practical, prudential connotations. Among the practicalities was what forgiveness does to ensure the continued existence of a fractured human community. (35)

Referring to the Middle Ages, Shriver speaks of the "Sacramental Captivity of Forgiveness." After 1500, Martin Luther experienced the church as a congregation of forgiven sinners, even having political implications, with a "theology of the spiritual 'liberty of the Christian man'" (Shriver: 53).

However, I see problems with Luther's understanding of the two kingdoms: Luther failed to set the kingdom of God above the kingdoms of the world. God's kingdom has an authority guiding believers as they sort out options in the secular and political orders. Disciples of Christ should give their highest loyalty exclusively to the kingdom of God. Yet as Shriver points out, Luther did recognize the place of forgiveness in social and political interactions. Shriver correctly focuses on the civil rights movement as an illustration of this in action.

Alan Paton's novel *Cry, The Beloved Country* was first published in 1946, just before unofficial apartheid became official in South Africa in 1948. The novel comes to its conclusion with the grief of Stephen Kumalo, whose son was to be executed for murder. He speaks of his fellow black South African Msomango, "who had no hate for any man" and who once said, "I have one great fear in my heart, that one day when they turn to loving they will find we are turning to hating" (via Shriver: 226).

From my own trips to South Africa, observing changes in the 1960s and 1970s, I have been amazed at God's answers to prayer in the gracious spirit of Nelson Mandela. He has not given way to resentment; he has found the dynamic freedom of forgiveness.

President Bill Clinton has told of awakening his daughter to watch on TV the momentous occasion when Nelson Mandela was released from prison. He told Chelsea that this was a historic event and that she should not miss it. Clinton observed a flash of anger on Mandela's face as he stepped out and looked at the people gathered. Then the anger disappeared. Years later, as presidents of their respective countries, the two men met, and President Clinton mentioned this to Nelson Mandela: "I want to ask, is it not true that I witnessed anger on your face, and then that it disappeared and has not returned?" Mandela replied,

> Yes. In prison I went to a Bible Study conducted by the son of a prison guard, and I made a commitment to Christ. Through this I

became a free man though a prisoner. That day, as I walked out of prison and looked at those faces, suddenly anger welled up in me at the thought of what I had been robbed for twenty-seven years, and then the thought came to me, "I was free when I was your prisoner, and now that I am free, I will not be your prisoner."

In resenting injury, we must not turn to vengeance. Instead, we are called to forgive and seek the positive course of action that the concern for right lays upon us. The work of any community is to discern how its members should hold justice and mercy in common, and then pass patterns of justice and mercy on to the future community. As Oliver O'Donovan says,

> Resentment of injured right must express its concern in effective action, which is to say, it must become vengeance; but vengeance cannot be just unless it renounces its character as purely private satisfaction and allows itself to become the matter of public judgment. Might, when it has not surrendered its coercive operations to the control of the public interest, is a damaging aggression upon community life; but the public interest itself is arbitrary and tyrannous unless it gives first place to the righting of wrongs. (129)

Justice that is punitive without reconciliation is little short of tyranny. Authentic justice seeks to correct the problem.

Paul instructs us to refrain from vengeance: "Vengeance is mine, I will repay, says the Lord" (Rom. 12:19; Deut. 32:35). Only God can deal with wrongs in the full meaning of righting the wrongs. Through Jesus, God righted wrongs at Calvary; in that public event, God confronted the world with his self-giving love and set things right—an action "effective through faith" (Rom. 3:23-26).

In correcting the problem, God is just in justifying the one who turns to Jesus. This is an aspect of the cross that takes on additional value for the global community today. Increased tensions between people are often stimulated by population increase, inequities of urbanization, and violence between ethnic groups.

Today many Christians find it difficult to understand the cross and its significant place in atonement, or to grasp reconciliation between us and God. Some see the cross only as the martyrdom of Jesus and speak of him as the first Christian. Others see the cross as the inevitable consequence of the clash between Jesus and the religious and political powers of his day. Still others see the cross as the price love always pays in suffering at the hands of those who live by the pursuit of power and control.

The Christian faith, however, has always seen the cross on one side as showing God's self-giving love, and on the other side as expressing humanity's sin in rejecting God. Among the numerous theories of the atonement, there is general agreement that at the cross, God was in Jesus, acting on behalf of humanity; in Jesus, humanity was put to death as the consequence of sin.

In the sixteenth century, Michael Sattler's tract "Concerning the Satisfaction of Christ" treats implications of the *satisfaction theory* of the atonement. He does not deal with how Christ made satisfaction for us with God, but rather with who benefits from this satisfaction. Sattler does not promote universalism or claim that all people are redeemed whether they respond in faith or not. Instead, he presents the view that there is a universal sufficiency, but it is efficient only in the lives of those who identify with Christ by faith. Rather than forgiveness being merely a forensic pronouncement (legal arrangement), as taught by many of his Protestant contemporaries, Sattler emphasizes that forgiveness is experienced in a faith identification with Christ (Yoder, 1973:108-119).

In *The Problem of Social Responsibility,* J. Lawrence Burkholder comments on the biblical basis for the Anabaptist conviction of an ethic of nonresistance as applied *agapē*-love:

> Clearly the gospel of redemption is first in the minds of the Anabaptists. Their starting point is the activity of God which was culminated in the historical event of the cross. . . . It is the response of the disciple who owes his salvation to Christ. It is the life of faith and gratitude. It is freedom to love, having been loved by Christ. . . . The active life of following Jesus and preaching the way of love was simply the inseparable result of reconciliation with God. (1989:63-64)

Most explanations of the atonement have failed to recognize the active dynamism of forgiveness and its cost as the essential in reconciliation. We can identify several prominent explanations:

• The *ransom theory*, given a more universal form in Gustav Aulén's *Christus Victor*, is the victory of Christ over the demonic in his death and resurrection.

• The *substitutionary theory* of Anselm presents Christ as the substitute for us in suffering death, as the consequence of sin.

• The *moral influence theory* of Abelard, in various forms, shows how the self-giving love of Christ as our supreme example calls the human spirit to respond to God in love.

• The *governmental theory* presents God as the Lawgiver, bound by justice to punish those who violate the law.

• The *dynamistic theory* is Christ's in-your-face confrontation with evil, a contemporary interpretation of the ransom theory.

• The *relational theory*, which I propose, affirms that the cross acts to extend reconciling grace to us. This explanation combines several of the concepts listed above, yet with the dynamic of forgiveness being the central aspect of the atonement. This relational theory is similar to what H. E. W. Turner, in *The Meaning of the Cross*, calls the "personal view" (59f.). It more clearly emphasizes reconciliation, that we who have gone astray have now returned to the shepherd and guardian of our souls (1 Pet. 2:24-25).

In this relational theory, Jesus took all that evil could do to him, yet spoke back to the human agents the words of forgiving and reconciling grace. The "mercy seat" is recognized as the OT model for reconciling love (Lev. 16; Rom. 3:25; Heb. 9:5). On a deep level, the self-giving Savior substitutes himself for sinners. He releases us from the power of the demonic and overcomes evil in the spirit of loving forgiveness. Jesus expresses God's love even to death, in forgiveness. He deals with sin in a justice that doesn't ignore it but sets up a real in-your-face confrontation with evil.

Paul says this is for all who believe: "They are now justified by his grace as a gift, through the redemption that is in Christ Jesus, whom God put forward as a sacrifice of atonement by his blood, effective through faith. He did this to show his righteousness" (Rom. 3:24-25). The cross combines the OT picture of the sacrifice and of the mercy seat, on which the blood of the sacrifice is sprinkled. The cross is the one place where God meets us in love that is just, dealing directly with our sin, and where we meet God in honesty, confessing the full nature of our sin as antagonism toward God.

The cross is the sublime demonstration of God's love, of God's grace, of God's character. His supreme act of grace is his self-giving love even to death. Here we are faced with the plan and pattern of the ages. Jesus is described as a Lamb slain before the foundation of the world (1 Pet. 1:20). Before creation, God chose to confront and overcome evil by the qualitative superiority of holiness and love. The cross is the grand exposé of all time: God was overcoming evil with good, exposing its perversion, in contrast to the quality of his love. The cross is God's timeless word to an unforgiving world, a word that transcends all cultures and times.

One of the most striking passages on the power of the cross is in Ephesians. Speaking to both Jews and Gentiles, former unbelievers and now believers, Paul claims Jesus Christ as our peace:

> He is our peace; in his flesh he has made both groups into one and has broken down the dividing wall, that is, the hostility be- tween us. He has abolished the law with its commandments and ordinances, that he might create in himself one new humanity in place of the two, thus making peace, and might reconcile both groups to God in one body through the cross, thus putting to death that hostility through it. So he came and proclaimed peace to you who were far off and peace to those who were near; for through him both of us have access in one Spirit to the Father. (Eph. 2:14-18)

Here reconciliation is clearly grounded in the cross. Reconciliation changes our relationship with God, and reconciliation is a power for social change: Christ makes Jew and Greek into one new humanity. Reconciliation creates a new peoplehood and provides a new fellow- ship in the Spirit. Reconciliation is not just individuals being recon- ciled with God; there is a crucial social dimension. The ultimate goal of reconcilation is a community of love, as God's people. Forgive- ness, reconciliation, and the cross are basic to the struggle for justice and restoration of relationships (Volf).

Christ has reconciled us by his blood at the ultimate cost to him- self. There is nothing shallow about the nature of God's salvation as forgiveness. This sacrifice is so sublime and yet so costly that we can never fully comprehend it. At best, forgiveness, the most costly and most difficult thing in the universe, is not fully grasped or adequately understood in the church. It needs to be shared as the good news of reconciliation in grace. Forgiveness is not simply a pronouncement of release; it is not something we receive and then run away with to keep for ourselves, nor is it something we can possess. Forgiveness is always in the context of relationship.

Forgiveness is the innocent one accepting one's own wrath at the sin of another and smothering that indignation in love. Forgiveness reconciles and releases people; it creates a new identity, a new relationship, a new lifestyle. Forgiveness renounces any quest to control another's life, but stands with the other and offers to help the other at personal cost. God does this in his forgiving love, expressed at the cross but extended in all time. In the cross, God has opened himself fully, personally, and intimately to us. The only genuine response for us is to open our lives intimately to him.

This emphasis and understanding of forgiveness explains my interpretation of the deeper aspect of the substitutionary meaning of the atonement. The focus is not on substitution as God judges, but on a self-substitution by God in forgiveness. *At-one-ment* (atonement) is the reality of the reconciling grace of God, at great cost to himself, in which he substitutes himself (through his Son) in suffering for us, in our stead.

Paul says, "In Christ, God was reconciling the world to himself." (2 Cor. 5:19). Charles Wesley catches the wonder of this in a hymn:

> And can it be that I should gain
> An interest in the Savior's blood? . . .
> Amazing love! How can it be
> That Thou, my God, should'st die for me? . . .
> 'Tis mercy all, immense and free;
> For, O my God, it found out me.

The substitutionary theory of the atonement is not to be discarded as an out-of-date view; it needs to be reinterpreted with contemporary understandings of self-giving love.

When believers receive God's love in faith, they enter a new way of life, in right relationship with God, as James Denny says:

The deepest thing we can ever know about God is that there is love in Him which bears in all its reality the sin of the world. And there is nothing superficial in what the NT calls faith, in its relation to this ultimate truth in God; on the contrary, faith exhausts in itself the being of man in this direction; it is his absolute committal of himself forever to the sin-bearing love of God for salvation. It is not simply the act of an instant. It is the attitude of a life; it is the one right thing at the moment when a man abandons himself to Christ, and it is the one thing which keeps him right with God forever. It is just as truly the whole of Christianity subjectively as Christ is the whole of it objectively. (291)

Redemption means that God has claimed us as his own, thereby releasing us from other contracts; now we are engaged in a covenant with God. The word *ransom* (*lutron*) appears in Mark 10:45: "The Son of Man came not to be served but to serve, and to give his life a *ransom* for many." The meaning of the root word is "to loose, loosen." The verb *ransom* (*lutroō*) occurs ninety-nine times in the Greek translation of the OT.

Yahweh is called "Redeemer" (Hebrew: *go'el*) thirteen times in Isaiah alone (as in 41:14). The related verb characterizes God's action in various passages: "I will redeem you with an outstretched arm" (Exod. 6:6). "With your strong arm you redeemed your people" (Ps. 77:15/16). This means that God delivers, with an "underlying thought of payment" (Morris, 1955:11, 17).

A sacrifice or substitute payment is a ransom price (Hebrew: *kopher*) for lives that are forfeit (as in Exod. 30:12; Job 33:24; Ps. 49:7-8). In Isaiah 43:3, God gives Egypt as the ransom price for his people. Thus we understand Paul's statement: "Our paschal lamb, Christ, has been sacrificed" (1 Cor. 5:7). As (Greek) *lutron* translates *kopher,* it means a substitute gift that covers a debt.

In Christ, we have God's act of self-substitution in dealing with our sin by extending expiation; God rescues us from living under his wrath and the power of darkness, the painful consequences of our wrongdoing (Rom. 1:18-32). God "has . . . transferred us into the kingdom of his beloved Son, in whom we have redemption, the forgiveness of sins" (Col. 1:13-14; Morris, 1956:9-59, 125-185).

The redeemed belong to the Redeemer, as shown in the account of

God's claim on the "firstborn" after redeeming them from slavery in Egypt (Num. 3:33-51). This remarkable story deals with one of the deeper aspects of the atonement, of redemption. God has redeemed the firstborn sons by instituting the Passover, in which the slain lamb's blood (symbol of life) is placed on the lintel and doorposts of the house. Painting the lintel and doorposts with substitutionary blood is a step of faith that God will do what he has promised. Seeing the blood, God's destroying angel will pass over that house, and the firstborn son will be saved from death (Exod. 12:22-24; cf. 2 Sam. 24:16).

Thus it happened; God spared the firstborn among the Israelites. Later, at Sinai, God informed Moses that the firstborn belonged to him: the redeemed belonged to the Redeemer.

In Numbers, God asks Moses to have Israel number the Levites, then to number the firstborn, and to make a trade. The Levites number 22,000, and the firstborn number 22,273. God negotiates the trade and sells the extra 273 to Israel for a price. This dramatically illustrates that the redeemed belonged to the Lord. The Levites now belong to him as priests, always a reminder that to be redeemed is to belong to the Redeemer.

In a similar way, we are redeemed by Jesus to be a "kingdom of priests," "a holy nation" (Rev. 1:6; 5:9-10; 1 Pet. 2:9). Again, the redeemed belong to the Redeemer. This understanding contrasts with the classical *ransom theory*, which focuses more on being bought from Satan than on belonging to the Redeemer. We are basically redeemed from our self-orientation, our self-centeredness compounded by the power of darkness, to belong to God in the freedom of grace.

As in this OT story of the firstborn, so Paul says to the Corinthians, "Do you not know . . . that you are not your own? For you were bought with a price" (1 Cor. 6:19-20). We now belong to the Redeemer. We have been brought into a covenant relationship, and in this relationship of intimacy, the Holy Spirit indwells our very selves. As indwelt by the Spirit, we are participants in the body of Christ with all other such Spirit-indwelt believers.

Special expressions of reconciliation appear in Israel's order of worship, set up later for the tabernacle rites. God prescribed significant rites for the Day of Atonement (Lev. 16): The high priest is to cast lots on two goats, present one as a sin offering, and present the other as the "scapegoat" of expiation (16:7-10, KJV). The high priest places his hands on the scapegoat's head and confesses the sins of the people; then this scapegoat is led into the wilderness and released to bear away their sins (16:21-22).

This symbol has received significant attention in theology, especially through René Gerard's writings: Jesus brought the process of scapegoating to an end. Some theologians regard this as the essential element of the cross, of the atonement wrought by Jesus' death; he became the final Scapegoat, and there is no other sacrifice for our sin.

God initiated the atonement: the offended One acted in forgiving love to reconcile the guilty one. As Paul says,

> God proves his love for us in that while we still were sinners
> Christ died for us. Much more surely then, now that we have
> been justified by his blood, will we be saved through him from
> the wrath of God. For if while we were enemies, we were recon-
> ciled to God through the death of his Son, much more surely,
> having been reconciled, will we be saved by his life. (Rom. 5:8-10)

The very fact that our salvation is tied not only to Christ's death but also to his life is in itself an affirmation of the positive ongoing aspect of this salvation as reconciliation with our Lord. Forgiveness establishes a new relationship, it removes the enmity, it engages us in a covenant of grace.

The reconciling power of forgiveness is made visible in a new dimension of human relations in the grace of God. There is no meaningful relationship possible between us fallible, sinful people without forgiveness, and there is no forgiveness without the innocent suffering for the guilty. This is true in marriage relationships, in parent-child relationships, and in friendships at all levels. None of us is perfect, and when we offend, the relationship is strained unless the other forgives us. In this forgiveness, we become participants in the love that suffers for us, or else the potential for reconciliation is missed. The substitutionary aspect of the atonement thus needs to be perceived from the more contemporary views of personhood and the psychology of relationships.

Too frequently some Christians think of the death of Christ as almost an economic transaction, a barter. Instead, we need to consider this more relational view of the atonement. The innocent one carries his own wrath over the sin of the guilty one and resolves it in love. Forgiveness frees the guilty, but at a cost to the forgiving One. God's forgiveness releases us to be free, but at a cost that God carries in himself. At the cross, Jesus in essence said, "Your problem is now my problem." He took into himself the problem of our sin, our rebellious estrangement, even to his death.

Soon after my wife and I moved to Washington, D.C., to plant the church on Capitol Hill, I had an interesting encounter with a man on the street. He was sitting on a bench, and I stopped to chat. Suddenly he asked, "Are you a preacher?"

"Yes," I replied.

He almost sneered: "What difference does it make in my life that Jesus died on a cross two thousand years ago?"

I looked at him, thinking of the theories of the atonement I had studied in theology. Then I asked, "Do you have friends?"

"Of course I have friends," he replied.

"If one of them is in trouble, what do you do?"

"Why, I help him out."

"But what if it gets difficult?" I pressed.

"You hang in there!"

"But what if it gets really difficult? When can you cop out?"

"Man," he said, "if he's your friend, you never cop out!"

I smiled. "God came in Jesus to be our friend. We were in deep trouble, but he hung in there with us. When could he cop out?"

The man looked at me in silence. Then it was as though lights went on in his eyes: "Is that why Jesus had to die?"

"That is one reason."

The man got up, squared his shoulders, looked at me with a smile, nodded, and walked off down the sidewalk. I watched him go and told myself, "He may not know it, but he has just been evangelized. One can never get way from the impact of knowing that God says, 'Your problem is my problem!'"

Sattler (as noted above) asked who rightfully grasps the meaning of the death of Christ. That meaning is experienced by a faith that brings us into a personal reconciled relationship with Christ. The Lutheran theologian-martyr Dietrich Bonhoeffer voiced a similar concern by contrasting "cheap grace" and "costly grace" (1951). When we presume on God's grace, we fail to understand it as his gracious acceptance of us in extended fellowship.

Forgiveness only functions within a relationship; forgiveness liberates the guilty for fellowship with the forgiving one. There is no such thing as release from guilt without reconciliation. Forgiveness is authentic only when it brings about reconciliation. It is never something we receive without response; we may not selfishly claim to have our guilt absolved without relating to the forgiver. Forgiveness is reconciliation, not simply getting rid of one's guilt.

To enjoy forgiveness, we must come back to God. As in the story of the prodigal son, God waits with outstretched arms to forgive and move beyond our offending actions. God is a Father who looks beyond the issue to the person. God would rather have us with our past and forgive us than not to have us at all.

This awareness calls us to distinguish sin and sins. Our basic sin is that of rebellion against God. This rebellion is corrected as we answer the evangelistic call to be reconciled to God by faith in Christ. But our sins show the perversions in our lives. These are not all instantly answered in the evangelistic call; they require the actions of sanctification, as we practice discipleship. Such a discipline uses the therapies of worship, nurture, and a loving community, often including therapy with counseling by trained professionals. Grace is always immediately available through the Holy Spirit in us and for us, and within the body of Christ.

As I have stated, Jesus as my Savior saves me today from being what I would be without him. Salvation is not just a matter that I have experienced; I am reconciled, and I am experiencing changes that are still enabled by his transforming grace.

We are "called to belong to Jesus Christ" (Rom. 1:6). It is a relationship of covenant, a reconciliation that issues in an "obedience of faith" (Rom. 1:5; 16:26). This covenant, correctly understood, is a relationship in grace, not a "work righteousness" seeking to merit God's acceptance. Instead, it is a walk in the righteousness or right-relatedness we are given in Christ. We do not deserve or merit relationship with God. Yet Christ accepts us in his love and reconciles us with the Father.

This relational concept of righteousness will move us beyond a legal or forensic view, and beyond a view of imparted righteousness, as though righteousness is an "it," something static. The Scripture says that God took the faith Abraham had and counted it in place of the righteousness he didn't have; this faith became the dynamic of the new relationship. Paul writes of this in Romans 4: salvation by faith is seen in the way Abraham shared God's grace by faith before rites of religion developed (circumcision), before deeds of good works were performed, and before the law was given.

Paul's readers might say, "Yes, but once the law was given, salvation came through the law." Paul has an answer: See how God treated David, king of Israel. When David had Uriah killed so he could take his wife, Bathsheba, he should have been condemned by the law. Instead, he was saved by the wonderful forgiving grace of God; this grace turned David's life around (Rom. 4).

Luther's discovery of justification by faith, Denney says, is a faith that "the moment it sees what Christ is and means, that moment it abandons itself passionately and unreservedly to Him." He adds,

> It is a crude way of putting this, to say that the interest of the Reformation was primarily religious rather than moral. But though it is crude, it is not untrue. No doubt religion must be ethical through and through, and it was through the needs of the moral nature, the need for repentance, that the eyes of the Reformers were opened to the true import of the gospel. But religion must in some sense transcend morality, or it has no [reason for existence]. It must deal with moral failure, and have power to renew the moral life when it has been discomfited and driven to despair. (296)

Protestantism, in its attempts to safeguard the religious aspect of faith, has often failed to call for a continuing life of faith, the "obedience of faith." Often it seems to lose the sense that justification by faith and the life of the new creature are vitally and intimately related. As Denney points out, "Faith tended to become intellectualized; faith was rather the acceptance of true thoughts about revelation than the sudden and irresistible conquest of the whole being by the Redeemer" (296). Redemption of a believer "ought to bring into his very soul, to lodge at the heart of his being, the spirit of him from whom the forgiveness comes" (136).

This is the lesson of Jesus' story in Matthew 18:23-35. The servant owes his lord a major sum of money, about the same as six million dollars today. He cannot pay on the principal or even keep up with the interest. His lord asks that he and his wife and children be sold as slaves; whatever they bring can be applied against the debt. The man falls down and pleads for mercy, and his lord has compassion and forgives him the entire debt. That is half the story; the one who has been wronged forgives the wrongdoer, and the guilty one goes free.

The second half of the story tells how the forgiven servant goes out and meets a man who owes him a mere twenty dollars, and demands repayment. When the debtor cannot pay, the servant has him put him into prison. In this servant's response to his debtor, there is a total absence of the grace he has received. No wonder the observers are incensed and report it to their lord, who calls that servant to judgment. Forgiveness releases us, but it also calls us to a sense of moral accountability for our behavior as well as to the privilege of forgiveness.

When Abraham Lincoln was a lawyer in Springfield, Illinois, he took a trip down the Mississippi River to visit New Orleans. The story is told that while there, he went to see a slave market and watched as people of color were brought out on the slave block and auctioned off to the highest bidder. They brought a young woman out, with clothing awry, hair disheveled, and eyes flashing anger as men examined her to decide on their level of bidding. Lincoln suddenly found himself so incensed that he began to bid.

Lincoln kept bidding as one bidder after another dropped out, and then he bought her. He walked down the aisle to the platform, took the rope that bound her wrists, and led her to the edge of the crowd. There he stopped and untied the rope. The young woman rubbed her wrists to relieve the pain and promote the circulation. Lincoln looked at her and said, "You are free to go."

She looked at him in amazement: "What's that, Massa?"

"You are free to go."

"You mean I can go where I want to?"

"Yes," he said, "you are free to go."

"Do you mean that I can say what I want to?"

"Yes," he replied, "you are free."

"I can think the way I want to?"

"Yes, you are free to go."

The tears began to run down her cheeks. She fell to her knees, clutched his ankles, and declared, "Then, Massa, I want to go with you."

This is the moral response of the thankful person who recognizes God's wonderful grace in releasing us. To be forgiven is to be set free. To be forgiven calls us in turn to walk in this freedom; that means walking with the One who forgives us. This is the amazing grace of God, the love that is self-giving to death. I rejoice in this. Denney says, "God would not have done justice to himself if he had not made himself known as a Savior" (156).

We need to use the more contemporary category of relationships as we approach justification by faith, a cardinal Christian doctrine. Righteousness is right-relatedness: reconciliation as a work of God precedes and undergirds our claim to justification by faith. As we claim the truth of this doctrine and rest in its provision, we need to enjoy the fact that our justification received by faith is a covenant in grace. This is transforming grace. As Paul says, "If anyone is in Christ, there is a new creation" (2 Cor. 5:17). Believers are living in a community of love, and a new world has dawned.

6

The Believers Church,
a Body of the Reconciled

*He is our peace; in his flesh he has made both groups into one
and has broken down the dividing wall, that is, the hostility
between us. He has abolished the law with its commandments
and ordinances, that he might create in himself one new
humanity in place of the two, thus making peace, and might
reconcile both groups to God in one body through the cross,
thus putting to death that hostility through it. So he came and
proclaimed peace to you who were far off and peace to those
who were near; for through him both of us have access in one
Spirit to the Father. So then you are no longer strangers and
aliens, but you are citizens with the saints and also members
of the household of God, built upon the foundation of the
apostles and prophets, with Christ Jesus himself as the
cornerstone. In him the whole structure is joined together
and grows into a holy temple in the Lord; in whom you also
are built together spiritually into a dwelling place for God.
(Eph. 2:14-22)*

IN THE EARLY 1960s I was studying for my Th.D. at Union Theological Seminary, Richmond. In the Th.M. stage of my work, I wrote
my thesis on "Conversion, a Comparison of Lutheran, Reformed, and
Anabaptist Thought." During my research, I made a trip to Goshen,
Indiana, and interviewed Harold S. Bender, one of the leading voices
in the Mennonite Church at that time.

"I am an evangelist," I told him, "calling people to conversion to
Christ, and you as a churchman are known for your emphasis on the

church and the life of discipleship. What would you say is the relation between conversion and church?"

Without a moment's hesitation, he replied, "Cause and effect,
cause and effect. There can be no genuine church apart from individuals first being converted to Christ."

Nevertheless, conversion often is not a simple dramatic changing
of direction, even if one point of commitment is highlighted. We tend
to think of those like the prodigal son or of Saul/Paul: once we went
our own way, but now we turn to walk with Jesus, going God's way.
But many have grown up within the community of faith and from
childhood have earnestly desired to walk with Jesus.

A sharp young woman lived high in an apartment complex across
the intersection from our church in Washington, D.C. When she completed her master of arts degree at the university, she also decided that
she was through with the church and religion. With this mind-set, she
came to the city in a teaching role. But each Sunday morning, she
looked across the street at the Washington Community Fellowship and
saw the couples and families coming and going with great joy and
enthusiasm.

After some weeks of observing people of this faith community, she
decided to come over and check it out. She never stopped coming. In
her commitment to Christ, she shared a winsome testimony and asked
to be instructed for baptism. My wife and I had the privilege of counseling and praying with her in Christian commitment, and I administered baptism to her in a Sunday morning service. She became a
participant in the community of faith, one of God's people who enriched each another and held each other accountable in living as disciples of Christ.

As far as we know, Jesus did not write a book; he created a community. So writes Lesslie Newbigin in *The Gospel in a Pluralist Society* (227). This is a community of worship, of faith, of truth, of fellowship, and of mission. The fact that any group of people can be
united in worship is in itself a witness to the grace of reconciliation.
Something is happening to call a group of individuals into a fellowship, into koinonia. The worshiping community is a witness to the
continuing activity of the risen Christ.

"The Christian claim," say Hauerwas and Willimon, "is that life is better lived in the church because the church, according to our story, just happens to be true. The church is the only community formed around the truth, which is Jesus Christ, who is the way, the truth, and the life" (*Resident Aliens*, 77).

God's work in history is the creation of a people for his Name. In Jesus, this people is a reconciled community. Through his Spirit, they know fellowship with God; by the same Spirit, they know fellowship with one another. This awareness creates a universal community. It crosses all racial, cultural, and national lines in a networking of the kingdom. The church as body has one head, the Lord Jesus Christ; just as he is universal, so the church is universal. It is the one body that is a global fellowship. By its presence the community of the reconciled changes the world. It is the primary means God uses to confront and call the world to himself.

In the current social context, we must rediscover the primacy of the church as a fellowship of the redeemed, a people of God, not buildings and institutional programs. We need to bring the church out from under the social and political orders and see it once again as God's highest order in the world. As God's redeemed people, the church is our first identification. We are called to be members of the body of Christ, a living dynamic fellowship. This covenant membership is our identity, our relationship, and our security.

There is no other movement in the world so important as the church. The more genuinely the church can live as the body of Christ, serving under his headship and extending his mission, the more we enrich our respective societies and enhance the good among humanity. God gives us grace to be "the salt of the earth" and "the light of the world" (Matt. 5:13-16). We do so, not by our own religiosity or ethnic strengths, but alone by the grace of God as we walk with Christ. Our goal is to know Christ better and to make him known to those about us.

When we live by God's commandments, love God, and love our neighbors as ourselves, we will be sharing Christ with our neighbors. We are witnesses that he is the Savior, for he is saving us and changing us. We are witnesses of Christ as the one Savior for all others as we invite them to join us in the body of Christ.

This truth is affirmed in Paul's letter to the Colossians:

> [God's beloved Son] himself is before all things, and in him all
> things hold together. He is the head of the body, the church; he is
> the beginning, the firstborn from the dead, so that he might come
> to have first place in everything. For in him all the fullness of
> God was pleased to dwell, and through him God was pleased to
> reconcile to himself all things, whether on earth or in heaven, by
> making peace through the blood of his cross. (Col. 1:17-20)

God is honored when the world sees his reconciling work in action among his people. God's primary program in the world is not
carried out through governments but through the church. In this
body of Christ, God is confronting the world with the living evidence
of his redemptive, transforming grace. With the exaltation of Christ
to God's right hand, God has in turn given Christ to be "head of the
church" (Col. 1:18; Eph. 1:22).

As members of Christ's body, we give honor to our head by showing that we are the people who share in the reconciling grace of God.
Spirituality is important, and religious precepts are of great worth;
yet the greatest life in the Spirit is our relationship with God himself.
We are called to join covenant with God and to walk with him (Gen.
5:22; 6:9). We cannot know Christ unless we are walking with him
in daily life (Luke 9:23; John 10:14; Denck).

This freedom and its responsibility are both individual and communal. As O'Donovan states, such

> freedom does not belong to us only as individual agents. Our
> communal action, too, is made free by the work of Christ, who
> is the first of a community of brothers. Human freedom consists
> not only in the power to act alone, but in the power to act
> together, as a cooperative fellowship. (163)

"Christianity presented itself to the classical world as a development of this Jewish faith," says Lesslie Newbigen, "but—unlike Judaism—it reached out in vigorous propaganda among all sectors of
the people" (1995:3). Ours is a mission of reconciliation, the building of a church that is open to all peoples. In this day of the global
village, we need a fresh awareness of the church universal, the expression of the kingdom of God in the world, the church as transnational, transracial, transcultural. The church is the one network

around the world that binds us together in a fellowship of mutual responsibility.

In this reconciled fellowship, we become agents of reconciliation in society, a role that is exciting and demanding but costly. We do society the most good when we maintain our integrity in a covenant with God and his kingdom. In this relationship, we become heralds of hope, agents of his peace, a people whose faith and love are qualities that spurn violence, tyranny, and injustice. This is in great contrast to what is done by political means, with violent responses to injustice, terrorism, and war. Samuel Huntington of Harvard has pointed out that wars of the future will be wars of civilizations. Hence, we do more for peace by bridging between peoples in a reconciling love than by any display of human power.

There is a special role for the church in the social order, to serve as an agent of reconciliation. It is always a global mission, for we are a worldwide community, a worldwide house, the "household of God" (Eph. 2:19). No other group has the potential for bringing together opposing ideologies under one allegiance to the one God and his universal kingdom. Earthly rulers continue to wield "the sword" (Rom. 13:4). Meanwhile, the church is responsible to live by the self-giving power of active love.

As in the days of the early church, we will be present as a people of God, at work in meeting human needs. There are thousands of Christian efforts in food and clothing distribution, finding clean water, organizing sewage disposal, providing medical treatment, and so much more. These ministries are a witness of grace, countering the violence of human greed that urges one group to destroy another.

In a 1988 Baptist-sponsored peace conference at Sjövik, Sweden, John Howard Yoder gave a sermon that he called "The Politics of the Lamb," explaining the new song of Revelation 5:9-10:

> You are worthy to take the scroll and to open its seals,
> for you were slaughtered and by your blood you ransomed
>   for God
>   saints from every tribe and language and people and nation;
> you have made them to be a kingdom and priests serving
>   our God,
>   and they will reign on earth.

Christ leads his church as lambs, in humility and innocence, to give of themselves as Christ gave of himself, for the salvation and reconciliation of the world. Yoder's presentation emphasizes the importance of being servants rather than superpowers, of self-giving love rather than status and dominance (via McClendon, 1994:98).

From Yoder's sermon, McClendon identifies the purpose of the reconciling work of Christ and his body: "In a word, what history is about is the formation of a new race of human beings, a race made of all races, a people made of all peoples." This royal people's rule can be distinguished from that of emperors and presidents precisely because love of enemies is its theme. Worldly rulers wield death-dealing power in mere triumphalism (1994:98-99).

"For the church to be a community that does not need war in order to give itself purpose and virtue puts the church at odds with nations," say Hauerwas and Willimon. They continue:

> Yet the church knows that this observation alone, and no other reason, puts it in the middle of a battle, though the battle is one we fight with the gospel weapons of witness and love, not violence and coercion. Unfortunately, the weapons of violence and power are the ones that come most naturally to us, so now we must ponder how we maintain the qualities needed to stay in this adventure called discipleship. (62)

In many areas, ethnicity, religion, and land are so interrelated that it is difficult to work at reconciliation between opposing groups. In a dreadful example to the world, the conflagration in Bosnia has left a bloody stain on history. On one hand, we see religious prejudices setting several groups at odds. On the other hand, nations seeking to help have themselves espoused a secularism that makes it almost impossible for them to understand the conflict; they are hardly able to help achieve a settlement.

Without endorsing secularism, the West needs to discover the realities of *secularity*. Genuine secularity is open to diversity, an official neutrality on religion, a concern for authentic humanness and for human rights. In contrast, secularism is a closed system, a narrow stance holding that "this-is-all-there-is." It becomes antireligious and incapable of openness and respect for diversity and the place of religion within the human family. The church, with an emphasis on freedom and voluntarism, can promote secularity in the sense of respect for humanness and human rights. At the same time, we promote a given faith in a style that is voluntary and respectful of each person's decision and of other religions.

Evangelism cannot thrive on arrogance. The church must avoid temptations to human power, to control a people or a society, and must share its faith in an evangelistic witness, calling hearers to voluntary commitments. Such an approach will refuse to create a Christian political party or to take over and enforce a "Christian" stance. Instead, we will call the community of faith to be a positive influence by being salt and light in society.

The pluralism of our times calls for the understanding and acceptance of diversity, while recognizing that there will be bigotry and persecution. In life, the way of the cross is a costly way of suffering love. It demands self-giving love in the service of Christ to others, and even more so in our pluralistic civilization.

Elton Trueblood has described the church as *The Incendiary Fellowship*, a people aflame for God, who share the suffering and meaning of the death of Christ. This may raise pictures from the history of martyrdom in the church, of beliefs so deep that people died for them; some were burned at the stake. Literal martyrdom comes to few of us in the Western world, yet the spirit of self-giving to the death of self-centeredness is a call to each of us. Peter reminds us that our call is to the "death route" in a dying-out to self-centeredness (1 Pet. 4:1-2). The way of grace is costly. It means giving up self-seeking and self-centeredness to take on a life of love, justice, equity, and peace for all peoples.

Self-giving love is at the core of the gospel; this unconditional love is expressed in the death of Christ on the cross. The evening before his death, sitting at table with his disciples, Jesus instituted the "new covenant," the communion that his followers share as a covenant fellowship. This is a eucharist of thanksgiving, a memorial of his passion, a communion of oneness in the body of Christ as we live in covenant relationship.

In the meaning of the Lord's Supper, this aspect of a covenant to keep even unto death is at its core. Look at the institution of the

Lord's Supper. Jesus said, "This is my body that is (broken) for you," and again, "This cup is the new covenant in my blood," "which is poured out for many" (1 Cor. 11:24-26; Mark 14:22-25). Since Jesus was sitting in his body, with his blood circulating, he was speaking with powerful symbols and personal realism. Thus he was saying, "I pledge myself to the death for you, to give you life and save you."

As we share the Lord's Table, we receive life and should also be saying, "I pledge myself to the death for Christ and his body." Paul says we are to examine ourselves lest we eat or drink unworthily, "without discerning the Lord's body." (1 Cor. 11:27-29), not taking seriously our covenant with Christ and his body, the church. We are a community of the reconciled, and our relationship is to live out this oneness and support for one another.

One basic problem is that our humanistic pursuits have not been placed under the lordship of Christ. Work, finances, social structures, political systems—all these are a necessary part of life. But they should be seen as servants rather than masters; we stand under the higher calling of our Lord. Secular roles will take on a new character when they are enriched by the quality of our walk with God.

We do not shirk from work. Instead, we handle work and management as good stewards of God's gifts. We do not withdraw from the structures that create stability in society; we see them as subservient to our higher calling of being a community of God's people. We do not oppose political processes. Yet we call people to recognize that our highest loyalty is not to a government; we render to Caesar only what is Caesar's, and render to God all that is God's, our very selves (Matt. 22:21). This text states our priorities. It is not an excuse for serving Caesar; it is a call to recognize the supreme claim of God upon our lives (cf. Acts 5:29).

The church is a special community within the world's social community, *The Community of the Spirit*, as identified in the book by C. Norman Kraus (Eph. 2:20-22). Kraus develops this concept as the essential nature of the new people of God. As we recognize the church as a community of the Spirit, we also take our place in it as a creation of the Spirit. True community is a gift, a gift from God: each sister and brother is a gift to each of us for our enrichment and fellowship. Christian community itself, as a dynamic fellowship, is a gift of grace. Our community is the special work of God by which we meet and relate to others in and through Christ.

Community does not mean a commonality that rejects structure, authority, and leadership; true community respects the need for institution and the different gifts that enable some to be effective leaders for the well-being of all. Some interpretations of community mistakenly pursue egalitarianism and appear to reject the diversity of gifts needed for an effective and aggressive ministry. Reconciling love enables us to celebrate the gifts in others rather than to compete with or reject another's abilities.

Dietrich Bonhoeffer presents this thesis on community in the little book *Life Together*. He emphasizes that in community we do not relate to each other directly; we relate in and through Christ. In these relationships, each of us is free and each is responsible. When we relate directly rather than in Christ, we may be tempted to dominate, intimidate, manipulate, or control another. But in and through Christ, such aberrations are challenged and defeated.

Similarly, the presence of Christ creates a transforming relationship for marriage, for family, and for the social context in which we live. The congregation is not a group withdrawing into a mystical experience of worship. It is a community that *as worship* lives out the meaning of faith in the social context of our life together.

Considering the many denominational differences in the church, we recognize that no one group has captured the kingdom. God's work is all that we can say about it, plus more than we can say. In a class lecture, John Howard Yoder said, "The Anabaptists were the most ecumenical people of the Reformation. On the basis of Scripture, they would meet anyone, anytime, and anywhere." We must ask, What is the meaning of their conviction for a believers church? What does this understanding of the church have to offer to other Christian understandings, and for worldwide fellowship?

In some manner, all churches are calling people to be believers. The term *believers church,* however, refers to a particular type of church that requires people to come to an understood faith for themselves. Their voluntary commitment in covenant is the ground for their membership in the congregation or church.

From the perspective of history, we learn that in the sixteenth century and since Constantine, people lived under the *corpus christian-um* (Christendom, political bodies purporting to be Christian: Constantinianism). They belonged without choice to the statewide church in an identity that was uniquely political; this involvement was from birth, as certified by infant baptism. In the Reformation era, the authorities counted the emerging emphasis on a believers church and believers baptism as a political threat, to be labeled and condemned as a heresy.

As a result, thousands of Anabaptists were martyred. They were the evangelicals of the Reformation; in contrast to most sixteenth-century Protestants, they became involved in evangelizing, in calling people to a personal commitment of their lives to Christ. Such evangelism was not known among Protestants or Catholics who lived with the *corpus christianum* view. The church, in the conviction of the Anabaptists, was a voluntary body of believers who shared regeneration by the Spirit of Christ.

In following centuries, especially in America, many denominations have adopted some forms of the believers church understanding. But one of the dangers of our denominationalism is that we become guilty of a *corpuscular christianum,* seeing our small group as the power to legitimize our values.

Various scholars, including Henry E. Dosker (Stone Lectures, Princeton, 1918-19), have suggested that the "free-church" movement had to wait for the New World before it could find freedom for exercising its convictions. Evidence shows that the free-church movement had a direct bearing on the creation of free societies in America. Also in North America, most denominations have caught up the basic concerns of the free-church movement. Even those practicing infant baptism have removed the political connotations; they baptize in anticipation of the child becoming a believer when old enough to understand the gospel and make one's own decision under the influence of parents and congregation.

Cris Sugden of Oxford, studying the growth of the church in what we call the two-thirds world, says it has become evident that the believers church is the dominant Christian movement (in Vinay). It calls people to respond to the gospel of Christ and accept baptism and a responsible role in the congregation of faith. In many cultures, doing so means a definite break from one form of life to take up a wholly new identity, relationships, and lifestyle.

I received a letter from a young man in India who had responded to the gospel in one of my meetings and broken from his Hindu past, committing himself to Christ. He told me of the remarkable inner peace and harmony he enjoyed. But he added, "Life is not so easy for me now that I am a disciple." For him and for many others, a commitment to Christ produces a new identity and a new life, and this identity cannot be hidden; hence, a commitment to Christ often brings tension and persecution.

The believers church is in itself a call to a firsthand relationship with the risen Christ. Existential Christianity means that the believer experiences peace with Christ as an actuality. It is wrong to describe the believers church as a form of primitivism, trying precisely to copy early church patterns as a religious exercise. Instead, I call it "primalism," engaging the primary faith-relation with the resurrected Christ, as experienced by the early Christians. This is not by copying them but by coming to Christ as they did.

Primalism calls for an in-depth awareness of the NT understanding of the church as expressed in three images:

• The church is *the body of Christ* (1 Cor. 12:27; Eph. 4:12).

• The church is *the temple of the Holy Spirit* (1 Cor. 3:10-17; Eph. 2:21).

• The church is *the people of God* in covenant with him (1 Pet. 2:9; Rom. 11).

In contrast to the believers church, the other sixteenth-century churches, both Roman Catholic and Protestant, were state-church in orientation, the *Landeskirche* (established church) to which everyone belonged. Since Anabaptists criticized them for not being a true church, for being a "fallen church," the other Reformers developed the doctrine of the invisible church. They distinguished between the church visible, to which everyone belonged, and the church invisible, the truly elect known only to God.

There may be some truth to this interpretation. But one problem with this view is that it allows people to claim membership in an invisible church and shirk their responsibility to make the church visible by living in faithful discipleship to Christ. They miss what we all need—joy in fellowship and mutual encouragement, edification, and counsel (Heb. 10:23-25; 1 Cor. 14:26-32).

By its nature, the true church is the church visible, the gathering of the regenerate who show Christ in their lives and thus make him visible to society. There is no invisible way of walking in faith; discipleship will always have visible expressions. One cannot be a true believer and retreat to a mystical claim of being elect without the election of being "in Christ." The in-Christ identity is marked by covenant and by a covenant lifestyle. The *church militant* is composed of visible people living by "the sword of the Spirit, . . . the word of God" (Eph. 6:10-17). The *church triumphant* is composed of saints of the centuries, who were faithful to death and are now invisible; they have left their impact on the church that is visible today (Heb. 11:1—12:1; Rev. 7:9-17).

What are the *marks of the church?* How do we know that a group who gathers in exercises of faith is truly "church" and not just a religious club? How do we recognize that a given community is truly the body of Christ? We can note various answers:

• Eusebius said, "Where the bishop is, there is the church."

• Martin Luther identified two marks of the church: "Where the Word of God is rightly preached and the sacraments rightly administered."

• John Calvin echoed Luther's two basic marks and added a third: the fencing of the Lord's Table, church discipline.

• The Anabaptists accepted these as marks but emphasized a dynamic community of the reconciled. They wanted the church to reflect more of the central meanings of being the body of Christ in every part of life.

Heinrich Bullinger, successor to Zwingli, wrote a book on the rise of the Anabaptist movement. In its appendix he quotes several Anabaptists on why they would not attend the state church. They answer that the church is a reconciled fellowship in which the participants share together the insights of the Spirit. The Anabaptists do not want to attend as spectators who just listen to a lecture and receive the sacraments. They cite 1 Corinthians 12 and 14, especially 14:23-26, where Paul expects various church members to take leading parts in worship services.

Being in this free-church continuum, I propose a contemporary view of the *marks of the church*. These may be recognized as internal marks, external marks, and universal marks.

Internal marks are the ways in which we who are in the church recognize that we are the church. These appear in two ways:

• Conversion: each confesses that Jesus is our Lord.

• Discipline: we hold each other accountable to live as disciples of Christ.

External marks are ways by which the world or community around us recognizes that we are the church of Christ:

• Evangelism: we demonstrate that we are Christ's disciples and love to share his life.

• Freedom from the powers: we live under the mandate of Christ alone and not by the idolatry of any nationalism.

Universal marks show evidence that we are not a cultural, ethnic, or sectarian club:

• Love as justice and peace, spread by our lives.

• Missions of service in compassion and identification with the powerless and needy in the world. Jesus said, "By this everyone will know that you are my disciples, if you have love for one another" (John 13:35).

Over the years, John H. Yoder has given much thought to the marks of the church (1984; 1992; 1998:12-13, 75-79). He developed a chart in which he identifies eight marks:

• Binding and loosing, sharing forgiveness and reconciliation, living in moral community (Matt. 18:15-20).

• Loving the brothers and sisters, sharing to meet needs, partaking of the Lord's Supper together.

• Teaching and testing messages by using "the rule of Paul" (1 Cor. 14:26-33; Acts 15), taking up our history anew.

• Following Christ in discipleship.

• Serving even through suffering.

• Praising God, giving thanks.

• Making disciples, baptizing, joining a voluntary covenanting community, living as the new humanity.

• Greeting the brothers and sisters, expressing unity, widening our experience of Christian fellowship.

In *Body Politics*, Yoder has a chapter on "the fullness of Christ" (Eph. 4:11-13) in a church where each member bears a "manifestation of the Spirit for the common good" (1 Cor. 12:7).

The epistles are especially relevant for an understanding of the early church, to which they were written. We also gain an understanding of the church from accounts in the book of Acts. In his Gospel, Luke does not use the word *ekklēsia*, though it does appear in Matthew (16:18; 18:17). In Acts, Luke uses *ekklēsia* at least two dozen times for those called to be a people of God.

Acts 2 presents the wonderful experience of Pentecost, when people gathered from all over the Roman world heard the gospel. The chapter concludes with specific reference to the nature of this new emerging church. It was characterized by (1) the apostle's doctrine; (2) fellowship; (3) breaking of bread, probably the Lord's Supper; (4) prayer; (5) signs and wonders; (6) mutuality in financial sharing, and (7) regular attendance at worship. The last verses of Acts 4 give a similar outline of the character of the church and say more about mutual aid in financial matters.

In the sixteenth-century, Felix Manz was on trial for his faith as a proponent of the believers church and was about to be sentenced to death. He was accused of teaching economic communism and answered, "No, I have not taught economic communism. What I have taught is that what is mine is the church's when my brother has need." This conviction has continued in the Anabaptist stream, especially among Mennonites.

Major programs support this conviction: Mutual aid associations help members in need. Mennonite Central Committee is a worldwide ministry of aid for the suffering and needy. Mennonite Disaster Service assists those who suffer loss. Large sales of donated material raise major amounts of money for relief and development projects around the world. In addition, many congregations and youth programs actively minister to the poor.

Our church on Capitol Hill, Washington, D.C., sought to fulfill this conviction by drawing from the pattern of Acts 2 and 4. The Jerusalem church "had all things common," and "there was not a needy person among them" (2:43-47; 4:32-37). Our group had several structured programs, and members performed much voluntary work.

The congregation took a special second offering each month in connection with our observance of the Lord's Supper; this went to a mutual aid fund, to assist those in need within the congregation. We arranged with a bank for loans to powerless persons in need, with the congregation giving an endorsement for security; thereby we enabled the needy to learn management in monthly payments and to build good credit records.

We also carried on deliberate discussions of financial matters in our covenant groups. The more successful could counsel those with less success, on how to be good stewards, including matters such as spending and giving patterns, adopting a child, renting or buying a house, or purchasing a car. These are samples of many ways churches can be creative in taking seriously the principle and practice suggested in Acts 2:44: "They had all things common."

Another significant passage on the character of the church is Acts 15. At that Jerusalem conference, Paul and Barnabas present a case for including Gentiles in the church without requiring them to be circumcised, as advocated by some from Jerusalem. Peter gives his witness about how God has included Cornelius as a Gentile. Finally James speaks, affirming this position. He quotes the prophets Isaiah and Amos, that God will rebuild the tent of David, and interprets this as God's extension of his people beyond ethnic Jews to include the Gentiles.

The conference decides not to ask circumcision of the new Gentile Christians but instead ask them to abstain from idolatry and immorality. They also voice a third concern, that the new believers also abstain from blood (Gen. 9:4; Lev. 17:10-14). Since the books of Moses are read in the synagogues every Sabbath, partaking of blood would offend those worshiping the Lord. This provides us with an example of the church's responsibility to work with integrity in a given context.

The earliest church grew north and west from Jerusalem. Acts follows the church through the arteries of the Roman world, to leading cities of art and commerce, and to Rome itself, the political power center. The church was not an activity carried out in secret or "done in a corner" (Acts 26:26). With deep conviction, believers spread the word across the Roman world. History students tell us that the church also extended east, south, and southwest, with even more people responding and developing churches in North Africa. In tracing the church to Rome, Luke shows how the early church confronted the culture and powers of its time.

Several other observations from the book of Acts help us think of the church at work in our time. First, the earliest church at Jerusalem did have, to some degree, community of goods (Acts 2 and 4). But consider the situation of the period. Hundreds of tourists in Jerusalem for the Pentecost festival had come to faith in Christ and had tarried in Jerusalem for fellowship; they needed aid for food and lodging. There is no evidence that when these new Christians carried the good news of the gospel back to their home communities, they took along the idea of community of goods or economic communism.

Yet Paul repeatedly called for believers voluntarily to help the needy (1 Cor. 16:1-4; 2 Cor. 8; Eph. 4:28). Today, Hutterite colonies and intentional Christian communities with things in common do challenge us toward faithfulness in sharing and helping the needy.

Acts also tells us how Paul encountered disciples at Ephesus who had likely been converted by Apollos, who before becoming a mature Christian was preaching the message of John the Baptist and his call to repentance (18:24—19:7). Paul asks these disciples, "Did you receive the Holy Spirit when you became believers?" This question places the experience of receiving the Spirit at the center of the happening that we call church. In his teaching on the Holy Spirit, Jesus calls us to awareness that the gift of the Spirit is the life of the church (John 14 and 16). Thus the Spirit in the church fulfills Jesus' promise: "Where two or three are gathered in my name, I am there among them" (Matt. 18:20).

Today, with the sense of living in a global village, we need to discover new ways in which the church can share across national and cultural lines as the global body of Christ. We are made aware of this universality every time we share in the Lord's Table. In response, we need also to find ways for responsible sharing of the resources of the North with the South. The Western world especially needs to share resources with the two-thirds world, which struggles to find the necessities of life.

For some time, I have urged my denomination to create an Anabaptist World Alliance as the pattern of our historic Mennonite World Conference. This could provide a way for us to become sister churches of equity and mutuality in the mission of Christ among the many different cultures where we exist. Our greater mission is to enable each other to be a presence for Christ as his disciples in our respective cultures.

One characteristic of our times is urbanization. All around the world, people have been moving to the cities. Today more than half of the world's six billion people live in cities; in most communities, half of them are under the age of fifteen. Think of the overwhelming opportunities for sharing the gospel. My friend Ray Bakke addresses this effectively in his book *The Urban Christian.*

From our experience in Washington, D.C., we have learned the excitement and joy of working in the inner city, with all of its diversity, multiculturalism, interracial relationships, social interchange, and deep human needs. A pastor needs to be clear on the core of the gospel, flexible in program and relationships, without controlling everything. Above all, a pastor must show a spirit that says, "We are here because we love and care."

The expression of genuine caring means that we open ourselves to share with other programs of caring ministries beyond our own. We are here to serve the people around us, not just to develop our own program. The city calls for contextualizing, for more openness to denominational diversity, and for more cooperative programs than are traditional in a strict denominational stance.

In our work in Washington, D.C., we could, with an evangelical spirit and faith, actually be more ecumenical in working with others than many ecumenists or mainline Protestants. We were doing this, not in denial of the diverse theological streams that make up the congregation, but in open and candid sharing of the values and weaknesses of each in their contribution to the community.

By sharing in a clear membership covenant, we found it possible to celebrate the unity of the body with the diversity of its parts. With clarity on how we work together, we were able to involve people in a common cause and fellowship. This happened even though they were from various denominations, a wide range of cultural backgrounds, and a variety of races and ethnic groups.

We designed a worship service to minimize performer-spectator tendencies and let the whole congregation participate in various ways (cf. 1 Cor. 14:24-33, 39-40; 11:5). We also found that polity can be adjusted to maximize participation. Thus we had a pastoral team of three, of several races and both genders; a board of elders to provide spiritual and theological guidance; a board of deacons to fulfill functional roles and guidance; and five commissions: worship, nurture, fellowship, stewardship, and missions. Members could thereby more freely participate in the ministries of the church.

Our goal was to be a congregation in fact and function, not just a casual assembly. As a community of the redeemed, this Washington congregation had several goals:

• First, we were seeking to be a community of the Spirit in our common walk as disciples of Christ.

• Second, we were seeking to be a community of nurture, encouraging and equipping one another to serve our Lord.

• Third, we were seeking to be a community of accountability, holding one another accountable to live our confession. Jesus taught that we are responsible for binding and also loosing one another, sharing moral discernment and guidance (Matt. 18:15-20).

• Fourth, we were seeking to be a community of compassion, of genuine caring and ministering to each other and to those around us, in the love of Christ.

• Fifth, we were seeking to be a community of interpretation, searching together for the mind of Christ as we interpreted the Scripture, for our lifestyle and for our relationship to the issues we face in our world.

As we hear the word from each other, the preaching of the Word takes a community focus and keeps us from succumbing to "the arrogance of one's own expertise," as someone aptly said. The exercise of listening together to the preaching of the Word is a great leveler, an experience that puts us all on common ground.

There is a danger that we may not be open to hearing the interpretation of the Word if we are too impressed by our own professionalism. If we regard preachers of the Word not as prepared prophets of God but as giving their own opinion, we will thereby miss the meaning of biblical preaching and the authority of the Word of God. The prophetic Word is more than a lecture; it is a presentation of the meaning of Scripture with a "happenedness." The intent of the passage happens again in the present moment. Further, the corporate act of hearing God's Word together is a major witness of our unity in placing ourselves under the authority of the Word of God.

The life of the congregation is expressed in at least the five functions mentioned above in which we share together as the body of Christ: worship, nurture, fellowship, stewardship, and mission. We participate in worship, including praise as celebration, prayer as communion, and proclamation as hearing God. This brings the community together in the presence of Christ. We direct worship to God himself. Our worship practice is corporate and not merely a social function of religious character.

There are aspects of devotion, worship, and mutual enrichment that happen in the larger group and cannot happen in the same way in a small group. For example, congregational singing is a great exercise of worship in which we share in a richer way than in a small group or in private devotion. Similarly, prayer has greater dimensions as a congregation shares its concerns and its intercession. This can also be said for fellowship and for service; a Christian group can become a genuine community in united action.

We should avoid becoming routine in our worship services. Yet there is value in a common understanding of the liturgy or order of worship. We do not want worshipers to be unduly distracted by innovations; instead, we want to enable them to focus freely on thinking of God and with God. If people desire change and innovation, leaders should announce simple details and lead with clarity so that worshipers are freely involved.

Congregational singing, corporate prayer, and hearing the Word together are engagements with God that in themselves are experiences of spiritual renewal. Music encourages worshipers to enter into a spiritual encounter with God; it carries our praise, aspiration, and commitment in a moving and powerful way.

In the earliest church, the disciples of Christ

> devoted themselves to the apostles' teaching and fellowship, to the breaking of bread and the prayers. . . . All who believed were together and had all things in common; they would sell their pos-

sessions and goods and distribute the proceeds to all, as any had
need. Day by day, as they spent much time together in the temple,
they broke bread at home and ate their food with glad and generous hearts, praising God and having the goodwill of all the
people. (Acts 2:42-47)

The summary passages here and at Acts 4:32-37 emphasize the core
of faith, community at worship, commonality in meeting needs, and
communication with others.

An essential unifying element in the worship of the church universal is the place and significance of the ordinances, often called *sacraments*. The Catholic Church has had at least seven sacraments. The
Protestant Church has held to two sacraments, baptism and the
Lord's Supper. In Anabaptist-Mennonite churches, not being sacramental, there has been a long history of referring to *ordinances*
rather than to sacraments.

However, in recent years Mennonites have tended to emphasize
two of these ordinances, baptism and the Lord's Supper. Yet they
think of baptism and communion not so much sacramentally as relationally. In fact, we view these symbols as relational and not onto-
logical (as things in themselves).

Baptism on confession of faith is a sign of the new life in covenant
with Christ and his church; baptism does not in itself automatically
mediate grace. As a sign, whether by pouring (a sign of the baptism
with the Spirit), or by immersion (a sign of dying to the old life and
being resurrected into a new life), the ordinance or sacrament is a
very unique symbol. In this sense the Anabaptist church is more in
the tradition of Zwingli, with what has been dubbed a "low view"
of the sacraments.

This is also true for the Lord's Table: the emblems are powerful
symbols or signs of the body and blood of Christ, and do not become
his actual flesh in us or to us. In the fellowship of the Lord's Table, we
in the Mennonite tradition see the emblems as communicating grace
rather than imparting grace in and of themselves. The Lord's Supper
is a eucharistic thanksgiving for the amazing grace of Christ and his
unconditional love which save us and reconcile us into one body.

In *The Lord's Supper in Anabaptism*, John Rempel maintains that
historically Anabaptists regarded the Lord's Supper as more than a

human act of remembrance. The bread and the cup "become the means of the church's union with Christ, of its participation in his body and blood." In and through the Lord's Supper, Anabaptists emphasize "faith, reconciliation, community, and mission." Balthasar Hubmaier

> explained the Eucharist as gratitude which takes ethical form (as Christ gave himself for me, so I can give myself for others) and links worship to mission. This thrust contributes to a Christian self-understanding which is other-centered, translating faith into love and thanksgiving into sacrifice." (Rempel: 225-6)

The communication of grace through the Lord's Supper emphasizes at least three things:
• The emblems of Christ's self-giving love even to death for our salvation.
• The communion of/with the Holy Spirit, who is the inner confirmation of the present meaning of the presence of Christ, of the love and self-giving of Christ.
• The communion of Christ's body, the church, in which we share the symbols as the expression that he is present with us, the church, his body, the body that shares the emblems of his redemptive sacrifice and participates in his mission.

When Jesus Christ instituted the Supper, he was alive on earth, and yet he said, "This is my body that is (broken) for you. . . . This cup is the new covenant in my blood" (1 Cor. 11:24-26). He was saying, "I pledge myself to the death for you." For us to truly partake of his communion, we need to say in covenant as his people, "I pledge myself to the death for Christ and his body." In this spirit of covenant, we "discern the Lord's body," our relationship as his people, when we take the emblems as powerful signs of the covenant (1 Cor. 11:27-29).

Since the church is composed of imperfect people, it will always be involved in both nurture and discipline for the integrity of relationships and of our witness. The goal of nurture is to build up the believers in faith and obedience, develop an informed congregation, and enable believers to give an answer for "the hope that is in [us]" (1 Pet. 3:15).

The goal of church discipline is the integrity and accountability of each person in a congregation and the restoration of relationship, where this has been spoiled. Such discipline is positive as well as negative. It is positive in helping members live the disciple's life in their respective vocation. It is negative in confronting and correcting such things as greed, self-centeredness, violent behavior, addiction, and sexual promiscuity.

The primary consideration in discipline is the integrity and witness of the local congregation in its social context, where the offending person is a member. The lack of discipline weakens the witness and service of the church, local and extended. But we must focus discipline especially on the healing of relationships. John Driver asserts that the purpose of discipline "will always be the restoration and reconciliation of the offending member" (1976:46). We must always do this with humility and compassion as we affirm together that we are the body of Christ.

Jesus spells out the process of discipline as a "binding and loosing" function for the church (Matt. 18:15-20). In earliest Protestantism, Martin Luther, Martin Bucer, and the associates of Zwingli recognized this "rule of Christ" but were lax in applying it. The radical Zwinglians, who became the Anabaptists, carried the concept and practice of discipline dynamically into the life of the believers-church congregations, in the voluntary church movement. The state churches noticed this challenge, and some of their leaders called for stricter discipline to keep their members from joining the Anabaptists (Bender).

John Howard Yoder provides guidance for us as we face the hazards of confrontation for church discipline:

> If you go about it in an open context, where both parties are free to speak, where additional witnesses provide objectivity and mediation, where reconciliation is the intention and the expected outcome is a judgment that God himself can stand behind, then the rest of the practical moral reasoning process will find its way. (1984:28)

God has vested responsibility in the church to demonstrate the reality of his kingdom breaking into society. The members of the local congregation are the feet and arms of the church universal, the agents of its witness and service. By worship, nurture, and fellowship, the local congregation helps its members grow into the likeness of Christ. The local congregation shares the witness of Christ to the people of a given society and thereby invites people to Christ and his church. This witness brings people to Christ on the common ground of the covenant of grace.

In the same service, it has been my privilege to baptize persons representing lower and upper levels of society (as the world measures the classes). Engaging the covenant of faith in Christ puts us all on the level of servants of one another.

The church is not primarily institution, though to be effective it must have structure. It is a people who walk together in community with God. The Holy Spirit gives evidence in the world of the reality of Christ's reconciling work by making the power of his redemption evident in the community of the reconciled. As a result, the local congregation will grow because faith is contagious; people observe our walk with Christ and then come to walk with us.

We are the true revolutionaries in society, speaking to the basic issues of modern life and calling people to a radically new life of participation in a community of fellow disciples of Christ. In and by ourselves, we are not culturally or ethnically God's people; our identification with Jesus as Lord and Reconciler makes us God's people. As Paul says, We are "in every place the fragrance that comes from knowing [Christ]" (2 Cor. 2:14).

7

A Spirituality of Discipleship

*We . . . worship in the Spirit of God and boast in Christ Jesus
and have no confidence in the flesh—even though I, too, have
reason for confidence in the flesh.*

*If anyone else has reason to be confident in the flesh, I have
more: circumcised on the eighth day, a member of the people
of Israel, of the tribe of Benjamin, a Hebrew born of
Hebrews; as to the law, a Pharisee; as to zeal, a persecutor
of the church; as to righteousness under the law, blameless.*

*Yet whatever gains I had, these I have come to regard as
loss because of Christ. More than that, I regard everything as
loss because of the surpassing value of knowing Christ Jesus
my Lord. For his sake I have suffered the loss of all things,
and I regard them as rubbish, in order that I may gain Christ
and be found in him, not having a righteousness of my own
that comes from the law, but one that comes through faith in
Christ, the righteousness from God based on faith. I want to
know Christ and the power of his resurrection and the sharing
of his sufferings by becoming like him in his death, if somehow I may attain the resurrection from the dead. (Phil. 3:3-11)*

PAUL TOURNIER, a Christian psychiatrist of Switzerland, has been
a significant voice for Christ. His books *The Meaning of Person* and
Guilt and Grace have blessed many with freedom and enrichment
for meaningful spirituality.

Gerald Mann says that as a young man, he heard Tournier speak
of being a freshman at University in Venice. On his first day in one

class, the professor asked whether any Christian was present. Tournier raised his hand, then looked around to see that he was the only person with a hand up. The professor responded, "You are a Christian. I want you to go to your room and write me an essay on why you are a Christian and bring it to my office."

Tournier went to his room and sat at his desk, trying to write an essay explaining why he was a Christian. Dissatisfied with his attempts, he scrapped what he had done and simply wrote an essay telling of his experience with Christ. He took it to the professor.

The gentleman sat silently, with his head bowed over the paper. Then he looked up with wet eyes and said, "I too am a Christian."

Tournier asked, "And when did this happen?"

"Just now," replied the professor, "as I was reading your essay."

Only one who walks with Christ truly knows Christ, and only one who truly knows him can walk with him (Denck). This premise for spirituality from the history of Mennonite thought has enriched my life and that of many others. Bonhoeffer states a similar premise: only the one who obeys truly believes, and only the one who believes truly obeys.

Spirituality for the disciple is always set in direct relationship with Jesus Christ. It is never simply a mystical exercise of transferred thought, nor is it ever achieved by withdrawal from life or by contemplating only one's own self. Spirituality is solidarity with Jesus, our risen Lord. Jesus is our Mentor in spirituality; he is the one person who always did those things that pleased the Father (John 8:29; Heb. 4:15). In the nineteenth century, Søren Kierkegaard spoke of this solidarity with the risen Jesus as "contemporaneity."

Many face the question "What does it mean to be spiritual?" and answer in terms of withdrawal from life and the material. But Jesus was not a hermit; the apostles did not live monastic lives. Though Jesus lived a celibate life and never married, he did not speak against Peter's marriage nor ask his disciples to take up celibacy. Jesus modeled the fact that one can have a full life apart from a lifelong sexual relationship in a commitment of marriage.

Spirituality for Jesus meant living in intimate relationship with the Father and placing the will of God or the kingdom of heaven above all other ambitions. Paul says spirituality, "spiritual worship," means "to present your bodies as a living sacrifice" and to have renewed minds, discerning "what is the will of God—what is good and acceptable and perfect" (Rom. 12:1-2). To be spiritual is to walk in the Spirit, in full identification with Jesus Christ.

The character of spirituality is not easily defined, especially when considered as mysticism, meditation, self-transcendence, and the like. Spirituality is often regarded as a withdrawal from the normal roles of life into a more "monastic" pattern that has been a calling for some. But when we study the person and life of Jesus Christ, we discover such characteristics as love, service, prayer, and self-giving. We need a renewed sense of spirituality as fellowship with God, as living in the Spirit rather than in the flesh, where selfish interests control one's life.

Dietrich Bonhoeffer has described this as *The Cost of Discipleship*, and David Bosch of South Africa calls it *A Spirituality for the Road*. A spirituality of freedom is the freedom to walk with Christ in his fellowship and in the fellowship of others without enslavements or addictions that pervert and limit one's life.

"Union with Christ," wrote John Murray, "is the central truth of the whole doctrine of salvation." These days, *spirituality* is almost the shibboleth of religion in general. Every religion has its own spirituality: Hinduism, Buddhism, Islam, Judaism, New Age, and Christianity—each emphasizes what it thinks to be the quality of in-depth spiritual experience.

Within the Christian church are varied forms of spirituality, calls to renewal, and exercises in spiritual disciplines. Nevertheless, the central core of spirituality is our union with Christ, as we connect with the transforming power of reconciliation with him. I call this the *spirituality of discipleship*, a full identification with Jesus, and solidarity with him. Paul explains God's intention for us: by God's call of grace, we are "predestined to be conformed to the likeness of his Son" (Rom. 8:29, NIV). For me, this has become the focus of all that can be said about spirituality.

One of the more relevant books on spirituality is by Dallas Willard: *The Spirit of the Disciplines*. He describes discipline in two categories, abstinence and engagement. Richard Foster's *Celebration of Discipline* is another that has helped shape perspectives on spirituality in the 1980s and beyond. His emphasis—from meditation to fasting, prayer, service, and more—calls us to a practice of spiritual disciplines.

Nevertheless, spirituality is more than a solitary person exercising disciplines of renewal. We are called to belong to Jesus (Rom. 1:6) and to love our neighbors as ourselves (Matt. 22:39). The love of neighbor becomes for us both expression and evidence that we are possessed by the Spirit of Christ and thus affirm the value of others. The discipline of love for others, including one's enemies (Luke 6:35), is the highest test of one's release from a self-seeking life. God gives us a spirit of loving one's neighbor as oneself. This call and character of love moves us beyond a private pietism to a quest for God's larger purposes for the human family.

In Protestant Christian history, special forms of spirituality emerge as better-known movements:

• Various forms of pietism, marked for a strong emphasis on the devotional life, yet quite individualistic and private.

• Holiness spirituality, emphasizing the baptism with the Spirit for inner sanctification in release from the sin nature.

• The Keswick movement, emphasizing victory in Christ with a deep sense of trusting all to his grace.

• The contemplative form of spirituality, using exercises of meditative identification with spiritual resources found in seeking God.

• The charismatic form of spirituality, with emotional ecstasy and engagement of the gifts of the Spirit.

• A revivalistic form of spirituality marking the church especially since the Great Awakening (from 1726). It appeared in the East Africa Revival (from the 1940s), and is still calling people to repentance and clarity in commitment to Jesus.

• A spirituality of discipleship, a solidarity with Christ that means walking with Jesus in the way, shown in both devotional and social ways.

In addition to these forms of spirituality, other voices have made additional contributions. These include especially the late Henri Nouwen, a Catholic writer who has been an instrument of the Spirit in refreshing the church. A. W. Tozer, of the Christian and Missionary Alliance Church, touched my life especially through his book *The Pursuit of God,* and later with *The Knowledge of the Holy.*

These writers stress that it is God's intention to conform us to Christ (Rom. 8:29). God does this through the Spirit at work in us, the action of God's transforming grace.

In my discernment, much emphasis on spirituality and on discipleship is too subjective, too much a work of renewing oneself, and too inclined to become a psychologized gospel. There often is a lack of objective identification with the incarnate Lord. By his intimate relationship with the Father, he calls us into the same close Father-son relationship, where we also call God "Abba" (Mark 14:36; Rom. 8:15; Gal. 4:6).

One remedy for individualistic patterns of self-renewal is worship in the corporate community, sharing in group prayer. This discipline calls us beyond self-interests that too often intrude into private prayer. I call for a spirituality of discipleship that is more objective, more wholistic, more focused on "walking with Jesus in the way" as a child of God. This walk involves meeting Christ in the Word, for the Christ is present in his word. As Bonhoffer said, "The story of Jesus, told in faith in the congregation, is the simplest sermon" (via McClendon, 1994:241).

David Bosch of South Africa has influenced my own thinking with his emphasis on *A Spirituality for the Road*. He speaks of walking with Jesus as servant relating to the master, and finding in the experiences of life the setting to demonstrate "the good and acceptable" "will of God" (Rom. 12:2). Bosch wants us to understand that the evangelistic impact of the gospel is felt most authentically when it is a call to walk with Jesus. This contrasts with offering a new form of mysticism alongside other forms of mysticism in various cultural religions. Being reconciled to God means that we now live in and by this new relationship, honoring God in faith and in action.

The word *spiritual/spirituality* is used some thirty times in the Scriptures, so a study of this term cannot be extensive. However, it is a concept that has the strength of the universal. In all religions it is used to designate one's affinity with the realm of the spirit, in contrast to the realm of the material. In Hinduism, for example, to be spiritual is to withdraw from the material.

When I was in Hyderabad, South India, the *Daily News* featured a successful business executive, sixty years old, who was renouncing his wealth and family relations to pursue the life of the spirit. The commitment and ceremony meant renouncing the billion rupees he had accrued in the first sixty years of his life. He said farewell to his wife and their family, with whom he would no longer relate. He discarded his clothing to walk naked as a "holy man" and eat only one meal a day, only what was given to him and he could receive in one hand. His withdrawal from the material orders of life was essential to his spirituality.

From the same setting, E. Stanley Jones tells of speaking with a Hindu holy man who said, "I gave up sex forty years ago." Yet, Jones later observed, "he talked about sex for the next forty minutes." Withdrawal from the material order does not in itself mean that one has found freedom from its immediacy. This tendency in our own thinking about spirituality permits people to believe they engage the spiritual when they are "in the house of God," but that living as fallen people in sin is unavoidable through the week. We need a renewal in understanding what it means to walk with God in the whole of life, in domestic, professional, and secular orders as well as our religious expressions.

We are called to show holiness in all of life (Eph. 1:4). The meaning of this holiness is wholeness, a life belonging wholly to God. Such was the thrust of William Law's *A Serious Call to a Devout and Holy Life*, which moved John Wesley so deeply. It is also the focus of the work by Thomas à Kempis, *The Imitation of Christ*, which touched the lives of so many, including the sixteenth-century church Reformers. There are devotional notes from early Anabaptists that reflect the deep spiritual satisfaction of a life in union with Christ.

One of the key passages in the Scriptures on this theme is Paul's statement to the church at Corinth. In 1 Corinthians 2 he emphasizes spirituality as directly related to the presence and work of God's Spirit, whom we receive by our relation with Jesus as our Lord. Jesus the Christ is the one who gives or baptizes with the Spirit; when we walk with Christ, we walk in the fellowship of the Spirit's presence. Discipleship is not legalistically copying the pattern of the historic Jesus, which we are incapable of doing on our own; instead, discipleship is sharing the intimacy of the Spirit given to us to glorify Christ in our lives. Paul says,

We have received not the spirit of the world, but the Spirit that is from God, so that we may understand the gifts bestowed on us by God. And we speak of these things in words not taught by human wisdom but taught by the Spirit, interpreting spiritual things to those who are spiritual.

Those who are unspiritual do not receive the gifts of God's Spirit, for they are foolishness to them, and they are unable to understand them because they are spiritually discerned. Those who are spiritual discern all things, and they are themselves subject to no one else's scrutiny.

"For who has known the mind of the Lord so as to instruct him?"

But we have the mind of Christ. (1 Cor. 2:12-16)

Personal Relationship with Christ

First, the spirituality of discipleship is based on a personal relationship with the Lord Jesus Christ. This mind of Christ becomes ours as we identify with him. Using Christ's mind, we think *with* God rather than *about* God. This mind is centered on Christ and his will rather than on the self-fulfillment of our will. It is far more radical than self-actualization; by being centered in Christ rather than wrapped up in our own self, we become a much better self, a more true self, an authentic self.

Paul testifies, "I have been crucified with Christ; and it is no longer I who live, but it is Christ who lives in me. And the life I now live in the flesh I live by the faith of the Son of God, who loved me and gave himself for me" (Gal. 2:19b-20).

The Swiss psychiatrist Paul Tournier probes into the meaning of being "crucified with Christ." In our lives as sinners, the ego has usurped the control of life and become the center of our lives. The real self, the capital "I," was shoved out of the center of our lives and to the periphery. When we are identified with Christ, the ego is crucified or rendered ineffective to control one's life; it is now shoved to the periphery. This happens by moving Christ into the center that the ego had been dominating.

What becomes of the "I" or true self? Tournier says the "I" is moved back into the center *with Christ:* "Nevertheless I live; yet not I, but Christ lives in me" (Gal. 2:20, KJV). Spirituality unites the true self with Christ. Now we live in solidarity with Christ.

To be spiritual is to have a mature relationship with Jesus that doesn't simply use him for guilt release, as a service agent who answers our prayer needs, an "insurance policy" that guarantees our future in heaven. Spirituality is to know Christ as present Savior; he saves me from being what I would be without him now. Christ is the understanding companion with whom I can walk in freedom and joy, the mentor who provides order or structure for my life in spirit and in deed. I eagerly accept the rigors of a discipleship that acknowledges his mentoring for all of life, the difficult as well as the joyous. Peter exhorts us,

> To this you have been called, because Christ also suffered for you, leaving you an example, so that you should follow in his steps.
> "He committed no sin, and no deceit was found in his mouth." When he was abused, he did not return abuse; when he suffered, he did not threaten; but he entrusted himself to the one who judges justly. (1 Pet. 2:21-23)

On this foundational truth, the fellowship of the church is created. The risen Christ confirms his presence and makes the church a spiritual community. The Spirit creates the "body of Christ" in which it is not "I" but "we," not "me" but "us."

Our relationship with Christ is a matter of covenant. On his side, it is the confirmation of the new covenant in his blood. On our side, it is a covenant even to death in fidelity to him. When we partake of the Lord's Supper we do so with responsible consideration of our relation to the Lord's body, the church, in which he is present (1 Cor. 11:27-29). We pledge ourselves even unto death for Christ and his body. If we partake with less than that integrity, we partake unworthily of symbols that Jesus instituted while sitting at table with his disciples.

Jesus said, "This is my body that is [given] for you." "This cup is the new covenant in my blood." Thus he pledged himself even unto death for us. In covenant with him, we pledge ourselves in turn. Spirituality involves us in surrender, in solidarity, in service for the love of Christ.

One cannot understand such an in-depth relation with Jesus without thinking of such terms as devotion, love, and prayer. Our response to the self-giving love of Jesus is to open our lives in love, in intimate relationship with him. Our devotion to the Lord is the response of our love to his love in the whole of our lives. We are not relating through constraint but in freedom.

In the intimacy of the Spirit, we share in the communion of prayer, in a conversation with the Beloved. Prayer is concrete engagement with God for purposes of transformation. In this sense, prayer is praxis. It becomes transforming action. This action relates us to a higher form of existence, that of loving fellowship with God. As response to divine grace, prayer evidences our ability to respond, our "respond-ability."

Clarence Bauman's *Anthology of Theological Reflection* (title: *On the Meaning of Life*) presents important insights on spiritual formation through prayer. I recommend his book and share a few statements from his chapter on the spiritual dynamics of prayer. Some he adapted from Martin Buber in *I and Thou,* and others from Abraham J. Heschel in *Man's Quest for God.*

• "Prayer is an act of spiritual obedience."

• "To pray in the Spirit is to transcend our ego and our mind in reaching for what is of supreme importance: God Himself."

• "One who prays experiences fundamental transformation of the ego; . . . in praying, I experience the boundless: the boundlessness of creation and the boundlessness of relation."

• "To pray is to cultivate mindfulness of God."

• "Prayer is not expedient, practical, or useful. . . . Prayer is not a need but an ontological necessity, an act that constitutes the very essence of man. He who has never prayed is not fully human." (Bauman: 35-38)

The Indwelling Holy Spirit

Second, a spirituality of discipleship requires the indwelling of the Holy Spirit. In the person of the Spirit, we experience the reality of Christ. This means that a spirituality of discipleship, of walking with Jesus in the way, is actually walking in the Spirit. In his fellowship we are gifted with "spiritual wisdom and understanding" (Col. 1:9).

Paul told the Galatians, "If we live by the Spirit, let us also be guided by the Spirit" (Gal. 5:25), or "keep in step with the Spirit" (NIV). Living in the Spirit is more than religious ecstasy, a subjective happening found in most religions. It is more than gifts expressing spiritual phenomena in one's life. In a popular term, it is more than warm fuzzies. Instead, walking in the Spirit means living in a discipleship of the Spirit, sharing attitudes and actions consistent with the Spirit of Jesus, and thereby honoring him.

The doctrine of the Trinity is to be understood more from the perspective of God's way of coming to us in our creatureliness than as the explicit definition of the person of God. A remarkable passage in Ephesians says, "There is one body and one Spirit, just as you were called to the one hope of your calling, one Lord, one faith, one baptism, one God and Father of all, who is above all and through all and in all" (Eph. 4:4-6). The doctrine of the Trinity is our attempt to explain the marvelous disclosure of God in our realm, the realm of the creature. God as Father, Son, and Spirit comes to identify fully with us.

The Scriptures speak of the communion of the Holy Spirit (2 Cor. 13:13). In some way this means an interchange of meaning and enrichment between us and God and each other. Communion implies dialogue or conversation. In recognizing the Spirit's presence, we surely are free to converse with the Spirit, and in this conversation our lives are laid open to him. In turn, the Spirit adjusts or conforms our lives to the will of God. The book of Acts often speaks of how early believers shared with and were led by the Holy Spirit (4:8; 6:3; 8:29; 10:19; 11:12, 28; 13:2; 16:7; 20:22-23). These passages call us to a more conscious recognition of the presence and conversation of the Holy Spirit.

From a biblical standpoint, we need to recognize the significance of John's statement that we are to try or test the spirits: "Every spirit that does not confess [that] Jesus [has come in the flesh] is not of God" (1 John 4:2-3). Our pneumatology or study of the Spirit is to be held in direct relation with our Christology: we know the Spirit of God in the same way we understand our Father God, as God is personified in Jesus the Christ. He said, "Whoever has seen me has seen the Father" (John 14:9), meaning, "If you want to know what God is like, look at me."

Identifying with the Pattern of Christ

Third, a spirituality of discipleship identifies us with the pattern of Christ. Spirituality as seen in the Incarnation is not a withdrawal from the material; instead, it makes all of life sacred. We find the norm of spirituality in the person of Jesus and recognize that he was a man among others, and a man for others. His spirituality was one of living and engagement: walking in obedience to the Father, always doing what pleased the Father, communicating with the Father in prayer, and honoring the Father in attitude and action.

Jesus did not withdraw from life: he worked, studied, built friendships, taught, served people, traveled his country, crossed cultural lines in communication, took short vacations, ate, got tired, wept, was tempted, and did things that show true humanness. *His spirituality is seen in that he set everything in its relation to God.*

Peter says believers are to follow the example of Christ, who entrusted himself to God and did not return abuse for abuse. Christ is "the shepherd and guardian of our souls" (1 Pet. 2:21-25). In this same tone, John writes, "Whoever says, 'I abide in him,' ought to walk just as he walked" (1 John 2:6). Paul similarly writes of his desire to be found in Christ, "not having a righteousness of my own that comes from the law, but one that comes through faith in Christ, the righteousness from God based on faith" (Phil. 3:9).

The *Confession of Faith in a Mennonite Perspective,* adopted in 1995, has an article on "Christian Spirituality" that says,

> We believe that to be a disciple of Jesus is to know life in the Spirit. As we experience relationship with God, the life, death, and resurrection of Jesus Christ take shape in us, and we grow in the image of Christ. In individual and communal worship, the Holy Spirit is present, leading us deeper into the wisdom of God. . . .
>
> We draw the life of the Spirit from Jesus Christ, just as a branch draws life from the vine. Severed from the vine, the power of the Spirit cannot fill us. But as we make our home in Christ and Christ abides in us, we bear fruit and become his disciples [John 15:5-8]. When we are in the presence of the Spirit, we also keep in step with the Spirit and show the fruit of the Spirit in our actions [Ps. 1; Gal. 5:22-26]. Our outer behavior matches our inner life. (69)

Priority for the Kingdom of Christ

Fourth, a spirituality of discipleship places priority on the kingdom of Christ. The kingdom is the rule of God; though larger than the church, God's rule is to be expressed in and through the church. God gives the kingdom and through Christ is building the church, using the "citizens" of the kingdom (Matt. 16:18; Eph. 2:19-22; 1 Cor. 3:10). We are responsible to structure the life of our congregations in accord with the rule of God. Hence, our spirituality is above all the demonstration of God's reign in our lives. As Markus Barth says, "Faith takes form in community and love, in confession and joy" (1971:69).

The *Confession of Faith in a Mennonite Perspective* also states,

> We believe that the church is called to live now according to the model of the future reign of God. Thus, we are given a foretaste of the kingdom that God will one day establish in full. The church is to be a spiritual, social, and economic reality [Acts 2:41-47], demonstrating now the justice, righteousness, love, and peace of the age to come. The church does this in obedience to its Lord and in anticipation that the kingdom of this world will become the kingdom of our Lord [Rev. 11:15; 15:3-4]. (89-90)

This priority of the kingdom led me to emphasize in our Washington, D.C., congregation, that discipleship is a Third Way of living. Amid pressures from the political right and/or the left, we are free to choose a path consistent with the kingdom or rule of God. On various issues, we may at times identify with the right, with the left, or with neither. We are guided by how we interpret the will of God as we see it in Scripture and as we are led by our risen Lord. This approach enables a mission of contextualizing; we are called to "become all things to all people, that [we] might by all means save some" (1 Cor. 9:16-23).

A spirituality of discipleship is a lifestyle that expresses the reality of Christ's presence in our lives, not simply in some mystical claims, but in a realistic Christ-centered order of life. We must always be asking, What does it mean that the Word became flesh and dwelt among us? How should this Word, Christ, be shown in us as we are conformed to his image?

Here are some characteristics of spirituality as we live by the rule of God:

> Humility and grace,
> Meditation and study,
> Prayer and communion,
> Faith and surrender.
>
> • • •
>
> Worship and praise,
> Love and fellowship,
> Obedience and the cross,
> Stewardship and simplicity.
>
> • • •
>
> Forgiveness and freedom,
> Integrity and purity,
> Equity and mutuality,
> Peace and justice.

Involvement in the Community of Christ

Fifth, a spirituality of discipleship is expressed by involvement in the community of Christ. Awareness of the larger church guards us against the narrow, limiting aspects of individualism. In the words of John Donne, "No man is an island, entire of itself; every man is a piece of the continent." Our life in faith is not a private experience but is life in the community of faith. We are made the better by the fellowship of faith in which we share. In turn, we participate as contributors in the community of faith.

We grow by doing, just as in a skill like playing piano or tennis. Just so, we grow by exercising ourselves in prayer, in worship, and in discussion of the meanings and implications of faith. Others in our community discover things in their walk with Christ that in turn minister to us.

Prayer, worship, and service to others are essential aspects of our sharing in the dynamics of being a people of God. In prayer, we confess that we are dependent upon God and his grace for our walk in his will; in prayer, spirituality is fellowship with God. Prayer is engaging conversation with our Lord. It is enjoying communion with him. I have found that prayer is far more than meditative thoughts in isolation; it is most effective when I pray over the Scripture, talking my way down through a passage as conversation with God. Worship, alone or with others, shows that we put the highest value on our fellowship with God.

James McClendon writes of knowing Jesus as acquaintance and friend. This is more than knowing about Jesus of Nazareth. It means knowing him through meeting him, sharing with him in worship, work, witness, and word. "Christian *worship* that knows its holy Object cannot be carried on by mere spectators or observers, however keen. Instead, in the remembering signs and in the dynamics of prayer and in all their worship, disciples engage One who meets them there" (1994:243). Thus worship itself is a witness of an authentic relation with Christ.

Worship in the gathered community is joining in celebration. We join the larger aspects of prayer with the consciousness of being "a priest at my brother's elbow," and we express this in the corporate setting. This means joining in the celebrations of great singing, lifting our hearts and minds to the Lord in praise.

Worship means hearing the Word of God with others; we witness and confess that as one united body, we each and all answer to the Word being presented to us. Spirituality is enhanced by this common act of accepting the discipline of the Word. Service is our deeds of love to those about us; it is the extension of our faith that "the Spirit of life" (Rom. 8:2), the spiritual, is of utmost importance. By our service, we encourage others and share resources with others to enhance their well-being.

McClendon speaks to the character of worship in answer to our Maker as having two definitive marks: "(1) Christian worship is a two-sided practice, divine and human, never just a monologue but a dialogue throughout; and (2) authentic Christian worship is never a path to power, never a way to control God or God's gifts" (1994: 374). Frequently worship fails these tests. McClendon correctly criticizes the tendency to turn worship into a therapy trying to impress its "audience," and the danger of perverting worship into magic in an attempt to extract favors from God or God's lieutenants, the "saints" (1994:374). Worship is intended to be response to God, not corporate self-arousal or entertainment.

Our community experience of worship helps us transcend individualism as we take part in spiritual exercises, praise, prayer, and proclamation. By engaging in the disciplines of worship together, we counteract individualism and open ourselves to the enrichment that comes from others, with their particular gifts of the Spirit. We recognize that the church, the redeemed community, is the body of Christ, and that each of us relates to the whole body; thus we become more complete in relationship.

Markus Barth says, "The communal form of response and praise called forth by God's judgment includes personal acts inside, at the periphery of, and outside the community." To these acts belong the following: (1) A turning away from evil ways and a turning toward the Lord (conversion). (2) Joining in the confession: "Jesus is Lord!" "God is one." There is "one Spirit." (3) Praying to God as "Our Father." (4) Singing hymns of praise. (5) Exhorting and consoling brothers and sisters in "a spirit of meekness." (6) Giving account to outsiders of one's faith (1971:69-70).

The community of faith in any culture is a witness for Christ. This community shows the meaning of being reconciled with God and with one another. Our new relationship in the redeemed community places into society something better: the quality of Christian living. In so doing, we actually improve the society in which we share. In fact, we do unbelievers the most good by maintaining our integrity and living out the love of Christ. This lifestyle gives even unbelievers something to compare with or use as a model, in pursuing the higher values of life. Christians may actually be mentors for others.

Similarly, in our evangelistic dialogue, we grow by meeting the challenge of other thinking people and seeking better ways to engage or answer them. This is a primary role in discipleship. Franklin H. Littell, a Methodist theologian, says,

> No words of the Master were given more serious attention by His Anabaptist followers than his final command: "Go ye therefore, and teach all nations, baptizing them in the name of the Father, and of the Son, and of the Holy Ghost; teaching them to observe all things whatsoever I have commanded you" [Matt. 28:19-20]. (94)

As disciples, we need to put our highest priority on obeying the great commandment to love God and neighbor. Then, as we exercise the great commission, we will do so with the right spirit and the right character.

The emphasis on witness is never an activity that excludes the primacy of the family. In the believers church tradition, we must place our children first in helping them come to an understanding of the faith, so they can make an informed decision. As with the early Anabaptists, so I believe that we are to be involved in the redemptive processes. This is an essential aspect of our spirituality: introducing people to Jesus Christ, who is the most important person in our lives. In word and deed, we are to demonstrate that being disciples of Jesus is the highest calling.

As J. Lawrence Burkholder says, "The Anabaptists . . . oriented their conception of discipleship in a kingdom which while historical is not of this world. Discipleship was confined to life within the committed community of believers which could theoretically exist without serious political involvement" (in Hershberger: 141). Their relation to the sociopolitical order was one of witness and of living out their discipline.

In 1964, as I ministered in India under the sponsorship of the Evangelical Fellowship of India, I learned the amazing story of Sadakar Memnon. He is the nephew of Krishna Memnon, secretary of defense under Prime Minister Nehru. Sadakar was attending university, studying under Radakrishnan, who later became the President of India. One day Sadakar called on his favorite philosophy professor and asked for the favor of being his disciple: he would cook his meals, run his errands, bring his sandals, and so on, if only Radakrishnan would be his guru, his mentor.

To his amazement, Radakrishnan replied, "I am not worthy to be your guru. Only one person in all of the world is worthy to be your guru, and that is Jesus of Nazareth."

"Jesus of Nazareth, he's dead and buried," said Sadakar. "I want somebody who is alive, someone I can talk to and learn from!"

"They say he is alive," his professor said. "I recommend that you get a NT and read it."

Sadakar left in anger. Later, out of curiosity as to why his professor would advise such a thing, he obtained a New Testament and began to read it. While reading, he met Christ, became a believer, went to a Christian church, and requested baptism.

Later he went back to his professor at the university to thank him for his counsel: "Dr. Radakrishnan, after your advice, I left your office angry; but later I got a NT and read it, and I met the Christ. I have become a Christian, and have been baptized, and now I want to serve him."

"Oh no, I didn't mean that," replied Radakrishnan. "You can believe in Jesus and still be a Hindu."

"Not the Jesus that I have met," said Sadakar. "He says, 'If anyone will come after me, let him deny himself and take up his cross daily and follow me.'" Sadakar took a Christian name, Paul Sadakar, and became a leading evangelist in India. He was known all across the country as a disciple of Jesus Christ.

8

Assurance Through
the Spirit's Inner Baptism

*Anyone who does not have the Spirit of Christ does not be-
long to him. But if Christ is in you, though the body is dead
because of sin, the Spirit is life because of righteousness. If the
Spirit of him who raised Jesus from the dead dwells in you, he
who raised Christ from the dead will give life to your mortal
bodies also through his Spirit that dwells in you.*

*So then, brothers and sisters, we are debtors, not to the
flesh, to live according to the flesh—for if you live according
to the flesh, you will die; but if by the Spirit you put to death
the deeds of the body, you will live. For all who are led by the
Spirit of God are children of God. For you did not receive a
spirit of slavery to fall back into fear, but you have received a
spirit of adoption. When we cry, "Abba! Father!" it is that
very Spirit bearing witness with our spirit that we are children
of God, and if children, then heirs, heirs of God and joint
heirs with Christ—if, in fact, we suffer with him so that we
may also be glorified with him. (Rom. 8:9-17)*

IN THE 1970s I had the privilege of being one of the speakers at the
Keswick Convention in Hong Kong. Another speaker was Stanley
Banks of Bristol, England, the president of a Bible college in that city.
He told of their old boiler burning out, leaving them without heat
and hot water. They prayed for God's help and began to solicit funds
to replace the boiler. When they received enough money, they hired
a plumber to put in a new boiler.

After it was installed, Banks and his staff gathered around for a dedication celebration. Banks turned on a spigot, expecting to see a gushing stream of steaming hot water, but there were only a few drips of water, a little jet of steam, and a few more drips.

He looked at the plumber, who told him to come back in several hours. When they returned, the plumber said they could go ahead with the service. This time, when Banks turned on the spigot, there was a gushing stream of steaming hot water. He looked at the plumber and said, "Please explain."

The plumber pointed to a shiny new pipe back of the boiler. "Do you see that pipe? It was so corroded you couldn't have stuck a lead pencil in it. The inflow of water was far too small for the outflow this new boiler can deliver."

Banks applied the story to many Christians with limited victory or fruitfulness. This happens because their connection with God is so corroded by things of this life that the inflow of the Spirit is too limited for spiritual success.

The gift of the Spirit, the baptism with the Spirit as we are reconciled in Christ, is the marvelous reality of the presence of God. Reconciliation means that our God is not a God far removed, but one who has moved into our experience. God did this in the Incarnation and especially at Pentecost, providing a continuing experience for all who receive him. "By this we know that he abides in us, by the Spirit that he has given us" (1 John 3:24). This wonderful inner witness that we share in God's reconciling grace is the inner word of the Spirit, making us aware that we are fully accepted in relationship. Our reconciliation is now!

The Anabaptists had a prominent emphasis on the gift and presence of the Spirit in their lives. In the Reformation, the theologian John Calvin stressed the inner witness of the Spirit as our assurance of God's electing grace. So do all true believers rest in this assurance. Calvin based this emphasis primarily on Paul's statement: "You have received a spirit of adoption. When we cry, 'Abba! Father!' it is that very Spirit bearing witness with our spirit that we are children of God, and if children, then heirs, heirs of God and joint heirs with Christ" (Rom. 8:15-17).

This is one of the marvelous ministries of God within us. The Holy Spirit assures us that we are in the family of God: "In the one Spirit we were all baptized into one body" (1 Cor. 12:13).

With all evangelical Christians, Mennonites emphasize the Trinity, the Threeness of our one God: Father, Son, and Spirit. However, as Christians we often fail to relate to the Spirit in the same way we relate with the Father and the Son. Yet it is by the presence of the Spirit that God dwells with us. By the indwelling of the Spirit, Christ abides in our lives. With this awareness, we should daily commune with the Spirit and benefit from his presence in our thoughts and prayers. A biblical view of the Trinity is that there is community in the Threeness of God. This is the God we know through Jesus Christ in divine Oneness (John 17:10-24).

There is no other experience confirming one's personal reconciliation with God that compares to the indwelling of the Holy Spirit. Being given the Spirit as the special presence of God in our lives as believers, we are sealed with the Spirit in our fellowship with God. We are to be continually filled with the Spirit, who is making us Christlike. The Greek of Ephesians 5:18 uses the present imperative: God commands that this infilling be a continuous experience. We are to walk in the Spirit, bearing the Spirit's fruit. As we abide in him, we are aware that the Spirit anoints us, bears his fruit in us, gives us gifts to glorify Christ, and enriches us with peace and joy. All of this is to bless the church as God's community.

This wonderful fellowship with the sovereign Spirit has for some people been altered by thinking of the Spirit as an "It," implying something we hold rather than recognizing that the sovereign Spirit holds us. The Spirit is our companion. Our relationship with the Spirit has the relational and emotional aspects of our companionship with him. The fruit of the Spirit expresses relational dynamics, in belonging, celebration, serenity, trust, esteem, reciprocity, integrity, respect, and restraint.

Paul's statement, "The Spirit himself/itself" (Rom. 8:16, RSV-NIV/ KJV) is to be understood not as a matter of gender; instead, the Spirit is person, "that very Spirit" (NRSV) with whom we participate. The Holy Spirit is the Spirit of God, the Spirit of Christ, the sovereign Presence who indwells us as believers to seal us in reconciliation with God.

Let us reflect on the person and work of the Holy Spirit:

• The Spirit of God is transcendent, yet imminent in our lives.

• The Spirit is universal in presence and yet immediate with us.

• The Spirit relates to us in the corporate experience and yet is personal in each of us who believe.

• The Spirit is sovereign and yet comes to us as a companion.

• The Spirit is an objective reality and yet while dwelling within us creates a subjective experience. The incarnate Christ, who is God-with-us, is now the risen Lord, present with us in the Spirit of God. By the indwelling Spirit, Christ continues to do his work within us. He perfects his will in us step by step, to be fulfilled in the final consummation at his return.

The person and work of the Holy Spirit creates the immediacy of reconciliation with God. Some theologians have asked whether mention of the Spirit is a reference to God's personal attributes or to the Spirit as person. Those who lack a strong conviction of the Trinity, of the Three-in-Oneness of God, tend to speak of the Spirit of God as simply the personal characteristic of the Divine. They think the Spirit is personal as love is personal, as courage is personal, as faithfulness is personal. But those of us who are Trinitarian in faith, take the references to the Spirit, especially in Jesus' teachings, as reference to the person of God as Spirit (John 4:24).

We understand the Spirit to be person, to be God himself. The Scriptures present the Spirit as the Third radiance of the Three-in-One God. Our knowledge of God is through his self-revealing acts in history, through the Incarnation, in which we meet God in Christ. Our knowledge of God also comes from our spirits being touched by the Holy Spirit in an intimacy that is beyond our articulation (Rom. 8:27-28). "To sum up this point," John Calvin wrote, "the Holy Spirit is the bond by which Christ effectually unites us to Himself" (*Institutes*, III.i.l).

God is transcendent, the God of glory and of grace, the awesome holy God, whom no one has seen face to face. Yet "it is God the only Son, who is close to the Father's heart, who has made him known" (John 1:18). The God who is totally "Other" yet speaks to us. God is holy, and no person can come into God's presence by one's own merit. God is, in his glorious majesty, so far beyond us that we cannot think adequately of him to interpret him. Yet this God has come to us in grace to make himself known. In Jesus, God became localized, concrete, and like us so that we could understand him and come to him.

Nevertheless, in thinking of God as localized in Jesus, it could not always be so. Jesus said it was necessary that he go away so that the Spirit could come (John 16:7). In this text, Jesus calls us to do transfer thinking, to move from the concrete to the universal. We now think of the transcendent God, of God as we know him in Jesus Christ, as present and active universally in the Holy Spirit.

When we speak of the Spirit as God present, we can relate to the Spirit as to personality, to One who has come to be with us. The Spirit comes to fill our lives and yet is distinctly a Sovereign Presence over and beyond us. In confessing the Spirit as an expression of the Three-in-One God, we thereby recognize that we do not know God fully apart from knowing the Spirit, nor do we know the Spirit apart from knowing Jesus the Christ. The manifestation of the Threeness is at the same time the Oneness of God, the God of community, reconciling us to himself.

Wilson Benton Jr. has spoken of our being in Christ, united in Spirit: "Without union with Christ by the Holy Spirit, there is no salvation. The Holy Spirit makes actual in us what Christ makes possible for us." This means that one cannot accept Jesus fully without accepting his gift of the Holy Spirit. And one cannot know the Holy Spirit other than knowing him as the Spirit of Jesus. In fact, there is no way in which one receives the Spirit other than in and through Jesus our Lord.

Nevertheless, many people have come to Jesus for salvation and received him without immediately understanding the full aspects of life in Christ. Some new believers do not yet understand the gift of the Holy Spirit, assurance of salvation, freedom from some enslaving sin, or joy in communion with other believers. As a result, there is a danger that new Christians may live for some time in a wilderness journey rather than entering his promise (Acts 2:38-39).

An even more subtle danger is that new believers may pick up or be introduced to forms of pseudo-spirituality and fail to experience the freedom of the Spirit. Lest we pursue other forms of spiritual phenomena, we are instructed to test the spirits. John wrote, "Every spirit that does not correspond to the Jesus come in the flesh is not of God" (1 John 4:2-3, author's paraphrase). Even sincere Christians may identify some phenomena of the psychology of religious experience as a new work of the Spirit simply because in it they achieve an emotional high. But the gospel of Christ is attested by his death and resurrection and by his gift of the Spirit; it does not need other attestations than solidarity with Christ.

The Spirit addresses us with a divine claim only through the Word, Christ, and not through any other word. When the Scripture speaks of Christ's divine authority after his resurrection, it means the authority of our sovereign Lord at God's right hand. Thus O'Donovan says,

> When the church has forgotten this, it has strayed in one of two directions: towards an excessive admiration of spontaneity, on the one hand, and towards an excessive reverence for tradition on the other. Of course, the Holy Spirit in the NT is seen to work also through spontaneity, in prophecy and ecstatic utterances; yet the attitude of the apostolic church to spontaneity is cautious. (141)

O'Donovan sees spontaneity and tradition as failing to bring the christological principle of criticism to the manifestation of the spirits: "Test the spirits to see whether they are from God. . . . Every spirit that does not confess Jesus is not from God" (1 John 4:1-3). O'Donovan observes, "What is tradition other than spontaneity in slow motion!" (141-2). The key to corrective measures is to recognize that over and beyond the sign of the supernatural in our midst is the calm sense of God's presence.

In addressing the woman of Samaria, Jesus said, "God is spirit, and those who worship him must worship him in spirit and truth" (John 4:24). The Greek text does not say "a spirit" but "spirit" in contrast to material. Here we are presented with the universal God, Yahweh, on whose form we dare not look yet who is present as the universal Spirit. God was Incarnate in Jesus; yet our Lord said, "It is to your advantage that I go away, for if I do not go away, the Advocate [Holy Spirit] will not come to you; but if I go, I will send him to you" (John 16:7). This is Jesus' promise, to send the Spirit; it was necessary that he go away so that the Spirit of God would be the immediate yet universal Presence.

Jesus spoke of the Spirit as person, similar to himself, and taking personal actions: "When the Spirit of truth comes, he will guide you into all the truth. . . . He will glorify me, because he will take what is mine and declare it to you" (John 16:7-15). He referred to the Spirit as another like himself, as "the Spirit of God" (Matt. 12:28), in much the same way as he referred to himself as "the Son of God" (John 11:4; 19:7).

Jesus' use of "he" should not be taken to mean gender, for God is beyond masculine and feminine. Neither would it be appropriate for the reference to the Spirit to be feminine, as that might seem to allude to a (pagan) "queen of heaven" (Jer. 7:18; 44:17-25). John, writing of Jesus as our "Advocate" with the Father, presents Jesus in his role of representing us, as our Mediator (1 John 2:1; cf. Heb. 4:15; 8:6; 1 Tim. 2:5). In turn, the Holy Spirit is God's Advocate for and with us (John 14–16; cf. Rom. 8:26-27); through his wonderful presence, God is in our consciousness. As God present with us, the Spirit is the "down payment" or "pledge" of what is to be known fully in our future with God (Eph. 1:14).

Following the resurrection of our Lord, he appears to his disciples and shares with them over a forty-day period. "He breathed on them and said to them, "Receive the Holy Spirit" (John 20:22). This text reminds us of OT references to the Spirit as the breath of God, the sovereign wind of God (Gen. 1:2; cf. 2:7). It also plays on multiple meanings: in Hebrew, *ruakh* means "wind/breath/spirit," and so does the Greek word *pneuma*.

Jesus' words to receive the Spirit are a command. He enjoins the disciples to open themselves to his gift of the Spirit. John closes his Gospel by referring to Jesus' specific promise of the gift of the Holy Spirit. This completes John's presentation of the teachings of Jesus about the Spirit (John 14–16). The passage points to a fulfillment of this promise on the day of Pentecost (Acts 2). This seems to be a more correct interpretation than to count John 20 and Acts 2 as different events in Jesus' act of giving the Spirit.

In the first chapter of Acts, Luke recounts the forty days in which the resurrected Christ has met with the disciples in seminar sessions. Jesus again reminds the disciples that they will be baptized with the Holy Spirit in a few days. On the day of Pentecost, something unique happens (Acts 2). Jesus as risen Lord baptizes his disciples with the Holy Spirit. The prophecy of Joel is now fulfilled as God pours out his Spirit on all flesh, men and women, young and older, powerful and powerless. This is unique.

The Spirit now fulfills the transformation promised in the new covenant prophesied by Jeremiah (31:31-34). This is an inner transformation or regeneration based on the finished work of Christ. Yet the Spirit affects more than the individual's experience. There is the creation of something new, the church, the body of Christ, "a habitation of God through the Spirit" (Eph. 2:22, KJV; 1 Cor. 3:16-17). This new community of the Spirit is the unique, dynamic, and transforming work of God. The Spirit is creating a people of God as a visible demonstration of the rule of Christ in the world.

Too often people have looked merely at the Pentecost phenomena of the tongues of fire, the sound of the rushing wind, and the people's speech in other languages than their own. These unusual symbols confirm that the experience is directly related to what was foretold by the prophets. However, the primary reality is not the symbols but the immediacy of God's presence in the Spirit. He has come, is there among them, and is now within them. This is true *now;* the Spirit is with us! Our reconciliation with God is so authentic and personal that God confirms it in us by his very presence in the Spirit. What a wonderful Savior, the Lord God!

Through the centuries, Christians have often debated over the relationship of the inner word and the outer Word. Those called Spiritualizers stressed the inner word of the Spirit so strongly that the outer Word, the Scripture, had a diminished authority. Authority thus came from subjective impressions. On the other hand, an emphasis on the outer Word of Scripture, the *sola scriptura* of the Reformation, too often treats the Bible in a legalistic manner, overstressing the "letter" of Scripture. This misses the "spirit of Scripture," the illumination of the Spirit. But the Spirit-inspired Scripture remains the authoritative Word of God, the one source for fully understanding the self-disclosure of God.

I believe we must hold the authority of Scripture together with the work of the Spirit functioning in the interpreting community of Jesus' disciples. We need to emphasize what I call an inerrancy of *meaning* rather than an inerrancy of words. This is not to minimize the importance of the study of words; we recognize that the inspiration of the Spirit was at work in the writer and led to choices of right words. Jesus said, "The words that I have spoken to you are spirit and life" (John 6:63).

Nevertheless, words are vehicles of communication, and they may be used differently, especially as they are translated across languages and cultures. Words are symbols of meaning; our task is to prayerfully discern the meaning the Spirit is conveying in, through, or by the word symbols. Again, this is not to minimize the Spirit's direction in the writer using "right words." Instead, we recognize that words in themselves are the vehicles of communicating the understanding that God desires. Our task in interpreting, in exegeting, is to seek the Spirit's guidance in grasping the meaning that is being communicated. There is a spirit of Scripture, and this transcends words (2 Cor. 3:3-6).

This is not a simple process, for mankind continues to search for meaning. In *Realms of Meaning*, Philip Henry Phenix, of Columbia University, speaks of four aspects of meaning:

• The first is reflectiveness or self-awareness, including the basic principle of duality or self-transcendence, enabling one to stand outside oneself and know things.

• The second is rule in logic or principle. Each type of meaning has its own rule: intention has meanings different from memory meanings, social meanings differ from artistic meanings, moral meanings differ from language meanings, and so on.

• The third dimension is selective elaboration, meanings with the inherent power of growth, leading to elaboration of the enduring traditions of civilization.

• The fourth is the meaning of expression, meanings that have civilizing power, that are communicable through symbols, identified with its referent, and also distinguished from it (21-25).

On this fourth level of meaning, the Christian community needs to think carefully about the relationship between symbol and reality. Some tend to idolize the symbol, to treat it as though in itself it mediates grace rather than communicating grace. The symbol always calls us to look beyond itself to the reality of which it speaks and in which it participates.

Religious symbols and metaphors give power to language. For example, the act of baptism or the elements in the Lord's Supper are symbols of covenant. Words are themselves symbols, and through these symbols we are called and enabled to reach out to the Lord. The words "baptism with the Spirit" speak of his divine Presence. For those who take Jesus as Lord, baptism with the Spirit is far more than a symbol; it is a reality. Jesus is the one who gives the inner witness of assurance, of peace, of joy in reconciliation.

The gift of the Holy Spirit and the immediacy of God's presence enable us both personally and corporately to experience his presence and his work. From the day of Pentecost onward, the language of the NT is a language of personal relationship. In his sermon at Pentecost, Peter quotes the prophet Joel: "God declares, . . . I will pour out my Spirit upon all flesh" (Acts 2:17). This personal relationship with the Spirit is the fulfillment of that toward which the prophet pointed. This relationship of reconciliation was to come in the last or final stage of God's redemptive work.

The writer of Hebrews says, "In these last days [God] has spoken to us by a Son" (Heb. 1:2). Likewise, Peter quotes Joel and focuses Pentecost as the fulfillment of God's full extension of grace for these "last days," last in the culmination of his work of salvation (Acts 2:16-21). It is for each of us to experience a new life in Christ, and in this relation we should each enjoy the gift of the Spirit and his transforming grace.

In the sixteenth-century Reformation, Zwingli taught, "There are two baptisms, the outer baptism of water that doesn't save or change anyone, and the inner baptism with the Spirit that saves and changes a person." He said this to minimize the issue of infant baptism. After dropping his earlier interest in believers baptism, he supported baptism of infants. Zwingli was saying that what really counts is the baptism with the Spirit.

This point of the inner baptism was accepted by his associates Conrad Grebel and Felix Manz as a meaningful part of their experience and faith. Then Zwingli chose to tie his reformation movement to the city council and thereby unite church and state for security. So these Radical Reformers broke with Zwingli and continued their quest for an authentic church of believers, in freedom from state control. Baptism for them was a "sign" of the new life in covenant with Christ, confirmed by his Spirit.

As this free church developed, the Anabaptists pursued many points of understanding the Scriptures as taught by the early Zwingli. The Anabaptists especially stressed personal commitment to Christ and walking in the resurrection (*Schleitheim Confession*, art. 1). Another conviction was this emphasis on the inner baptism with the Spirit. They believed that the Spirit calls and transforms a person, that the Lord Jesus baptizes each believer with the Spirit. By the Spirit's work, one is brought to Christ; only by the Spirit's work can one walk with Christ. Their convictions on the order of discipleship grew out of this reality of relationship with Christ.

Menno Simons, a sixteenth-century Anabaptist leader, wrote,

> No, outward baptism avails nothing so long as we are not in-
> wardly renewed, regenerated, and baptized with the heavenly fire
> and the Holy Ghost of God. But when we are the recipients of
> this baptism from above, then we are constrained through the
> Spirit and Word of God by a good conscience which we obtain
> thereby, because we believe sincerely in the merits of the death
> of the Lord and in the power and fruits of His resurrection, and
> because we are inwardly cleansed by faith. (125)

Jesus taught that just as John baptized with water, so he (Jesus) would baptize with the Spirit (Acts 1:5-8). The Spirit is our baptism, and the one doing the baptizing is Jesus. The Spirit does many things: convicting, calling, regenerating, sanctifying, anointing, illuminating the Word, giving us his fruit and his gifts. But the Spirit does not baptize us with himself; Christ gives the Spirit to us as this baptism.

The word *baptism* means to be brought under the control of a superior power or influence. Thus we have a variety of expressions: baptism with suffering, baptism with fire, baptism with water, baptism with the Spirit, baptism into the death of Christ, and baptism "in the one Spirit" into "one body" of Christ (1 Cor. 12:13). This last text tells us that the Spirit is creating one body.

Paul also writes to the believers of Ephesus, "There is one body and one Spirit, just as you were called to the one hope of your calling, one Lord, one faith, one baptism, one God and Father of all, who is above all and through all and in all" (Eph. 4:4-6).

In the church today, we need to rediscover the realities of life in the Spirit. We need renewed understanding of what it means to receive the gift of the Spirit from Jesus. In the Spirit, Christ is present with us. This is a reality for us both as individuals (1 Cor. 6:19) and as a corporate body or community of the Spirit (3:16). In 6:19, Paul says that one's very body becomes the temple of the Spirit. In 3:16, Paul emphasizes the community of believers as a temple of the Spirit.

This community reality will keep us from reducing the church to social, institutional, or political processes. Each congregation, as one unit of the larger church, is a community of the Spirit, a temple of the Holy Spirit (1 Cor. 3:16), "a habitation of God through the Spirit" (Eph. 2:22, KJV). This is especially liberating for Western Christians who tend to major on organization, structure, and program more than spirit, fellowship, and diversity. Each of us can share this freedom to live as participants in a community of the reconciled.

The Spirit is present in the corporate body and also present for each believer. One's very body "is a temple of the Holy Spirit within you, which you have from God" (1 Cor. 6:19-20). Paul holds this in relationship with the corporate body: "In the one Sprit we were all baptized into one body" (1 Cor. 12:13). In other passages, Paul speaks of the Spirit being the seal or security of our relationship with God, and of the Spirit being the inner witness that we belong to God (e.g., 2 Cor. 1:22; Eph. 1:13; 4:30; Rom. 8:16).

In his commentary on Romans, John R. W. Stott introduces chapter eight by emphasizing that Paul speaks to the believer's security more than to the believer's sanctification. This arises from the conclusion of the chapter, where Paul affirms that nothing can separate us from the love of God that is in Christ Jesus our Lord. Such is also the meaning of being sealed with the Spirit (Eph. 1:13); the Spirit protects or keeps us in the fellowship of Christ.

The Lord has defeated the one who has now only the power we give him to harm us. We are told to resist the devil, and he will flee (James 4:7). Our security is in the presence of the Spirit of Christ. Our victory is by walking in the Spirit, not ignoring, quenching, or grieving the Spirit, but by knowing his presence and power in the actualization of our reconciliation.

In addition to inner baptism with the Spirit and outer baptism with water, the Anabaptist tradition recognizes a third baptism, one of suffering and blood (Klaassen, 162-170; van Bracht, 234; *Confession of Faith in a Mennonite Perspective*, 46-49). This baptism is our identification in cross-bearing, our participation in the suffering that comes with the encounter of God's kingdom and the realm of darkness, selfishness, and evil. Jesus speaks of his cup of suffering and his baptism of overwhelming disaster, and says his disciples will experience both (Mark 10:38-39; 14:36; Luke 12:50; cf. Isa. 43:2).

To the Colossians, Paul makes a difficult statement: "I am now rejoicing in my sufferings for your sake, and in my flesh I am completing what is lacking in Christ's afflictions for the sake of his body, that is, the church" (Col. 1:24). The church shares the suffering of the cross as we engage the world in thought and evangelistic witness, calling people to the way of Christ. We witness for Christ and take our stand openly as his disciples, knowing that those who are hostile to Christ will transfer hostility to us.

Thus Paul says, "All who want to live a godly life in Christ Jesus will be persecuted" (2 Tim. 3:12). Peter reminds believers of their calling to follow Christ's example in suffering for the gospel (1 Pet. 2:19-24). The sixteenth-century Anabaptist Conrad Grebel said, "Christ must suffer still more in his members, but he will strengthen them and keep them steadfast to the end" (Harder: 293). Yet Jesus says, "Blessed are you when people revile you and persecute you and utter all kinds of evil against you falsely on my account. . . . Your reward is great in heaven" (Matt. 5:11-12; cf. Rom. 8:7).

In gratitude for God's amazing grace, we should honor all that the Spirit does in our lives as believers. It is his work to call us, convict us, regenerate us, indwell us, seal us in fellowship with God and each other in the church, anoint us for power, illuminate our minds to perceive truth, fill our lives with grace to be Christlike, bear fruit through us, gift us with abilities to do the work of God, liberate us to enjoy the walk with God, and use us as spokespersons with the gospel and the word of love, peace, and justice.

All that we experience of God, provided for us in Christ, is mediated to us by the Holy Spirit. In Galatians 5:22-23, Paul writes of the "fruit of the Spirit," which I have paraphrased:

The Fruit of the Spirit Is Love

Joy is the celebration of love.
Peace is the practice of love.
Patience is the preservation of love.
Kindness is the expression of love.
Goodness is the action of love.
Faithfulness is the loyalty of love.
Gentleness is the attitude of love.
Self-control is the restraint of love.
The fruit of the Spirit is love.

This greatest passage on love in Paul's writings is set between two chapters of 1 Corinthians that deal with the gifts of the Spirit (12 and 14). The reason for this may be suggested in 12:31: "Strive for the greater gifts," or "Covet earnestly the best gifts" (KJV). Here the same form of the Greek verb "strive" or "covet earnestly" (KJV) may be indicative (as in NIV note) or imperative, as usually translated.

If indicative, Paul is describing the behavior pattern he wants to correct in chapters 12–14: individuals taking pride in their spiritual gifts (cf. 1:7). We could read, "You Corinthians are always seeking the better gifts." Paul follows this observation with his statement: "And (yet) I will show you a still more excellent way" (NRSV/KJV). This excellent *way* follows and is poetically portrayed in the beautiful passage on love (1 Cor. 13). Love rather than competition is the whole context or *way* of exercising spiritual gifts. Without love, the gifts have no usefulness. With love, believers should seek not so much the "greater gifts" but simply "spiritual gifts" (14:1).

Possibly "strive" in 12:31 is imperative (as in 14:1, 39). Paul is commanding believers to seek spiritual gifts that are better/greater for building each other up than tongues (14:6, 17, 24, 31). Tongues are not forbidden but must be exercised only with restraint, interpretation, and good order (14:27, 39-40). We are to rely on the Spirit for the wide range of gifts manifested in speaking ministries, administration, wisdom, power in ministry, grace for living, and service. Love is the only context for expressing all the spiritual gifts (12:31—13:13; Fee: 623-5).

Then in 14:1 Paul says, "Pursue love and strive for the spiritual gifts." The same Greek verb form for "strive" in 12:31 is repeated as possibly imperative in 14:1 and 39. In chapter 14, Paul explains how the gifts of the Spirit should be used for the profit of all, not to promote self. These gifts are to be received for the good of the church and not for puffing up individuals (12:7; 4:6-7).

As Hebrews also says, "God added his testimony by signs and wonders and various miracles, and by gifts of the Holy Spirit, distributed according to his will" (Heb. 2:4). The significant phrase is "according to his will" (cf. 1 Cor. 12:11). Gifts must be used for calling unbelievers to account (14:24) and "for building up" the church, "so that all may learn and all be encouraged" (14:26, 31). Paul repeatedly refers to the fact that the work of the Spirit is for the good of the body, that everyone may profit as we enable one another to become more Christlike. God enables his people with grace and power to do his will and perform his work.

In his letter to the Galatians, Paul speaks of the counteracting power of the Spirit in overcoming our tendency to sin:

> Live by the Spirit, I say, and do not gratify the desires of the flesh. For what the flesh desires is opposed to the Spirit, and what the Spirit desires is opposed to the flesh; for these are opposed to each other, to prevent you from doing what you want. But if you are led by the Spirit, you are not subject to the law. (Gal. 5:16-18)

This remarkable passage is often misinterpreted. The Greek verbs in this passage are in the present tense, thus meaning, "The self is continually desiring to have its way," and "The Spirit is continually present and desiring for us to go God's way." These two are opposed to each other. But the Spirit is always present "to prevent us from doing what the self desires (what we want)." This is our victory, the counteracting power of the Spirit to claim us for God and keep us from surrendering to evil. The transforming power of grace is at work in the lives of the reconciled—a truth often missed by commentators.

The Spirit's liberating victory in the lives of Jesus' disciples witnesses to those about us that salvation is a transforming reality. His counteracting power enables us to live in victory over the sins that beset us. The Spirit witnessing through us to the new life is a reality. In the early 1950s, I was the pastor of a Mennonite Church in Sarasota, Florida. During the winter of 1952, William Culbertson, president of Moody Bible Institute, Chicago, visited friends in Sarasota who attended our church. I invited Culbertson to preach at a Sunday evening service, and he shared this truth as he spoke from Jesus' words about the Holy Spirit from John 16:

> Nevertheless I tell you the truth: it is to your advantage that I go away, for if I do not go away, the Advocate will not come to you; but if I go, I will send him to you. And when he comes, he will prove the world wrong about sin and righteousness and judgment: about sin, because they do not believe in me; about righteousness, because I am going to the Father and you will see me no longer; about judgment, because the ruler of this world has been condemned. (John 16:7-11)

Culbertson emphasized that the Spirit doesn't just float around doing his work; he does it in and through believers. The Spirit convinces the world of their sin of unbelief by showing the meaning of belief in our lives. He convinces the world of righteousness by showing the righteous quality in our lives as believers. He convinces the world of judgment by showing in our victory that Satan is defeated and that those who come to Christ are free. This striking exegesis stresses the dynamic aspects of the Spirit's work through the church. As the body of Christ, we make Jesus' rule visible to the world. This is our joy, our mission, and our privilege.

Hallelujah, what a wonderful Savior, what a marvelous and thorough reconciliation, and what a wonderful saving relationship!

9

A Community
of the Third Way

You are a chosen race, a royal priesthood, a holy nation,
God's own people, in order that you may proclaim the mighty
acts of him who called you out of darkness into his marvelous
light.
  Once you were not a people,
    But now you are God's people;
  once you had not received mercy,
    but now you have received mercy
  Beloved, I urge you as aliens and exiles to abstain from the
desires of the flesh that wage war against the soul. Conduct
yourselves honorably among the Gentiles, so that, though they
malign you as evildoers, they may see your honorable deeds
and glorify God when he comes to judge. (1 Pet. 2:9-12)
  So, whether you eat or drink, or whatever you do, do
everything for the glory of God. Give no offense to Jews or
to Greeks or to the church of God, just as I try to please
everyone in everything I do, not seeking my own advantage,
but that of many, so that they may be saved. Be imitators
of me, as I am of Christ. (1 Cor. 10:31—11:1)

INDIVIDUALISTS SEEK to have their own way; it is no small mir-
acle when they are brought together in fellowship. I heard of two
brothers who lived on adjoining farms, but they were at odds. For
months they had been estranged, not speaking to each other. One day
a young man stopped at the elder brother's farmhouse. He needed a
job and asked if there might be some work he could do for the

farmer. Looking at his chest of tools, the farmer asked about his skills, and the young man said he was a good carpenter.

Suddenly the farmer had an idea. He pointed to the next farm where his younger brother lived: "Do you see that farm over there? That is my brother, and we are not on speaking terms. Things were well until he took a bulldozer, cut into the bank at the reservoir, and ran that stream of water down through the meadow between us. Yes, I'll give you some work. There is a pile of lumber by the end of my barn. I'll hire you to build a solid fence between us. Build it eight feet high, and then I won't need to be looking at that farm."

The farmer went to town and said he would see the carpenter in the evening. The young man went to work, but not in the way the farmer had instructed. He spent the day building a bridge across the stream. When the farmer came home in the evening, he was amazed to see the bridge, beautifully done, stretching across the stream, with braces, handrails, and all. But there was no fence.

Just as he was about to object, he saw his brother coming down across the field to the bridge. As the farmer also walked toward it, his neighbor called out, "You are some brother, to build a bridge like this so we can get together." He started across the bridge. The older brother paused, then also walked onto the bridge. The two brothers embraced and were reconciled. The farmer turned to thank the young man and ask him to stay and do other work, too.

The carpenter replied, "No, I need to be moving along, I have other bridges to build."

Community is the social and spiritual dynamic of reconciliation. It is not a partisanship created around a stance either to the right or to the left; it is a *Third Way,* a community that desires to know the priorities of the reign of God. Previously, we have emphasized that the church is above all the body of Christ and a community of believers. It is important that we understand community as a dynamic relationship. The kingdom, Jesus said, "is not coming with things that can be observed." It is the rule of Christ as a spiritual dynamic (Luke 17:20-21). Similarly, we do not think of community as organization.

Community is not created. It is a gift from God. Community is participation in grace, a oneness that comes by our common center, fellowship with Jesus. As a people of God, we are called to community, to the fellowship of his Son. This fellowship forms the true essence of the church, not an institution but a fellowship of the reconciled. The biblical emphasis is on *koinonia*, on fellowship in the Spirit. Our community is a witness to spiritual quality even within the larger society of relativism and secularism.

As our congregation developed on Capitol Hill from 1981, we found that to be a people of God in the inner city called for a deep sense of community. This was a dynamic of the Spirit, a gift of grace, and not just a social gathering of people with ethnic ties or geographical proximity. We came together across cultural, denominational, racial, and ethnic lines and found our common ground in the worship of Jesus Christ.

This dynamic of relating to each other in and through Jesus Christ gave us a sense of belonging. We enjoyed fellowship at the level of the spirit, and not merely on the psychical or emotional level. This relationship gave us freedom and power to be a community of the Spirit within the larger community surrounding us, to be a people of the Third Way.

The first priority for our congregation was and is to understand and do the will of God. We took seriously the words of Jesus: "Strive first for the kingdom of God and his righteousness" (Matt. 6:33). We sought to know what it meant to live by the will of God in the context of the inner city, but also among a people who boast of being the most powerful people in the most powerful city of the most powerful nation of the world.

We had to keep asking what it means to be a servant in a social milieu where the usual quest is for power and control. Jesus said, "You know that the rulers of the Gentiles lord it over them, and their great ones are tyrants over them. It will not be so among you; but whoever wishes to be great among you must be your servant" (Matt. 20:25-26). Humility of this magnitude is actually the cost of living by the Third Way.

What I call a community of the Third Way finds its character in and from the kingdom of God. His kingdom, or rule, determines the character of his people. His rule has priority in the lives of his disciples, resulting in a lifestyle that may well be called a style of the Third Way. I began using this term in the early 1980s as one focus among others for my ministry in our congregation in Washington, D.C. It has offered a perspective on life that enables our people in their various occupations to ask the in-depth questions of what is consistent with the will and kingdom of Christ.

Our people came from both sides of the political and social spectrum, yet many became less partisan, not identified with either right or left but with the way of the kingdom of God. As disciples, we can be neither rightist conservatives nor leftist liberals in lockstep. Instead, we can live in loyalty to Christ, a loyalty that lets us select from right, left, or middle, going by primary considerations of faithfulness to the kingdom of God. We are given freedom amid the partisanship of our society, a freedom to engage people in dialogue, whatever their position in the pluralism of our times.

Paul Lederach's 1980 book of sermons on *A Third Way* helped introduce that term to Mennonites. At Denver in 1985, during an inter-Mennonite conference, my paper focused on the Third Way as an approach in evangelism. It supplied the title for the book Henry Schmidt edited from papers presented at this conference on evangelism: *Witnesses of the Third Way*. The term *Third Way* has become more commonly used in Mennonite circles and now is even the Internet address for a Mennonite ministry and information website (www.thirdway.com).

Many in our society want issues to be answered with a simple right or left position, conservative or liberal, so they can follow their leanings. But Jesus did not simply accept two choices, such as whether to be a Zealot or to cooperate with Rome. He stood in the Third Way, the way of the kingdom of God. For many people, there is too much ambiguity in this; they want black-and-white answers and do not want to live by principles that call for a difficult interpretation in each of life's situations.

When Jesus taught us to turn the other cheek, this is a Third Way. It is not retaliation or surrender; instead, it is a response in freedom. Turning the other cheek is the Christian's style of operation. It shows that we are free to decide our course of action. We are not bound by simply reacting to the way others treat us, eye for eye, and so on. But we act in response to what we have become in Christ and have learned of his principles of love and justice.

As Walter Wink says,

> The question here . . . is how the oppressed can recover the initiative and assert their human dignity in a situation that cannot for the time being be changed. The rules are Caesar's, but how one responds to the rules is God's, and Caesar has no power over that. (*Engaging the Powers*, 182)

This is the character and freedom of Third Way living.

When Jesus stood before Pilate, he faced the governor's question, "Are you the King of the Jews?" Jesus could either deny his kingship or make a political claim that would be threatening to Pilate. Instead, Jesus expressed the Third Way of the kingdom of God: "My kingdom is not from this world," not in the character of this world order. "If my kingdom were from this world, my followers would be fighting to keep me from being handed over. . . . But as it is, my kingdom is not from here" (John 18:33, 36). Jesus presented Pilate with a totally different stance to handle.

This interchange gave Pilate a glimmer of insight into Jesus' meaning; he asked, "What is truth?" Even if he asked cynically, he at least recognized this as the real question (18:38). In this exchange, we see the uniqueness of Jesus as the One who is "the way, and the truth, and the life" (John 14:6). Walter Wink develops this theme in a chapter on "Jesus' Third Way: Nonviolent Engagement" (*Engaging the Powers*, 175-93).

We need to ask real questions on the issues and not simply go with the flow of society. In the midst of intense partisanship, a few people would not simply vote the party line; they sought to follow the (higher) right in another way. On the Gulf War, Senator Mark O. Hatfield, a deeply committed Christian who understands the perspective of the Third Way, voted against U.S. military involvement. He stated publicly on television and at personal cost that we were only there because of our thirst for oil; we could do other things that would not take the lives of thousands of people.

Yet many Americans seemed to understand only an aggressive approach. On TV, they viewed the war as almost a game and admired the precision of U.S. military technology. But they had little awareness of the suffering inflicted on so many ordinary citizens. Rwanda and Bosnia have presented us with the incalculable cost of human tyranny and suffering. Nevertheless, many Christians insulate themselves from the reality of such atrocities by taking seriously only what is immediate for Americans: our own "national interest." We ought to concern ourselves with God's greater kingdom interests in the global community and utilize America's resources for the well-being of all peoples.

As Christians committed to the practice of nonviolence, we believe the church is called to live by the mandate of Christ; the state answers to the mandate of the people. We are not necessarily calling the state to be pacifist—though why not give it a try? Instead, we are calling the state to live up to the highest level of its own claims. The church is called to nonviolence. We are witnessing to the state by urging it to seek justice for all people alike, and work through humane negotiation rather than brute force. Through our lifestyle in the practice of love, we make it easier for the state to achieve this purpose.

Not being pacifist, the state can at least be committed to the principles of the so-called just-war approach, even though many of us do not see the possibility of a just war. Even so, we ask that the state take its claims of just war with utmost seriousness and conduct itself at least on this level. In turn, we ask churches that support a just-war theory actually to speak, in the face of war, on whether the practice is just. At the invitation of the Lutheran church, John Howard Yoder presented a series of lectures published as *When War Is Unjust*. This is an example of a major Protestant church taking the issue seriously.

Many evangelical voices advocate views of the extreme political right. Still others try to counterbalance this by speaking from and promoting a position that is over against a "rightist" position and often appears to be "leftist." There is another way. Joshua counseled the Israelites, "Be very steadfast to observe and do all that is written in the book of the law of Moses, turning aside from it neither to the right nor to the left" (23:6; cf. Deut. 5:32; Prov. 4:27).

Paul M. Lederach comments,

> That counsel from Joshua is most appropriate for us today, especially for those in the Believers Church tradition who profess to follow Jesus in a radical way. The pressure is on us to move,

sometimes to the left (liberal) and sometimes to the right (conservative). Indeed, if we take seriously the life and teachings of Jesus, the world will sometimes see us as liberal. At other times we will appear to be conservative. (*Gospel Herald*, 2/28/95)

I heartily agree. As a pastor and evangelist, I have found that such an approach is ultimately relevant. Many in our congregation have sought to discern the way of God's reign and thereby remain free to accept or reject positions of either right or left.

As a reconciled people, we know something about the cost and meaning of reconciliation. In its spirit, the church should reflect the Spirit of the Master, seeking not to control but to serve (Mark 10:42-45). Believers do this not so much to prove a point as to participate with each other in the love of Christ. The late David Thomas of Lancaster County, Pennsylvania, has said, "It is more important that we see together than that we see alike!" The dynamic of harmony becomes our most effective witness to the peace of Christ among us and through us.

Reconciliation with God includes our being reconciled to all that God is doing in our neighbors, whether friend or enemy. Jesus calls us to love God with the whole of our being, and to love our neighbors as ourselves (Mark 12:30-31). When we open our lives to God, we open our lives to what God is doing in our neighbors, whether friend or enemy. Reconciliation calls us into a new community, a fellowship of faith that is our primary association in society. This relationship will include people we like as well as those we find it difficult to understand.

One of the problems in Western society is our individualism, our loss of a sense of community. This individualism is a characteristic of human nature; it is also thought by some to have a particular relationship to the doctrine of justification by faith as the consequence of individualistic faith. But we should note that the priesthood of believers in the Reformation tradition is not only our direct association with God; we may well understand it as our privilege of being a priest and serving at another's side.

Others of us see the roots of Western individualism just as strongly in the Enlightenment and the individualism of humanistic thought.

Whether there is a direct relation to the Reformation or not, expressions of religious faith have become more individualistic; they will probably become more individualistic in the new century, with its socially pluralistic and multicultural nature. In contrast, God calls his people into community, a community of the Spirit, of the Third Way, and of grace. Our togetherness is an essential part of our covenant with Christ, on the common ground that each of us alike is totally dependent upon his grace.

Earlier we considered the visible and the invisible church. In Scripture, one does not find reference to the church militant as anything other than visible Christians living by the sword of the Spirit (Eph. 6:10-17). Only the church triumphant is the invisible church (as in Heb. 11:1—12:1; Rev. 6–7). The church militant is made up of those who identify with Jesus Christ as Lord. This identification becomes a lifestyle that makes the church visible.

The church is a light to the world that is not hidden under a basket (Matt. 5:15). As believers, we do not walk incognito, as though our identity with Christ is hidden; we are a "new creation" now (2 Cor. 5:17). Of this transformed people, Peter writes, "You are a chosen race, a royal priesthood, a holy nation, God's own people, in order that you may proclaim the mighty acts of him who called you out of darkness into his marvelous light" (1 Pet. 2:9). We are witnesses of God's grace and his continuing actions in the world. What is God doing in our time? God is building his kingdom, as made visible in the church.

The contemporary church, especially in America, seems to minimize the uniqueness of being a special people in the world, a people of the Third Way. In large measure, the church has identified with cultural religion. Evangelicals have almost uncritically accepted right-wing agenda that includes a conservative political stance. Liberals or ecumenical churches tend to left-wing positions but are less aggressive or "evangelistic" about their stance. Others of us, including many who are "progressive" evangelicals, are seeking Third-Way answers. We are asking, What is the way of the kingdom of Christ for today?

We look for clues in the writings of Jacques Ellul, Lesslie Newbigen, Jim Wallis, Ron Sider, Walter Wink, and others. In our day of pluralism, global village, and ethnic struggles, they call us to seek first the kingdom of God. Lesslie Newbigen's *The Gospel in a Pluralist Society* and Hauerwas and Willimon's *Resident Aliens* challenge the church to rediscover the truth of our calling to be God's people as aliens in our world.

To be effective as the church, we must begin thinking more relationally. We are called to be a people of God, and the church is people, not primarily organization or structure. We are a people in solidarity with Jesus, a people who walk with Jesus "on the way" (Mark 8:27). Each congregation of disciples becomes a fellowship of people who may not have all of the answers as to a Third Way. Yet they live in the excitement of searching and finding the way of Jesus beyond the more easily articulated options.

Each congregation becomes a covenant community with responsibility for the nurturing, discipling, and maturing of each member. Lesslie Newbigin says that as the community of disciples, we read the Bible together, "standing in the confessional circle" (1995:101). For a community of faith to become a people of the Third Way, we must become a hermeneutical community, together interpreting the Word and the will of God. As we follow this "congregational principle," we will more clearly define the local church as our primary fellowship of accountability. Particular aspects of life together in Christ make this fellowship dynamic:

• The local congregation is a community of the Spirit, called, regenerated, and transformed by the Spirit. The work of the Spirit in the community continues to sanctify the people who have been redeemed by the blood of Christ. His claim upon us is that we belong totally to Christ.

• The congregation is a community of worship, engaging in dialogue with God, declaring his worth-ship, and honoring him in celebrating his presence among us as we hear his Word and respond in prayer and praise.

• Such a congregation is a community of nurture. We understand one another in our walk as disciples, growing beyond our comfort zones, encouraging and equipping one another to serve Christ better.

• Such a congregation is a community of accountability, holding one another accountable to live out our confession, both for our own sake and for the sake of our witness to society. We are a people who have entered covenant with the Lord, and we continually challenge one another to integrity.

• This congregation is a community of compassion where there is genuine caring. Ministries of caring are developed for and with each other in the community of faith. With the congregation, we carry out ministries of service in our society across racial, ethnic, and class barriers, using the bridge of love.

• Such a congregation is a community of interpretation. We seek together for the mind of Christ as we interpret both the Scripture and the application of that Scripture to our lifestyle and to the issues we face in our world. This community hermeneutic helps us to transcend the individualism that marks our society, and to find the Third Way of the kingdom.

• Such a congregation is a prophetic expression, in word, in work, and in witness. It demonstrates that a people in Christ can live by the character of God's kingdom. Through our prophetic role, we extend the exercise of interpretation beyond ourselves into the world around us; it is our responsibility to make sure that people truly hear the Word of God in our social and global setting. As a community of the reconciled, we will extend the grace of reconciliation to groups beyond our circle.

It is always humbling to take part in a contextual interpretation of the Third Way. If we recognize the leading and discernment of the Spirit among us, we cannot be opinionated. The Spirit enables us to hear the Word of God in the Scripture as God's word written. In this hearing, our faith is vitalized and hope is actualized.

While we are personally justified by faith in our covenant with Christ, we are also a part of the redeemed community. This fellowship enriches us by moving us beyond an individualism that isolates us from others, creates a competitive stance, or makes us seek to dominate and coerce others. In contrast to the self-orientation marking our society, we become involved in a Christ-orientation that actualizes the togetherness of the Spirit.

In local congregations, we must find grace to show the unity of the body with the diversity of its parts. We need to see diversity as a gift rather than a problem. We recognize that each of us alike is created in the image of God. Yet we are not alike; in service we have different gifts and different cultural contributions to make.

To fully benefit from God's grace, we must accept the image of God revealed in every person, across all lines of gender and racial differences. We recognize differences without placing one above the other; we seek equality as we respect the different gifts the Spirit has given for the profit of all. Equality does not mean sameness, but value. In recognizing this value, our sense of equality becomes the key to harmony and mutual esteem.

There is no biblical evidence to justify one race or gender thinking of itself as above the other. As to race, we need a greater appreciation of the unity and variety with which God has graced humanity. The Bible speaks of "the human race" (Job 15:7) being "from one [ancestor/blood]" (Acts 17:26, NRSV note). All are called to receive salvation through Christ and join the new humanity (Rev. 7:9-10; 14:6).

As to gender, male and female are both alike created in the image of God (Gen. 1:27). In the average congregation, nearly 60 percent are women and 40 percent are men. This mix calls for teamwork in ministry; it is not adequate for men to do all the leading, nor is it good for men in a congregation to hear only men and not hear the word of God through the insights of women. Teamwork in ministry is one way to avoid competitive roles and to demonstrate the unity of the body of Christ (see Faith Martin).

As a people of God, we seek to hold evangelistic and social responsibilities together in the congregation and in its ministry in the community. Just as the Word became flesh and dwelled among us (John 1:14), so we are to put into flesh, express, and live out the will of God. We are social beings; we cannot retreat from social aspects of the gospel into a pious mysticism or private piety. Just as Jesus emphasized being responsible to one's neighbor, being a neighbor to the one in need, so we extend the understanding of the evangel by deeds that authenticate our words (Luke 10:25-37).

Our concern for the poor, our emphasis on justice, and our actions of love are all an extension of the grace of God through us. We are to be merciful, as our Father in heaven is merciful (Luke 6:36). People will believe our message when they see its truth showing through our lifestyle.

In most communities, more men and woman have professional roles. This factor opens increased opportunities for sharing the witness of faith as we carry the gospel into our professional world. A sense of the dynamic of presence, of being there as a presence for Christ, will enable us to be evangelistic in a gracious social pattern. Theodore Wiedel has said, "Evangelism is presence, service, and communication," and I accept that order. We earn the right to be heard as we relate to people in a style like that seen in the Master himself, a style that is respectful, loving, empathetic, and direct.

The contemporary evangelical church tends to see evangelism as a function, as verbally confronting people with the gospel. Instead, evangelism should first be a loving acceptance of others in the spirit of Christ. Francis of Assisi said, "Preach the gospel all the time. If necessary, use words!" We are first a presence for Christ. Our total lifestyle of discipleship is a witness to the gospel that changes us, even though we must then use words to explain that Jesus is the one who makes the difference. An alive congregation is a witness that is salt and light to the world (Matt. 5:13-16). We enrich society through the quality of the faith we share.

Congregations are made up of families, and as such we have a ministry to one another. Many voices impact our youth; at a particular stage of personality development, the adolescent needs to prove oneself over against the parents. Hence, it is important for developing young adults to have mature believers as friends, in addition to parents, mentors with whom to relate in the community of faith. No family should go it alone; the congregation should share in family dynamics in ways that build intimacy and respect in a larger and an accepting circle of friends.

Not all participants in a fellowship are married. Congregations need to find meaningful ways to include singles in the social aspects of their life together. This can also provide a proper context for people of mixed sexual inclinations to find social benefit that will help them to walk in the victory of Christ, leading celibate lives. Dietrich Bonhoeffer reminds us that one way to promote sexual purity is to enhance the sharing of fellowship in which we see each other as sister and brother rather than as sexual objects.

A community of the Third Way will help the congregation, especially the youth, to engage life from the stance of God's reign. This means to have clear priorities, to delineate principles that are transforming and free, and to establish loyalties that rise above political and social party lines. The evangelical church should move beyond being a political one-party group. Anyhow, we do not believe we will bring in the kingdom by political votes but by being a presence for God's reign. Attempts to build a "Christian party" will pervert the universal nature of the Christian gospel. If we politicize Christianity by party spirit, we radically alter its character.

The gospel calls us to be faithful to our Lord. We recognize that he carries forward his purpose throughout the church, even amid evils in a given society. In *Christian Reflections*, C. S. Lewis said that if one gives ultimate loyalty to a nationalism, a party, or a class, one has already given to Caesar what belongs to God.

We must be realists about the political process and the gifts with which people are endowed. We are blessed to have a good number of people of faith in political roles. But we need to recognize that there are many born-again Christians who are not qualified or called to political office, and who would not be good politicians or give insightful service to society. There also are many wonderful people in the world who are not in our community of faith; among them are gifted people who may make good politicians.

As Christians, we agree that we should have, as Lincoln said, "a government of the people, by the people, for the people." We do not place the matter of the rise and fall of Christian ideals in the hands of any political system. We do not subordinate the church to any political system. Instead, we accept responsibility as Christ's servants to teach and invite people to commitment to him. We call people to practice the highest ideals by joining us in discipleship of Christ. A secular (religiously neutral) government can be a good government, but a secular church is a compromised church.

We can be good citizens without endorsing everything the government does. Paul called the early church to pray for rulers, even though the emperor was an atheist and opponent to the Christian faith. Citizenship is a privilege, but we fulfill our role of relationship to government best by being good citizens whose prayers, integrity, and quality of life become our greater contribution.

My father-in-law, Lloy Kniss, was born into a Lutheran home and joined the Mennonite church as a young man. His new insights into biblical teaching on war and peace led him to take a firm stance of nonviolence, what the church called nonresistance. In World War I, he was drafted into the army; provision for conscientious objectors was not developed until World War II. With his convictions, as he entered the army, he refused to wear the uniform or carry a gun, so he would not be participating in war.

Kniss was treated in a rough way. Army staff threatened his life by showing him an open grave and mounds of dirt. He was told that his buddies were buried there for refusing to cooperate, and that the open grave was for him. They beat him and called him in for many rough interrogation sessions. He maintained a respectful attitude toward his persecutors but did not surrender his stance.

After months of this, Kniss received an honorable discharge and took the train to Pittsburgh, to return home to Johnstown, Pennsylvania. When he stepped off the train at Pittsburgh, he was surprised to meet the sergeant who had treated him with such meanness. In tears, the sergeant said he had come to the train station to find Kniss and apologize for the way he had been required to treat him.

In all the years I knew my father-in-law, he never spoke a word of criticism or disrespect for government. He simply believed that Jesus as his Lord led him to take a stand for nonviolence. Kniss recorded his experience and faith in *Why I Couldn't Fight*.

The Third Way provides freedom for people to follow their convictions. In turn, it creates a special vitality for the congregation in its relation to social and political decisions. But this way of kingdom priorities also safeguards the integrity of the congregation itself. As E. Stanley Jones has emphasized, we don't build the kingdom; God gives us the kingdom (Luke 12:32). Christ builds his church with our help, and we are to work in harmony with the kingdom (Matt. 16:18; 1 Cor. 3:10; Eph. 2:19-22).

In Washington, D.C., we shared the Lord's Supper the first Sunday of each month; this practice reminded us of the priority of the kingdom for our congregation and its worldwide relationships. Thereby we affirmed our commitment together to the Third Way of God's kingdom. We did not find this to be routine but a fresh and meaningful experience each time, enriched by patterns people brought from a variety of churches.

As we shared the emblems, we focused on our common relation with Christ. An Orthodox priest told me that when members of his church partake of the sacrament, they share with the Anabaptists this strong emphasis on the community of faith as the expression of the body of Christ. The service is not only a memorial service, as in most Protestant churches; it is especially a covenant of fellowship with the body of Christ, the church. In its various forms, observing the Lord's Supper is one continuing practice of the church as God's own people from the time of Christ to the present.

As people of the Third Way, we regard the church as our primary frame of reference. We form an interpretive community in which we seek to express the way of the kingdom of Christ amid the ideologies and parties of our society. This community seeks to avoid the idolatries of an enslaving materialism in our identity as a people of God, using but not abusing material resources. We educate for kingdom thought amid the secular orders and seek to avoid the syncretism of civil religion and of mere subjective humanism. As a people of the Third Way, we confess that we are already members of the kingdom that God is building.

The church as a people of the Third Way is a community of the reconciled and of the reconciling. Our unity with diversity shows this reconciliation to the world (2 Cor. 5:18-19). As such, it is a unity enabled by the Spirit, a common commitment to Jesus Christ, and a common worship of the one God and Father of our Lord Jesus Christ.

This kind of congregation grows through worship as celebration, enriches itself by nurture in becoming an informed congregation, enhances community by overt acts of fellowship for mutuality, extends its caring by mutual aid as people have need, and invites others to faith in Christ by its evangelistic witness.

My wife, Esther, was born in India as the daughter of missionary parents, Lloy and Elizabeth Kniss. They served in Mohadi, a jungle village fifty miles from Dhamtari. Nearby they had close missionary friends with the same church board. At the mission compound were several villagers who helped the missionary family in many ways. One of them was their cook, Suti.

Each morning the mission leader would call the workers to join in morning prayers. Suti, a Hindu, resisted this, but the missionaries insisted that she at least attend even if not taking part; this was their policy for all the workers. She resented this deeply and began her pattern of protest. There was no toaster, and she put the bread over the hot coals just before morning prayers. When prayers were over, the toast was burned black.

The missionary family agreed to say nothing and to daily eat the burned toast. After several weeks, with no retaliation or negative spirit toward her, Suti came to them in tears. "There is something in your religion that I don't find in mine. Your attitude of love even when I've treated you with such meanness is more than I can understand. I need to know this Jesus whom you serve." Suti came to Christ not by a lot of words but by the beautiful expression of grace in the lives of this missionary family.

The Christian church is made up of people who identify with Christ and walk with him. This church, as the people of God, seeks by word and deed to serve God's reign in society. Our mission is to show God's reconciling love to all people, across all class, ethnic, racial, and nationalistic structures. In Christ, all peoples are enabled to be one people, a people of God. In passages such as Psalm 67, the OT shows a yearning that all nations would join Israel in recognizing God's "saving power." In the NT, this is happening as a unique aspect of the body of Christ. We are called in Christ to transcend all social and political divisions, to be one new humanity through the redemption accomplished in the cross (Eph. 2:14-18).

The Third Way is not simply a strategy; it is loyalty to Christ. It means faithfulness to Jesus above every other secondary loyalty. This is made clear in the story of Jesus asking Peter, "Do you love me more than these?" (John 21:15-19). Out of fear, Peter has denied three times that he knows Jesus. After Jesus is crucified, Peter's guilt and despair are enormous. The resurrected Lord acts to reclaim Peter and reinstate him in the circle of the apostles. This shows that life for Peter and for all of us is based on God's transforming grace. Forgiving grace, yes, but more than this—grace that transforms us in relationship.

As Jesus questions Peter, we observe therapeutic steps of honest confession and self-understanding. First, Jesus asks, "Do you love (*agapaō*) me more than these?" The comparative word form in the Greek is ambiguous: *these* may be focused with a gesture to the other disciples, placing Peter in his place among them; or by a gesture to the fishing boats, placing before Peter the priority of serving Christ above his business.

Peter answers that he has affection for Jesus, using the word *phileō* for offering friendship rather than the word *agapaō* for sacrificial love. A second time, Jesus asks Peter, "Do you love (*agapaō*) me?" This means that Peter needs to face himself and answer, not in comparison with anyone or anything, but in authentic self-understanding. Again he replies that he has affection for Jesus (*phileō*). In each instance Jesus does not reject him, but says, "Feed/tend my sheep/lambs."

Yet this is not the full intent of Jesus' dialogue with Peter. He presses Peter to the full realization of what he is saying. The third time Jesus questions, "Do you offer real affection (*phileō*) to me?"

The text says Peter feels hurt because Jesus asks a third time (echoing Peter's triple denial), or perhaps that this third time Jesus uses the word *phileō*, offering affection rather than *agapē* love. Jesus is challenging Peter to genuine honesty and self-understanding. Peter cries out, "Lord, you know everything; you know that I love (*phileō*) you." This marks the basic honesty upon which Jesus can build a lasting relationship; he extends his commission to Peter.

What an amazing dialogue! Peter then looks at John and asks, "What about this man's commission?" (John 21:21, paraphrased). Jesus says, "What is that to you? Follow me!" He holds Peter to the integrity of his own confession and warns him against comparing himself with another. There is no authentic relationship with others when we avoid the integrity of the ethic of love in our own lives.

In this account the risen Christ calls us to an ethic for the new community. It is an ethic of liberating love toward God and toward our fellows. We learn this love from God in Christ and receive it from God through the Spirit of Christ. It is a love in freedom, freedom to walk in the family of God, and by the action of love to extend this family to others. In the liberty of Christ, we will treat all others in the spirit with which Christ has treated us. In his acceptance, we will witness to the joy of his love and of his fellowship. We will never harm someone for whom Christ died (1 Cor. 8:11); we wish, instead, to help them become fellow disciples of Christ. This is Third-Way living.

Ellul emphasizes that freedom operates with two axes, love for one's neighbor and love for the glory of God. In living as "strangers and pilgrims," the "aim of Christian freedom is not that society should be better or should function better. Betterment may well come about; we may expect or hope for it; but it is simply an added gift when Christians are living a genuinely free life" (1976:299).

Martin Dibelius says the gospel brings a social demand:

> The gospel is not a social message but it functions as a social demand. . . . The vision of the coming of God's kingdom shapes this demand. . . . What we have here is not a program for reorganizing the world but marching orders for every age. (*Botschaft und Geschichte* [1953], 178; via Ellul, 1976:299)

Finally, I share several ideas from Walz on a threefold orientation of freedom lived out in the world:

> First, [the church] has an evangelistic role. . . . This does not mean bringing non-Christians into the church but carrying the church to them. . . . The second orientation is missionary. This is not quite the same thing as the evangelistic orientation. The objective here is presence rather than conversion. . . . The third orientation is mediation. This follows from the second. Christians must stop judging or moralizing on activities and institutions so that they can be agents of their sanctification by the sacrifice of Jesus Christ. (via Ellul, 1976:299)

Any society is made better by having Christians present, believers who live in the freedom of Christ and relate in a freedom that expresses love for neighbor and the glory of God.

10

An Ethic of Freedom
in Righteousness

For freedom Christ has set us free. Stand firm, therefore, and do not submit again to a yoke of slavery. . . . For through the Spirit, by faith, we eagerly wait for the hope of righteousness. For in Christ Jesus neither circumcision nor uncircumcision counts for anything; the only thing that counts is faith working through love.

For you were called to freedom, brothers and sisters; only do not use your freedom as an opportunity for self-indulgence, but through love become slaves to one another. For the whole law is summed up in a single commandment, "You shall love your neighbor as yourself." (Gal. 5:1, 5-6, 13-14)

IN THE FALL of 1984, Esther and I accompanied Duke McCall and his wife to the former Soviet Union. McCall, as president of the Baptist World Alliance, was there to celebrate the hundredth anniversary of the Baptists in Russia. We were invited to be present with the Baptists as they recognized the two hundredth anniversary of their neighboring Mennonites in Russia.

Catherine the Great had invited the Mennonites to Russia. They were currently identified as members of the All-Union Council of Evangelical Christians-Baptists, the Government's recognized association of Protestant churches. This was before *glasnost,* and restrictions were everywhere; Christians were not free to share hospitality with us in their homes. KGB (State Security) police were present, to check what the American visitors were saying.

One Sunday morning, I preached in the great Baptist church in Moscow and was impressed with the wonderful choir and the packed building, with people standing in the aisles in rapt attention. I commented on the good service to my translator, Juri Puang. He said, "Yes, and there were many visitors." I responded that it was a remarkable attendance. He repeated, "There were many visitors, do you know what I mean?" Then I understood; he was telling me that KGB informers were well represented.

We could sense the yearning for freedom, and our hosts demonstrated it in an unusual way. When we went to the hotel dining room for meals, one of the pastors would stand and pray in a loud voice so all in the room could hear. He would ask for God's blessing on the meal, upon us as we shared, and upon our friends around us. Then we enjoyed the meal together. At the conclusion, another pastor would stand and again in a strong voice would give God thanks for the meal we had just eaten. They showed the freedom of the spirit in which they served the Lord, an inner freedom where social and religious freedom was forbidden.

In Christ we are called to freedom. Our Christian experience is not primarily moralistic. It is first and always a relationship, a fellowship with Christ. It expresses the covenant and character of reconciliation. "If we walk in the light as he is in the light, we are having fellowship one with another, and the blood of Jesus Christ his Son keeps cleansing us from all sin" (1 John 1:7, author's trans.). Ethics for the disciple of Christ is the personal extension of this fellowship, this freedom, this solidarity with Jesus.

As Christians, we commonly expect to enjoy a freedom of spirit in our personal life or piety; yet I perceive that we have not adequately related this freedom to ethics. For the Christian, ethics should take as normative the new life of discipleship, following Jesus Christ. A major issue for the church is how we can regard the life and teachings of Jesus as normative for Christian living. The emphasis on justification by faith has raised questions as to how we relate belief and behavior, faith and obedience, law and love.

I answer from this theological perspective: we relate ethics to Christology in the same way we relate salvation to Christology. We are saved in relation to Jesus, and we conduct ourselves (behave) in relation to Jesus. Christian ethics is therefore more relational than moralistic, more personal than structural.

To think of ethics in terms of reconciliation, we must appreciate God's transforming grace, his active work in our lives to enable us to pursue his intention for us. We see this grace as God calls Abraham and later interrupts Abraham's act of obedient faith in preparing to sacrifice Isaac. God is saying that his people must not follow a cultural pattern of human sacrifice. We also find this transforming grace in the Word of God spoken by the prophets. Ultimately, transforming grace is displayed in the Incarnation.

With a central Christology in the Anabaptist tradition, emphasizing the new creature in Christ, ethics is integrally related to our solidarity with Christ. But this solidarity is more than an inner piety; it means walking with Jesus in life. This Christocentric ethic has its power and its character in a direct relationship with Jesus; he works in us by his Spirit.

Before going further, we need to define an ethic of freedom. The term *freedom in righteousness* means a special quality of freedom. It is relational, a freedom of redemption. God has exhibited his new and perfect humanity in Jesus Christ, and now he shows this new humanity in those of us who share in the work of the Holy Spirit (O'Donovan: 101). It is not a humanistic freedom of autonomy, but a freedom in grace. In this freedom, the Holy Spirit's presence effects—for both the individual and the redeemed community—a freedom for the possibilities of grace.

The phrase *freedom in righteousness* clearly places possibilities before us. This righteousness, right-relatedness, is God's free response in righteousness and faithfulness. Paul shows this relationship for ethics: "God is at work in you, enabling you both to will and to work for his good pleasure" (Phil. 2:13, adapted). Our choosing and working for God's pleasure is our responsibility, as made clear in the Greek syntax, and is made possible only by the work of God within us, bringing about free expression.

In the condition of fallenness, humanity has turned freedom into unfreedom or slavery, the bondage of sin. But this is our condition, not our confession. Paul writes, "For freedom Christ has set us free" (Gal. 5:1). The bondage of sin is destroyed, and the Holy Spirit brings us into union with authentic humanity that is in fellowship with Christ. Freedom is related to authority; our authority is now the authority of Christ, the authority of Christ as Truth (John 14:6). Paul says, "There is no authority except from God" (Rom. 13:1); this authority evokes free action from us.

As O'Donovan writes,

> Created to exercise free choice, mankind is bound to the terms of creation and remains, even in a state of alienated freedom, a race of free agents. Nevertheless, fallen man does not live freely; for, as a free agent, he is bound to the choices he has made for unfreedom. . . . The work of the Spirit as "witness" to the objective deed of God in Christ, and his work as "life-giver" who restores freedom and power to mankind enthralled, are not two distinct works but one. For man's thrall is precisely that he has lost touch with reality. (109)

How does ethics relate to reconciliation? From my understanding of Anabaptist thought and emphasis, I have come to the conviction that the key is this: when we are reconciled, we have a new freedom in grace. This is a freedom by solidarity with our Lord. As a result, we now behave or act in this liberating relationship. We have a freedom to be and to become mature in Christ (Eph. 4:13-15), a freedom to live righteously. "Sin will have no dominion over you, since you are not under the law but under grace!" (Rom. 6:14).

Hence, this is an ethic of freedom, but not over against other elements of ethics such as love, discipleship, gratitude, obedience. Instead, the Spirit integrates and inspires these various perspectives.

Ethics in the believers church tradition has been commonly spoken of as an ethic of discipleship, of following Jesus in life. But this is only possible in the freedom of his grace. Further, following Jesus as disciples means that we see Jesus as the Word of God to us in his life, his spirit, and his words. Accepting Jesus as our mentor, our example, means that he becomes the standard of ethical behavior (1 Pet. 2:19-23). But in saying this, we cannot mean that we simply copy him; we need transforming liberating grace.

As sinful people, we have oriented our lives around ourselves rather than around God. We need a Savior-Liberator, one to reconcile us to God. Jesus is that Savior. We are saved in relationship with him, and as saved people we live in relationship with him. We live the new life in the freedom of his love.

An ethic of love is also a common emphasis among contemporary Anabaptists. This is true in some form among numerous other groups. As Augustine says in the conclusion of his *Enchiridion* (Handbook), a person is not known by what he believes, nor by what he hopes, but by what he loves (135). Augustine took this further: "Love God and do as you please." He apparently meant that those who love God will live to please God. An ethic of freedom in love is more than Luther's adaptation of Augustine's statement, that in the assurance of grace we "sin boldly so that God may forgive boldly and his grace be magnified."

Anabaptists stress freedom to walk in the will of God and to do so in fellowship with God, by participation in grace. Justification by faith means that we are accepted in our intent to do the will of God, even in our limited and imperfect obedience. The ethic of love will bring freedom to ask the basic question in every situation: "What is the course of love? How does *agapē* love act in this situation?" This ethic is set in the context of the freedom of grace. We will seek a relationship with others that will enhance their freedom for fulfillment in life.

Jesus said that the greatest commandment is to love God with the whole of one's being, to open one's life totally and intimately to God. This involves one's heart or affection, one's mind or attitude, one's soul or ambition, and one's strength or activity. Further, Jesus said that the second commandment is like the first, to love one's neighbor as oneself, that is, to open one's life to what God is doing in the neighbor, whether friend or enemy (Matt. 22:36-40). This love, the fruit of the Spirit in one's life, is the spirit of the disciple. Jesus said, "By this everyone will know that you are my disciples, if you have love for one another" (John 13:35).

As we love, we are liberated from self-centeredness; we can only love truly when grace has liberated us. In this freedom, Jesus gives us a "categorical imperative" (see Kant in chap. 11, below): "In everything do to others as you would have them do to you" (Matt. 7:12). We are to love others the way we would be loved.

From their writings and witness, we may conclude that an Anabaptist ethic is based on the freedom of Christ. Ours is a freedom to walk with Christ in the gracious acceptance of his grace. As Paul told the Galatians, "For freedom Christ has set us free" (Gal. 5:1). In this we recognize the primacy of grace, the fact that God extends both forgiving grace and transforming grace.

Eduard Schweizer affirms this view: "The effect of Christ's death is the effect of a deed of love bringing its fruit in a human life which is touched by it" (70). J. Lawrence Burkholder has also written of this freedom in the ethic of nonresistance: "It is the response of the disciple who owes his salvation to Christ. . . . It is freedom to love, having been loved by Christ" (1989:64).

Without the freedom of Christ, life would be bondage in sin (Rom. 6:14). There would be none of the meaning that we enjoy in Christ, none of the fellowship we enjoy with other believers in the reconciliation of Christ. Jürgen Moltmann says,

> Life without freedom has two special perils. We experience an outward hostility against which we can no longer defend ourselves, so we creep into our shells and protect ourselves against the hostile world outside through indifference and callousness. . . . But in doing so we are blocking our own vital energies. Our self-esteem diminishes. . . . We become inwardly submissive. This submission then becomes dependence, and dependence makes us irresolute. Our lack of initiative develops into general apathy. We stop living. (1992:104)

Immanuel Kant listed "God, freedom, and immortality" in a single sequence and made them to be mutually justifying: without God there is no freedom, and without freedom there is no God. We are "free for freedom." Moltmann comments that this emphasis is seen in the Liberation Theology of Latin America; he sees it as "the first convincing outline to combine belief in God and the will to be free as the biblical traditions enjoin" (1992:109).

As evangelicals, we need to take more seriously the last half of Ephesians 2. Here Paul grounds the redemptive and the ethical in Christ's cross. He holds the two together and shows that the greatest social change we can imagine—reconciliation between Jew and Gentile—is made possible as redemptive grace is extended into the social realm.

There are many tracks of ethical thought. Among them one finds an emphasis on Theocentric ethics (Gustafson), Christocentric ethics (John Howard Yoder), utilitarian ethics (human centered), an ethic of gratitude as one's response to God's grace (Lutheran), an ethic of obedience to the law or will of God (Reformed), an ethic of discipleship (Anabaptist), and so on.

I define an ethic of discipleship as freedom in solidarity with Christ. As such, it is too profound to be defined by any one word. It is an ethic of holiness in essence and character, an ethic of love in relationship and self-giving, and an ethic of freedom in spirit and being. An ethic of freedom undergirds and focuses the varied expressions of Christian ethics and builds solely on the grace and freedom granted us in union with Jesus Christ. An ethic of freedom is relational, arising from reconciliation. An ethic of freedom does not control, coerce, or manipulate but relates to others in the freedom of grace.

God's grace creates freedom in our lives as new beings in Christ. This includes freedom for victory over the dominance of sin, as Paul writes, "Sin will have no dominion over you, since you are not under law but under grace" (Rom. 6:14). Hence, we recognize that a basic emphasis in this transformation is regeneration; we are made to be new creatures in Christ, "a new creation" (2 Cor. 5:17). In this new creation, we are brought into freedom in Christ, a freedom in right-relatedness or righteousness.

As we are made into a new creation, we have the freedom to own God as Father, to walk with Jesus as disciples, and to live in the love of the Spirit. The early Anabaptists held this truth, as shown in their writings and in their call to obedience and holiness of life. As Clarence Bauman writes, "With this imperative of freedom, our total existence is at stake. Obedience to Christ's call can only be rendered in freedom or else it is not obedience" (102).

As I write, I am on a five-week preaching-teaching mission in Japan. A missionary friend in Hokkaido hosted Esther and me and arranged a beautiful cultural experience for us in sharing a tea ceremony. We watched the exquisite, coordinated movements, the smooth flow of transitions from one aspect of the ceremony to the next. Thereby we came to understand what our friend Mary Beyler meant by the "freedom of the discipline." Once we know the discipline, we can act with freedom within it. So it is with the freedom of discipleship, the freedom of grace. Obedience is not a legalism of works; instead, it is the devotion of relationship.

Paul says, "It is for freedom that Christ has set us free." In the same verse, he also instructs us, "Stand firm, then, and do not let yourselves be burdened again by a yoke of slavery" (Gal. 5:1, NIV). Repeatedly the apostle Paul affirms the liberty of the new life in Christ: "Now the Lord is the Spirit, and where the Spirit of the Lord is, there is freedom" (2 Cor. 3:17). This privilege is a relationship of openness rather than defense, of love rather than rebellion, of joy rather than the depressing aspects of perversion.

It first is a liberation to be, to belong, to become. But it is also a freedom from estrangement, from rebellion, from self-centeredness, from the perversion of one's life. When I first read Jacques Ellul's book *The Ethics of Freedom*, I found a positive response in my spirit. Here was an approach to ethics that was personalistic rather than moralistic, yet calling us to a high level of morality. The ethic of freedom is an ethic of righteousness, right-relatedness. God sent his Son and condemned sin in the flesh, "so that the just requirement of the law might be fulfilled in us, who walk not according to the flesh but according to the Spirit" (Rom. 8:3-4).

Thus ethics for the disciple of Christ is not a moralism but a fellowship. Pursuing the "right" is the pursuit of this relationship of love, both toward God and toward neighbor. The disciple makes ethical decisions in a positive response to the will of God. Our obedience of faith is the fidelity of relationship.

Jürgen Moltmann speaks of freedom and liberation as the biblical emphasis on exodus and resurrection. He sees this in Paul's words: "Where the Spirit of the Lord is, there is freedom" (2 Cor. 3:17). Moltmann relates this to the OT presentation of the exodus as God the Liberator (Exod. 3:1-15). Exodus means participation in covenant; in this relationship, the Spirit liberates us for life. Moltmann states three aspects of this freedom:

- Liberating faith—seeing freedom as subjectivity.
- Liberating love—seeing freedom as social, for "the person who

claims freedom for himself must respect the same freedom for other people."

• Liberating hope—seeing freedom as our future (1992:114-119).

While living in the inner city of Washington, D.C., for fourteen years, we needed to apply this ethic to many situations and issues:

• Helping a congregation recognize and promote the freedom of women and equality between men and women as known in Christ.

• Helping people confronted by violence to understand "tough love" in holding people accountable; finding ways to use nonviolent resistance in handling individuals prone to violence.

• Helping people with homosexual desires to respect themselves, respect the freedom of others, and not impose their inclinations on others and violate their freedom to live with celibacy in wholesome relationships.

By freedom we thereby enhance the lives of each other in grace. Love gives us the freedom of right-relatedness and of self-giving; such love can be trusted. We can live in freedom when and where we know that love is always seeking our well-being.

The resurrected Jesus, as noted above, focused this freedom of love in asking Peter the question each of us must answer: "Do you love me?" The ethic of the disciple is the liberating power of love, freedom in love. It begins by first establishing a freedom of relationship between us and Christ, between us and God. It further creates a freedom of relationship between us and others, providing unity with diversity. It also creates a freedom for disciples in the world by giving us a calling or mission. That calling liberates us from becoming enslaved to some lesser cause.

We need to experience this freedom in at least five areas of life:

Fellowship with God

First, an ethic of freedom means that we are free in Christ to enjoy fellowship with the reconciling God. Since we first are born into unfreedom, we must become free by the grace of God. We are not innocent: we are guilty of alienation from God, and we are burdened by the whole past experience of the human race (Rom. 5:12). The world talks about freedom, but freedom is difficult to understand outside of an awareness of God's grace. We only know freedom when we move from the question "freedom from what?" to the question "freedom for what?"

Believers are free to walk with Christ in his reconciling love. This opens the way to a totally new life, a life of freedom for what we know to be the good. Paul writes of this in Romans 7; though the law points to the good, one is not free to live by the good simply by knowledge but only by the freedom of the Spirit. As Helmut Gollwitzer says, "We are all free when and to the extent that we stand in obedience to the love of Christ."

John writes of this in the opening of his first epistle: Whoever claims to have fellowship with God and walks in darkness is dishonest. But if we walk in the light as God is in the light, we and God are having fellowship with each other (1 John 1:5-9). Earl Palmer says, "The Lord who is the light for the roadway is also our companion on the roadway" (30).

In Romans 5 Paul treats the problem of sin and how Adam's transgression really affects us all. Jesus' work was to correct what happened through Adam's transgression. His work of reconciliation restores what humanity lost in the Fall (Rom. 5:12-19). As we come to Christ, this fallenness is our condition, but it is not our confession or stance in faith. In the reconciling work of Christ, our relation with God is restored; our confession is that Christ counteracts the effects of the curse on Adam.

Working in us, Jesus overcomes consequences of Adam's sin. Christ is correcting our pride and self-centeredness, pursuit of dominance, quest to control others, injustice and inequity in relationships such as with racism, the competition of genders, and mistrust and misuse of one another. We do not build a position for ethical behavior on fallenness, on fallen humanness, or on behavior described but not prescribed in the judgment upon sinning humanity (Gen. 3:14-19); God gives humanity up to suffer the consequences of their sins (Rom. 1:18-32). Instead, we have been redeemed in Christ and reconciled to God and his purpose for us. Therefore, our ethic is built on the freedom of our new life in grace.

As we share this freedom in righteousness, the central characteristic of life is *agapē* love, the unconditional love of God and the anointing of love from God. Love is the manner and spirit of ethical behavior. It is the character of righteousness. In one sense, love is justice-righteousness spread around. But we are incapable of this freedom of love in and of ourselves. Only as we are liberated from self-centeredness are we able to love, to relate with intimacy to another, and to share authentic caring with those around us.

In the Sermon on the Mount, Jesus summarizes this in the golden rule: Act toward others as you would have them act toward yourself (Matt. 7:12). Bruce M. Metzger points out that while the negative form of the golden rule was around long before Jesus' time, he gives it as a positive course of action (161). In the love of God, we come to understand what love really is; in the grace of God, we are brought to share in this love. Once we know God, the love of Christ is "shed abroad in our hearts" (Rom. 5:5, KJV). As a fruit of the Holy Spirit (Gal. 5:22-23), Christ's special quality of *agapē*, unconditional self-giving love, is extended through us.

Another perspective on freedom in righteousness, freedom in right-relatedness, is seen in Jesus' teachings on the spirit and implications of spiritual restoration, in the Jubilee. In the synagogue at Nazareth, Jesus finds the text from Isaiah that announces the jubilee of freedom (Luke 4:16-21; Isa. 61:1-3). After reading the passage, Jesus says its meaning is being actualized in his ministry. Jesus gives it a deeply spiritual as well as a social meaning; it includes good news to the poor, freedom to the captives, and deliverance to the blind and the oppressed.

According to John H. Yoder, "The Jubilee year or Sabbath year included four prescriptions: (1) leaving the soil fallow, (2) the remission of debts, (3) the liberation of slaves, (4) the return to each individual of his family's property" (1972:64). This was a wholistic renewal or restoration in life, the time of the Lord's favor. Yoder develops a whole chapter on the significance of the Jubilee and the freedoms that it extends (1972:64-77).

The sixteenth-century Anabaptists sought and taught this freedom for the church in contrast to the Constantinian state-church practice. They also sought the liberty to be a believers church, with membership by voluntary choice. The Anabaptists emphasized the privilege to share material goods with the needy: "What is mine belongs to the church if my brother has need" (Felix Manz). They also sought a freedom for the peasants, who were oppressed and overtaxed. Their quest for freedom was not a (worldly) political revolution but a spirituality of righteousness in which all people were treated justly. They lived, and even died as martyrs, with the conviction that such justice would change society.

Jacques Ellul decries the fact that

> in the sixteenth century the Reformers were far from being liberators, as may be seen from Luther's attitude to the peasants, or from that of Calvin in Geneva, or from that of both of them to the Anabaptists. Hence, in spite of Protestant propaganda, the Reformation did not represent a victory for freedom or its establishment. (1976:88)

Nevertheless, the Anabaptists did recognize this call for freedom: first, in the freedom for individual decisions of faith; second, in liberty from any coercion by the state; and above all, freedom to live as disciples of Christ in a voluntary believers church as a new social order.

The Anabaptists made many appeals to governments and ruling authorities for liberty to live by their own understanding of the Scripture and by their own conscience. In his Princeton lectures, Henry E. Dosker interpreted their vision as ahead of its time; only in the new world did social and political development allow freedom of conviction in the social orders. Even then, genuine freedom was not adequately integrated into an evangelical theology.

In his review of history, Jacques Ellul admits that the church has been known more for its authoritarianism than its quest for liberty. He comments on modern missions:

> Was not this liberation achieved only at the expense of the imposition of a crushing and meaningless moralism, of an association with colonialism in a continent like Africa, of a destruction of social structures, and of the entry of, e.g., Christianized black peoples into a new spiritual universe which was no less oppressive, although for different reasons, than that which it replaced? (1976:89)

In critique, Ellul emphasizes that true freedom exists only in Christ and for those who confess Jesus Christ as Lord and Savior. The church needs to assume its liberty and live in the freedom of Christ.

Fellowship with Others

Second, in an ethic of freedom, we are free in Christ to live in fellowship with others, in covenant with one another (1 Pet. 2:16-17; Gal. 5:13-15). Fellowship with God means that we are in the family of God; we participate in belonging with a new people. The uniqueness of an ethic of freedom is that this freedom is always to be set in the context of community. This dynamic, setting liberty in the milieu of our life in Christ, safeguards freedom from individualism and enables the full development of the individual without self-centeredness.

In the reconciled community, Christian freedom finds expression through a discipline of responsible action. Paul quotes libertines at Corinth who say, "All things are lawful for me," and replies, "But not all things are beneficial; . . . I will not be dominated by anything" (1 Cor. 6:12). In his treatment of freedom where there are differences of conscience (Rom. 14; 1 Cor. 8), Paul resolves issues by two special considerations: (1) the centrality of the lordship of Jesus Christ (1 Cor. 8:6), and (2) concern for others in the body of Christ.

"Take care that this liberty of yours does not somehow become a stumbling block to the weak" (1 Cor. 8:9). Freedom in reconciliation invests the community with the responsibility of discernment, enabling us to move together in the will of God.

Freedom is discovered as reality in our reconciliation with God in Christ. The reconciliation leads to us becoming a "new creation." This new creation means that we have a new Lord, a new motive, and a new purpose. It also means that something new has happened at the center of our life by the presence and transforming work of the Spirit. The more prominent perspective of faith for the believers church was not forensic or legalized justification or a hope that one is among the elect. Instead, they affirmed with Paul, "If anyone is in Christ, there is a new creation: everything old has passed away; see, everything has become new!" (2 Cor. 5:17).

We are new creatures in a reconciled relation with God. God's love is mediated to us by our Lord, "the glorified Christ, . . . the suffering servant, the Lamb always slain before God" (Ellul, 1976:83). Such a christological ethic is centered in reconciliation, in this new creation. This is a new life in the Spirit modeled after the Savior himself; he is our norm for life in the will of God.

How shall we explain an ethic consistent with the Anabaptist tradition? For me, it means a definition that combines the reality of reconciliation, the experience of regeneration, and the freedom of grace as deliverance in Christ (Rom. 6:14). We need serious reflection on the implications of the Fall. How much of what Adam lost in the Fall has been restored in and by Christ for his followers?

This restoration affects our (1) relation with God, (2) each other, (3) oneself, and (4) creation. In each area, we need to recognize how Christ has overcome the curse of the Fall (Rom. 5:12-19; 2 Cor. 5:21). We must take seriously the liberation brought by Jesus as a freedom of conscience, freedom for the church to be the church in society, and freedom to incorporate his liberating Jubilee in our experience (Luke 4:1-11).

As one who professes Christ as Lord and seeks to live as his disciple, I believe the ethic of "love as a lifestyle" is biblical and essential to Christian living. However, the ability to love, to live by the self-giving love of *agapē*, is only possible by the grace of God and not through human ability. Hence, such love presupposes our being in Christ, our participation in God's transforming grace. Therefore, since we understand salvation as reconciliation with God in Christ, being righteous by faith (Rom. 1:17) means being in right relationship with God. Hence, the concept of an ethic of freedom in righteousness is the biblical focus.

This is consistent with the sixteenth-century Anabaptists, who sought the freedom of Christ in society; it also is especially relevant for us today in the Christian community. As we move into the new century among the many cultures ruled by God, we need to emphasize the freedom of reconciling grace.

Ellul borrows from Karl Barth and affirms an outline on an ethic of freedom: (1) prayer, the freedom to talk with God; (2) confession, the freedom to claim Jesus as Lord; (3) Sabbath, revitalization in rest and worship that puts work in its proper place; and (4) the reading of Scripture, letting the Word of God confront us (1976:120). On this latter point, we know that we do not have perfect knowledge of God. Yet in Christ, we are free to speak of God and with God even though we speak imperfectly. We do this in faith; only the person who is in Jesus Christ knows the freedom of being in grace.

From my point of view, I propose six more characteristics:

1. Walking in the Spirit is the privilege of the reconciled. In this relationship, we experience the changes the Spirit works to conform us to the image of Christ.

2. Discipleship, walking in solidarity with Jesus in life, is a relationship that sets us free among the powers, both social and political. Only those who are nonconformed and nonresistant are truly free in society.

3. Love as a spirit of openness and self-giving in relationship with others can be experienced in the intimacy of Christ.

4. Witness as sharing out of one's personal covenant with Christ, in a spirit of openness to others and shared in a witness dialogue. We must hear others authentically but in turn expect them to hear us with the good news of Christ.

5. Service in freedom is the enabling of others by the giving of oneself. Service roles are not simply from altruism or condescending kindness, but are authentic expressions of mutuality.

6. Worship, the freedom to display the core value in one's life, brings enjoyment of the reconciliation by which one stands in the circle of God's family.

These points help us declare and celebrate being children of God. However, no list of terms adequately conveys the full dimensions of an ethic of freedom based on Christ. We are not following a set of laws. We are relating to a personal Savior who is our Mentor and our Mediator, who mediates the will of God to us in any situation in life. A christological ethic of freedom in reconciliation finds its character in the person and spirit of Jesus.

It is always simpler and easier to operate by rote-thinking and legalism. Yet when we do so, we miss the higher level of liberty in relationship. Human nature tends to legalism: we like systems we can master or by which we can measure our lives. Legalism focuses on codes; freedom focuses on people and their value in community. We are to be a people of God not only in name but also in practice, living in loving support of one another. Freedom in God's love calls us to unity as expressed in the unity of God. Jesus prayed that we might be one as he and the Father are one (John 17). For us, as disciples, this is a relationship of freedom to be and become in unity with God and with our community of faith.

This ethic is a covenant of love, a relationship with God that is the trust of discipleship. Freedom in relationship is the influence of God's grace in our lives as we walk with Jesus. We do not simply copy Jesus' life as our Mentor; from where does the strength come for us to copy the life of Jesus? Instead, we walk *with* Jesus in grace as his disciples; our identification with him shapes our lives. We cannot walk with Jesus, walk in his Spirit, without knowing that this means a call to live beyond ourselves, to live other than for ourselves.

Freedom from Slavery to Sin

Third, in this ethic we are free in Christ for life beyond the limiting dominion of sin (Rom. 6:14-18; Gal. 5:1). This liberty in grace includes a realistic understanding that sin is always there, "crouching at the door" (cf. Gen. 4:7, NIV). But God provides us with victory over sin and sets us free. This freedom brings the objective and the subjective aspects of salvation together in our experience.

Since we believe that an experience of salvation in the grace of God brings us into a new relationship with God, we must ask how and with what character we express this new life. I am not talking about works that one performs to gain acceptance by God. God has already granted this acceptance through his grace. But I am speaking of an ethic of covenant response, of a responsible relationship of liberty in love.

We acknowledge that salvation is by grace through faith, that God has come to us in grace and called us to himself; thus we are excluding any human merit to achieve his grace. Nevertheless, we do not exclude integrity in our covenant response; the very nature of this relationship calls for integrity. Since the experience of grace brings us into an actual right-relatedness, a righteousness that is in Christ, it follows that this new relationship is not a balancing act between faith and works. Instead, it is simply "faith working through love" (Gal. 5:6).

Roland Bainton quotes Martin Luther as saying, "Faith is a living, restless thing. It cannot be inoperative. We are not saved by works; but if there be no works, there must be something amiss with faith" (331). This is evidently what James means in saying "Faith by itself, if it has no works [of love], is dead" (James 2:17). Yet Luther would scarcely have used James to make his point! Douglas John Hall adds that faith leads us to practice love and seek to understand the faith:

> Faith in the God who is love (1 John 4:8) moves us to love the other—namely, everything upon which the window of faith opens. The same faith which expresses itself in the love of God and the neighbor impels us to embrace the totality in our understanding. . . . That faith manifests itself in the love of understanding is the meaning of Anselm of Canterbury's famous phrase, *fides querens intellectum*, faith seeking understanding. If it is truly faith, Anselm insists, it will seek to understand what is believed. (1991:255)

To think with Christ is to understand how he would have us order our lives in relation with him. Since we are reconciled to God in Jesus, we must pursue the questions of what difference that makes in our lives, our minds, our wills, and our affections. What direction does this new relationship bring into our lives? How do we work out righteousness in the freedom of Christ? Menno Simons wrote,

> It is clear that the regenerate do not willfully live in sin, but through faith and true repentance were buried by baptism into the death of Christ, and arose with him to a new life. Also, those who have the Spirit of the Lord bring forth the fruits of the Spirit. (97)

Walking with Christ is to walk with him as we know him in Scripture, the whole Jesus Christ, who demonstrated the word and will of God in his earthly life. Thus John claims Jesus as our pattern of obedience: "Whoever says, 'I abide in him,' ought to walk just as [Jesus] walked" (1 John 2:6). In the marriage covenant, I am free to walk with Esther in the intimacies of our life together; likewise, in covenant with Christ, I am free to walk with him in daily life.

A high view of the Scriptures, as divinely inspired, will not let us misinterpret Paul's teaching on being justified by faith in Christ; we cannot take it as some pronouncement apart from covenant with Christ through the faith that he accepts us. Justification is grounded in reconciliation as a faith-identification with Jesus.

Stanley Hauerwas affirms, "What makes Christian ethics Christian is the overriding significance of Jesus" (1983:72). Hauerwas emphasizes the centrality of Christology in Christian ethics: the teachings of Jesus on following the will of God, and an ethic of the kingdom of God and his righteousness. This is the ethic of the new covenant, showing what it means to be reconciled to God in faith and life. It is a life of love expressed in faithfulness to the God of covenant.

Jesus says, "Apart from me you can do nothing" (John 15:5). Thus it doesn't matter how high one may set the ethical standards in terms of principles; the fact is that such standards, left to themselves, are only laws. But when our ethics are placed in relationship with Christ, they show the intimacy and influence of his Spirit at work within and through us. Our ethical behavior at best is the representation of a covenant with Christ and an enabled integrity in this covenant. The lack of ethical concern and clarity is a violation and a denial of the covenant and our faithfulness.

Our walk in covenant is a walk in the intimacy of grace, and our ethic is our participation in grace. Some church people make the mistake of separating ethics from the in-Christ relationship. They fail to see that believers' relationship with Christ includes relating to his example as Jesus of Nazareth *and also* sharing the in-Christ relationship that frees ethics from being merely a matter of moralistic deeds. If we separate ethical action from Jesus, our behavior is by human strength. If we hold the ethical teaching of Jesus in the freedom of grace, we walk in the Spirit.

Paul tells the Romans,

> I beseech you therefore, brothers and sisters, by the mercies of God, to present your bodies as a living sacrifice, holy and acceptable to God, which is your spiritual worship. And do not let the world squeeze you into its mold, but be transformed by the renewing of your minds that you may demonstrate what is the

good and acceptable and perfect will of God. (Rom. 12:1-2, adapted from NIV/Phillips)

This remarkable text holds God's mercy and God's expectation together; it holds God's forgiving grace and God's transforming grace in harmony. The goal is that we may demonstrate the good and perfect will of God in our lives. Paul emphasizes an ethic of right conduct, but it is a conduct that grows out of a right spirit, a spirit issuing from a right relationship.

Free to Live in Love

Fourth, this ethic means that we are free in Christ to live in *agapē* love (Luke 6:27-36; Rom. 12:9-21). We follow an ethic of freedom in righteousness, shown in love that does not violate or seek to control others, in holiness of life or Christian integrity, in justice that seeks to set things right for others, and in peace as praxis for the total well-being of others. John writes, "Whoever does not love does not know God" (1 John 4:8).

The Hebrew and Greek words for justice and righteousness mean either or both, depending on context; here the concepts are held together. John writes, "All who do not do what is right are not from God, nor are those who do not love their brothers and sisters" (1 John 3:10). Hebrews says, "Pursue peace with everyone, and the holiness without which no one will see the Lord" (12:14). The tone and the language of these texts is imperative but not legalistic. We are commanded to follow; yet we are a people on the way, without pretending to achieve perfection.

In the sixteenth-century, Menno Simons wrote,

> For true evangelical faith is of such a nature that it cannot lie dormant, but manifests itself in all righteousness and works of love; it dies unto the flesh and blood; it destroys all forbidden lusts and desires; it seeks and serves and fears God; it clothes the naked; it feeds the hungry; it comforts the sorrowful; it shelters the destitute; it aids and consoles the sad; it returns good for evil; it serves those that harm it; it prays for those that persecute it; teaches, admonishes, and reproves with the Word of the Lord; it seeks that which is lost; it binds up that which is wounded; it

> heals that which is diseased and it saves that which is sound; it
> has become all things to all men. (307)

Jesus elaborates on this freedom by his emphasis on love as the
fulfillment of the law, in his Sermon on the Hillside (Luke 6:17-49),
and in the Sermon on the Mount (Matt. 5–7). These passages present
an ethic of righteousness, but a righteousness in relationship rather
than a righteousness by rules. Jesus stresses an attitude or spirit as
the way to express this relationship of righteousness. He has not
"come to abolish the law or the prophets, . . . but to fulfill" them.
He fulfills the law by giving us its full meaning (Matt. 5:17).

Therefore, Jesus is able to say, "It was said, . . . but I say" (Matt.
5:21-22, 27-28, 31-32, 33-34, 38-39, 43-44). In this context, Jesus
says, "Unless your righteousness exceeds that of the scribes and Pharisees, you will never enter the kingdom of heaven" (5:20). We are called
to move beyond a Pharisaic code to a righteousness of spirit, a right
relationship known in love. This is the liberty of Christ's disciples.

Freedom bases its claim on the authority of God, as he is heard
and understood in the hermeneutical community, the church (Acts
15). This authority regards all people as equals. Jesus said, "You are
not to be called rabbi, for you have one teacher, and you are all students" (Matt. 23:8). In the lifestyle of Christ's disciples, we live by
God's authority. We therefore renounce any use of power that would
impose our will on another. Instead, we live by God's will, calling
people to accept his authority voluntarily.

This means living by the primary authority of the divine Spirit
rather than chiefly by some institutionalized practice. Yet the
hermeneutical community knows and tests this direction of the Spirit (1 Cor. 14:29; 1 Thess. 5:21). If we do not test a spiritual voice, we
will simply be acting out our own subjective judgments (1 John 4:1).
We stand together under the authority of the Lord and his Word in
faith, action, preaching, and serving by a spirit of equity. It is risky
to do this with respect for voluntarism, but it is the risk of freedom.
However, in love we cannot coerce another's faith; we must wait for
their adult, voluntary decision.

Church discipline has been swept away from all but the sectarian
Protestant communities. O'Donovan observes that discipline

does not exist first to serve the penitent; it exists to enable the church to live a public life of integrity. The community as a whole will decay, and lose its sense of its gospel calling, if its public life is not free to express the gospel, . . . the gospel of God's forgiveness of sin in Jesus Christ; so that any authentic church discipline must be centered on the reconciliation of the sinner rather than on his punishment. (168-169)

This emphasis on the freedom of the community in relation to the freedom of the individual is quite significant in pastoral ministry. It calls for compassionate disciplining relations with individuals involved in such things as addiction, sexual immorality, homosexual practices, roles of violence and militarism, or economics of greed depriving others of fair opportunities for meeting their human needs. The community of faith, as it stands in the freedom of Christ, is responsible to hold individuals accountable for their unfreedom. This is the way of love.

Free to Live by Christ's Reign

Fifth, this ethic sets us free to live by the kingdom of Christ rather than by the cultural orders (1 Cor. 8:1-13; Rom. 14:13-17, 20-23). The ethic of freedom is for disciples of Christ and cannot be truly followed by those outside the fellowship of Christ. As Jürgen Moltmann has said, "Christocentric ethics can only be discipleship ethics. It is an ethic for Christians in a state, but not a Christian ethic for the state. It is political ethics for the Christian community, but not Christian politics for the civil community" (lectures at AMB Seminary, Elkhart, Ind.).

Discipleship recognizes that Jesus Christ is Lord; all power in heaven and on earth has been given to him. As his disciples, we walk with him "on the way." Under his lordship, our beliefs are both the enrichment and the stability of the community of faith and also our public proclamation.

The ethic of freedom has major social implications. We are called to extend the ministry of reconciliation in society. Freedom is a call for justice for everyone, to enable all persons to know and share the benefits of liberty in their roles in life. In this freedom, we avoid injustice to any and all people and seek to behave justly toward all. For my evangelical friends, freedom calls us to extend the ethic of freedom into the realms of human rights, and to treat the powerless and the minorities with expressions of enabling love. Such liberty transcends racism, respects the dignity of all peoples, and seeks to enhance the well-being of all.

This ethic begins with each of us who are disciples of Christ; it makes a good impact on the world around us, for the sake of God's reign. As Christ liberates us, we in turn will be liberators, free from tending to abuse others, from coercing others to achieve our own selfish interests, and from being addicted in our own lives (sexual, drugs, alcohol, nicotine, etc.), with negative consequences for self and others. Our freedom is guided by mutuality; in our freedom we should never violate the freedom of the neighbor. As disciples of Christ, when we truly follow freedom in grace, we make a healing impact on our society; we become the "salt of the earth" and "the light of the world."

In 1951 H. Richard Niebuhr published *Christ and Culture,* a classical work on the sociology of religion. He presented five different ways in which he saw Christians relating to cultural issues:

1. "Christ against culture" appears as the position of radical Christians who take literally John's words, "Love not the world" (1 John 2:15). Niebuhr saw it in the lifestyles of the monastics, Anabaptists (Mennonites), and Quakers, among others.

2. "Christ of culture" represents the position of the medieval Scholastics and of the Social Gospel (ca. 1870-1920). Building on Acts 15, they show Jesus as the Messiah of society.

3. "Christ above culture" stands for the conservative point of view, a synthesis represented by Thomas Aquinas and based on Jesus' statement "Render . . . to Caesar the things that are Caesar's, and to God the things that are God's" (Matt. 22:21, RSV).

4. "Christ and culture in paradox" labels a dualistic approach built on the doctrines of sin and grace, with sin as the human part and grace as God's part. Luther follows this in his "two-kingdom" perspective.

5. "Christ the transformer of culture" is based on John 3:16; the separation between the church and the world is bridged by a conversion that can transform culture. Augustine of Hippo, John Wesley on social holiness, and H. Richard Niebuhr represent this position.

In a lecture at a Think Tank sponsored by the Coalition of Christian Colleges and Universities at Washington, D.C., Stanley Hauerwas of Duke University asked whether Niebuhr's categories go far enough in challenging our culture. His models may have done more harm than good. This seems especially true when we analyze his category of "Christ against culture." Niebuhr has missed several important points:

1. In many situations, we do the world the most good by simply maintaining our integrity.

2. Culture itself is neutral, yet people share it in a way that tends to idolatry; such expressions need to be exposed and rejected.

3. The Incarnation shows that Christ could become human without being sinful. Therefore, we need to expose and reject aspects of culture that manifest sin rather than grace.

4. This selectivity in culture—by a community of God's people who live by his kingdom—is itself a transforming influence in society. Even the lives of unbelievers in a society are enriched by the presence and quality of the Christian community among them.

I have had the privilege of some association with Dr. Cheryl Sanders, professor of Christian Ethics at Howard University Divinity School, Washington, D.C. In a lecture on ethics and race, she proposed adding to Niebuhr's outline a sixth approach: "Christ transcending cultural barriers." Sanders noted how Jesus—a Palestinian Jew, a Middle Eastern man, not a European—was able to minister to the Samaritan woman, the Canaanite woman, and the Greeks. His ministry was multicultural. This impresses me as a relevant approach to social aspects of living out our faith in a day of tribal or ethnic groupings.

Samuel P. Huntington of Harvard terms ethnic groupings as the coming pattern. In "The Clash of Civilizations?" he expects that

> conflict between civilizations will be the latest phase in the evolution of conflict in the modern world. . . . During the cold war, the world was divided into the first, second and third worlds. Those divisions are no longer relevant. It is far more meaningful now to group countries not in terms of their political or economic systems or in terms of their level of economic development, but rather, in terms of their culture and civilization. (22-3)

As our guest at another Think Tank in Washington, D.C., Lesslie Newbigin of England emphasized the freedom of the gospel in a pluralist society. From his own experience of more than forty years as a missionary in South India, he stressed the unique power of the gospel of Christ to release people in any social setting to walk with God. This is an actualized salvation of living in love, a change of relationship with God, who is known and enjoyed through our faith response to him. We should go about our mission of sharing Christ by deed and by word in the liberty that shows Christ has done a special work in overcoming the fatalism keeping many people in bondage.

Jacques Ellul stresses this truth as well: "There is now one possibility of vanquishing and surmounting, or rather escaping fate. This is giving oneself to Jesus Christ in faith. To do this is to break free from the circle of fate" (1976:77).

The misuse of the freedom God gives us is a subtle temptation of life. This is essentially the temptation in the garden to which Adam and Eve succumbed (Gen. 3). The tempter, by appealing to their interest in their own self-fulfillment, led them to use their freedom for selfish ambition. The misuse of freedom shows in the claim of autonomy, the extension of one's pride. This autonomy leads to attitudes of atheism: "No God as far as I am concerned" (Ps. 14:1, literal trans.).

Such misuse of freedom is ultimately self-destructive. Suicide is a misuse of liberty. It may happen due to mental and emotional disturbance that does not allow a person to conduct life in a balanced way. Yet it is the ultimate sin against oneself in a false freedom that says, "I can do with my life what I will." Killing, the taking of the life of another, is an even more serious sin; it extends one's freedom into others' spheres of life and removes them for the sake of one's own desires rather than respecting their space. Sin is unrighteousness: the failure to live in the rightness of relationships with oneself, with God, and with neighbors.

At Montgomery, Martin Luther King called his people to "not only avoid violence of deed but violence of spirit." An ethic of doing what is right to any person calls for love in practice, a participation in the self-giving love, the *agapē* of God. This is a love that gives without asking "What's in it for me?" True compassion never condescends but empowers, enabling others to maximize their own potential.

This kind of love never intimidates, manipulates, coerces, or violates another. Such love is an ethic for enriching the other. Thus it crosses all barriers at cost to oneself, transcends all racism, tribalism, and nationalism. It rejects feelings of superiority from any strength of one's gender, talent, wealth, education, or personality. An ethic of righteousness builds on the fact that we see in each person the *imago Dei* (image of God, Gen. 1:27), and that we treat each person as of supreme worth in the presence of God.

An ethic of freedom in righteousness is liberty to be, to become, to belong in the whole of life to Christ, who has redeemed us and reconciled us to God. With Charles Wesley we sing,

> Come, thou long-expected Jesus! born to set thy people free,
> from our fears and sins release us, let us find our rest in thee.
> Israel's strength and consolation, hope of all the earth thou art,
> dear desire of every nation, joy of every longing heart.
>
> Born thy people to deliver, born a child, and yet a king,
> born to reign in us forever, now thy gracious kingdom bring.
> By thine own eternal Spirit, rule in all our hearts alone.
> By thine all-sufficient merit, raise us to thy glorious throne.

11

Love Overcoming Evil
with Good

*I appeal to you therefore, brothers and sisters, by the mercies
of God, to present your bodies as a living sacrifice, holy and
acceptable to God, which is your spiritual worship. Do not be
conformed to this world, but be transformed by the renewing
of your minds, so that you may discern what is the will of
God—what is good and acceptable and perfect. . . .*

*Let love be genuine; hate what is evil, hold fast to what is
good; love one another with mutual affection; outdo one another in showing honor. Do not lag in zeal, be ardent in spirit,
serve the Lord. Rejoice in hope, be patient in suffering, perse-
vere in prayer. Contribute to the needs of the saints; extend
hospitality to strangers.*

*Bless those who persecute you; bless and do not curse them.
Rejoice with those who rejoice, weep with those who weep.
Live in harmony with one another; do not be haughty, but as-
sociate with the lowly; do not claim to be wiser than you are.
Do not repay anyone evil for evil, but take thought for what is
noble in the sight of all. If it is possible, so far as it depends
on you, live peaceably with all. Beloved, never avenge yourselves, but leave room for the wrath of God; for it is written,
"Vengeance is mine, I will repay, says the Lord." No, "if your
enemies are hungry, feed them; if they are thirsty, give them
something to drink; for by doing this you will heap burning
coals on their heads." Do not be overcome by evil, but overcome evil with good. (Rom. 12:1-2, 9-21)*

DOING GOOD always outshines evil, but it is not necessarily always victorious over evil in the short run. Yet *the good* lives on. This is seen ultimately in the cross of Christ and his death by evil hands.

From southern Russia of the early 1900s comes a remarkable story of Aaron Rempel, a wealthy Mennonite farmer and estate owner in the community of Gnadenfeldt. A grandson published the account in the *Los Angeles Times*, and I have confirmed it through another of Aaron's grandsons.

Rempel was a prominent and successful businessman in his community and beyond. His estate was so well-known that the czar of Russia would come to go hunting on his estate. In the days of turmoil that marked the beginning of the Marxist revolution, the White Army at first would defeat the Red revolutionaries, put their prisoners in boxcars, and ship them off to Siberia.

One evening Rempel passed a railroad siding while walking home with groceries for his family. He saw a boxcar full of men.

One man called out to Rempel, "Sir, we're so hungry; we've been in here all day with nothing to eat. Can you help us?"

With Christian care, Rempel walked over to the boxcar and began shoving his bread, cheeses, and sausages through the cracks.

The man inside took them and passed them around. "Thank you," he said.

Rempel responded, "God bless you."

Months later the tide of the struggle changed. The Red Army totally defeated the White Army, put their prisoners in boxcars, and shipped them to Siberia. Within a few months, as the Marxists took over the country, the Red Army rounded up Mennonite farmers in that area, put them in boxcars, and shipped them to Siberia.

Rempel went from wealth to poverty, from position to weakness. Yet in Siberia he was still the entrepreneur: he saw the need for a warm drink and began shipping tea in from Mongolia. Soon he had a good business going. But to his neighbors, he was guilty of capitalism. Envious of his success, they had him arrested.

As the trial progressed, it was evident that he really was guilty of capitalism. Finally the commissar told him to step forward to be sentenced. Rempel stepped forward, fully expecting the sentence to mean his execution.

The commissar said, "I think we have met before."

"No, your honor," Rempel replied, "we have never met."

"Yes, I think we have. Were you ever in Gnadenfeldt?"

"Why yes, I lived there," Rempel admitted.

"Do you remember an evening when a man called to you from a boxcar, and said, 'We're so hungry; we've been in here all day with nothing to eat'?"

"Yes," Rempel said, "I remember that."

"And what did you do?"

"Why, I went over to the boxcar and shoved my bread and cheeses and sausages through the slats."

"And what did you say?"

"I think I said, 'God bless you.'"

The commissar said, "Yes, we've met before; I was that man. I'm not going to sentence you. If you like, I'll sign papers for your family to emigrate."

"Oh sir, thank you," Rempel said. "I also have brothers here. Would you sign those papers for all of the Rempels?"

Thus all of that clan of Rempels migrated to Burbank, California, where I picked up this story. When he did the good deed, little did Aaron Rempel know what the future consequences would be. As disciples of Christ, we live by the good no matter what the outcome.

On the back of my pastoral calling card, for years, I have presented the following statement: "If love were possible without the gospel, we would need no gospel; if love is not possible by the gospel, we have no gospel; that love is possible by the gospel is what Christian discipleship is all about." This captures the power and meaning of the gospel in its spiritual and social dimensions. This is reconciliation spiritually and socially.

The church must constantly hold together the evangelistic and the social aspects of our faith. I believe the evangelical community needs to take a stronger stand on the implications of the gospel for the social dimensions of our mission. The so-called mainline denominations also need a clearer emphasis on the evangelistic focus of our mission.

Newbigin speaks of the illusions of the liberals in acting as sovereign explorers formulating questions: "We are not honest and open-minded explorers of reality; we are alienated from reality because we have made ourselves the center of the universe" (1995:104). We do not learn to know God simply by philosophical reflection. Just as we know a personality through someone's life story, so we learn to know God in the story of his acting in love. By understanding the nature of God's love for all people, we can discern the course of love in our mission to the human family. The evangel is the good news of this loving and gracious God who acts to reconcile us in Christ.

The essential unity of the evangelistic and the social aspects of the gospel is to be found in the centrality of reconciliation. By his Word and presence, the Holy Spirit actualizes the meaning of reconciliation with Christ. In doing so, he creates in us a new dimension of *agapē* love, establishing love as a lifestyle. This calls for more than subjective interpretations of "union with Christ," as often appearing in private piety. Instead, Christ calls us to active self-giving, with the goals of serving, enabling, and enriching others. In emphasizing the primacy of love, I interpret evangelism as everything that makes faith in Christ possible for a person.

While ministering in Tanzania, I came to know the work of a Catholic missionary from France, Bernard Joinet. In his pamphlet "A Stranger in My Father's House," he tells of what it means to be an expatriate working as a guest in Tanzania. As a disciple of Christ, he said the most compelling lesson he learned was "to serve people as they want to be served and not as we want to serve them." If we serve as we want to serve people, we are still the boss, still in charge, not fully servant. Service is the way of love in action, building bridges to others, contributing to their lives because of their intrinsic worth.

Freedom is love in action. Love extends justice; it never violates another. It seeks the other's fulfillment as well as our own. The following is a summary of the quality of freedom expressed in love:

> Freedom in deliverance;
>   from self-centeredness,
>   from pride and arrogance,
>   from addiction and misuse of passion,
>   from sexual perversion,
>   from tyranny and abuse,
>   from racism and prejudice,
>   from hostility and violence. . . .

• • •

Freedom for love;
   to live in the openness of love,
   to be vulnerable,
   to be innovative,
   to build bridges,
   to forgive another,
   to serve as enabler,
   to meet in and through Christ. . . .

• • •

Freedom to walk with Christ;
   for life in the Spirit,
   for victory over self-seeking,
   for the fruit of his indwelling,
   for the exercise of his gifts,
   for life in community,
   for daily discipleship,
   for the witness of his grace.

Reconciliation means that God is a God of love more than of law. He reaches beyond issues to people, and cares about us more than caring about what we have done. When we understand negative commands in light of God's love, we can see a positive power even in them. God sets boundaries by his laws; at the same time, he gives us freedom for creative living inside of those boundaries.

An illustration of God's love and mercy is found in the OT tabernacle, in the most holy place. Here the law was placed in the ark of the covenant, and thus under the mercy seat! In the NT message, we learn that this mercy seat, this place of propitiation, is our meeting place with God at the cross. We come to Christ as "the atoning sacrifice for our sins," a costly grace in the cross (1 John 2:2). Yet God's love is accompanied by God's law. God's holiness includes his laws and provides content for God's love.

I have enjoyed lectures by my professor Paul Scherer, Lutheran pastor-theologian, and I recall his statement: "There is love in law and law in love. That there is love in law is evident when you ask any parent, and that there is law in love is evident when you ask any spouse" (class at Union Theol. Seminary, Richmond, 1961). God's act in giving the law was an act of love, directing and securing a relationship of covenant. But when that same law becomes an end in itself, it becomes the enemy of love.

Love is more than a subjective emotion. It is a positive action of intimacy. In this intimate relationship, love is the expression of freedom—a freedom to walk with God not on the human level of mutuality but as receiving his power and grace. This grace from God establishes the love-relationship with him.

When love is conditioned by holiness or the wholeness that comes from God in grace, it is an honest caring. This love is a relationship of integrity that seeks the best for the other. In *Agapē and Erōs*, Anders Nygren explains how *erōs* can describe a human movement toward God, and *agapē* is shown in God's act of coming down to humanity. The word *erōs* is not used in the NT, though it was the common Greek word for passionate love, with a lover wanting to fulfill one's own need. In contrast, the NT writers chose the rarely used word *agapē* to denote God's movement to us in total self-giving love, a love even unto death.

This quality of self-giving love was ultimately displayed in "the terrible agony of Son, Father, and Spirit on Golgotha" (cf. Finger, 2:78). God loves, and God suffered in giving his Son; the Son loves, and the Son suffered in giving his life for us; the Spirit loves, and the Spirit suffers and continues to suffer in giving himself to us and with us. God's work of redemption is an eternal self-giving love of reconciliation. What amazing love!

As Nygren says,

> Agape is God's grace: salvation is the work of divine love. Agape is unselfish love, it "seeks not its own," it gives itself away! Since God is Agape, everyone who is loved by him and has been gripped and mastered by his love cannot but pass this love on to his neighbor. (210, 216)

Peter praises God's unselfish love with the astonishing claim that we are given grace to be made "participants of the divine nature" in escaping moral corruption (2 Pet. 1:4). When Jesus speaks of this new nature, of our being perfect as our Father in heaven is perfect, he is identifying impartial love (Matt. 5:43-48).

This self-giving love expressed in Christ becomes for us the Jesus-model for behavior. He gives a new commandment that we love as he loved, in service and in self-giving even to death (John 13:34). His example becomes a relevant social ethic of a higher quality of ethics than the approach of mainstream Protestant ethics, which does not emphasize Jesus as the norm (Yoder, 1972:11-25).

According to John, we are to live as Jesus lived (1 John 2:5-6). We are to love as he loved: "Whoever does not love does not know God, for God is love" (1 John 4:7-12). The Incarnation is the extension of this love into the human arena in all of its reconciling power. As people are engaged in meeting Jesus, they are introduced to a new awareness of a God of reconciliation.

J. Lawrence Burkholder says, "Love has the advantage of going straight to the heart of the Christian ethic. . . . It is a fact of social existence that love must take the form of justice if it is to be effective" (1989:223). This is the ethic of freedom in its social implications. But in making justice a criterion of Christian social strategy, we must be careful that we do not separate our pursuit of justice from our discipleship to Christ. Stanley Hauerwas reminds us, "The church must learn time and time again that its task is not to make the world the kingdom, but to be faithful to the kingdom by showing to the world what it means to be a community of peace" (1983:103).

To make love a lifestyle, we base ourselves on the very acts of God, who is love. God's actions in human history and on behalf of humanity are actions of love, even unto death. As we have seen, God's love is the total self-giving demonstrated in the Father giving the Son, the Son giving himself even to death, and the Spirit giving himself totally to us in the work of grace. He has bound himself to us to create the church as the body of Christ. The Spirit's work is to glorify Christ in us.

People often ask, "If God is sovereign, why doesn't he reach in and correct the problems in the world?" In response, we can ask, "How does God work? How does he show his sovereignty?" How does God act when his nature is love, when he offers grace and extends himself into our lives primarily as the Reconciler?

We study Scripture and reflect on the nature of God in his holiness, justice, love, and integrity; thereby we learn that God does not manipulate people, violate personalities, or coerce us. Furthermore,

God could have destroyed the devil long ago by exercising his superior power. The Scriptures have convinced me that God's sovereignty is not a deterministic authority but a uniquely self-determined way of functioning. God is sovereign, and he alone decides how he will act. The profound biblical truth is that God functions to overcome evil with good, to overcome evil by exposing it through its contrast with his holiness and love.

Let us examine the thesis that God overcomes evil with good:

• First, God the Father has chosen to destroy or overcome evil, not by exercising his superior power but by expressing his superior character: qualities of holiness, love, and justice. God continues to break into human experience to display the superior quality of his grace, and he does so in and through the lives of his people.

God brings many influences to bear on individuals in calling and offering providential direction. He brings many Christian voices into our lives as witnesses or influences for the good. He allows many circumstances for their impact upon us. However, in God's calling in grace, there is still the paradox of human freedom, leaving us with the choice as to what we will do with God's call. God is patient with us in our limitations, respecting our intrinsic worth. He works in correction without coercion.

If then God does not simply overcome evil by exercising his superior power, how does God continue his work today to overcome evil? Paul tells the Christians in Rome to overcome evil with good (Rom. 12:21). In my theological study and experience, I understand that this is how God has worked and continues to work in overcoming evil with good.

When I was a lad, my dad told of a workman who became his enemy out of envy because my dad had been promoted to be foreman instead of himself. When a cutback in work happened, several employees were laid off, including this man. Morning after morning as my dad went to work, this man would be among those at the gate, hoping for a job.

One day my dad created several more jobs for his crew and went to the gate to hire extra workers. He chose one and then turned to his enemy: "Bob, get your tools." This act earned the man's respect.

Years later I was preaching in that city, and a man came forward in the invitation to respond to the gospel. First he asked, "Do you know Clarence Augsburger?"

"He's my dad."

"He is why I'm here," the man said.

God does not overcome evil by exercising his superior power but by showing his superior quality of love and holiness and justice. Any thinking person ought to be able to look at evil for what it is, then look at the quality of God's work for what it is, and readily make a choice for God's grace.

Speaking of God as a God of love, we recognize that love does not use force. Instead, love is a spirit of selfless acceptance. Love does not give us the content but the manner of action. The content is to be found in the Incarnation, as God acts to identify with us:

> For God so loved the world that he gave his only Son, so that everyone who believes in him may not perish but may have eternal life. Indeed, God did not send the Son into the world to condemn the world, but in order that the world might be saved through him. (John 3:16-17)

• Second, when Christ as the Son of God confronted evil, he chose no other way than to overcome evil with good, just as God overcomes evil with good. Jesus chose to overcome evil with the quality of his love, his mercy, and his justice. In the garden of Gethsemane, he told his disciples that he could have called for twelve legions of angels to deliver him from his enemies (Matt. 26:53). He could have overcome evil by exercising superior power over them. Instead, he chose to manifest the superior quality of his love even to death.

Jesus' death was the supreme sacrifice for us, as he gave his life for our redemption. He showed this ultimate love in forgiveness, absorbing the hostility of his enemies even to death. While we were enemies, Christ died for us (Rom. 5:6-10); his *agapē* even to death is the qualitative manifestation of love that expresses and extends the reconciling grace in the heart of God from Creation morning.

On this issue of overcoming evil with love, Luke presents a difficult text (Luke 22:35-38). In the upper room and before going to the garden, Jesus tells the disciples that this hour is different from earlier when he sent them out as his witnesses (9:3; 10:4). Now he tells them to take a purse, a bag, and a sword—essentials for travelers of that day. Must they be ready for flight, for living by their own resources while coping with hostility?

The disciples say, "Look, here are two swords."

Jesus replies, "Enough."

What does Jesus mean here? Some readers take this as justifying use of the sword. But if Jesus means to endorse armed protection, he would hardly say that two short swords are enough. In the same scene, Jesus even rebukes a disciple who tries to defend him with a sword and heals an injured slave's ear (22:49-51; Matt. 26:52).

Likely Jesus is using striking metaphors to tell the disciples they need to be ready for the beginning of a crisis. They must be spiritually prepared to face persecution as they carry on Jesus' ministry (Acts). The word "enough" is simply a way of saying, "Enough of that! You don't understand me anyhow."

Jesus may have wanted swords to appear on the Mount of Olives because he is fulfilling prophecy by being counted among the transgressors (Isa. 53:12; Luke 22:37, 52). Coming to arrest him are soldiers armed with swords along with temple police armed with clubs (Luke 22:52; John 18:12). Jesus does not respond in kind; he even stops a follower from using his sword in defense.

Jesus' pattern of behavior stands over against the conduct of others. He heals that slave's ear and thus lives true to his teachings: "Love your enemies, do good to those who hate you" (Luke 6:27; 22:51). Jesus accepts arrest, suffering, and death rather than even threatening to inflict injury on others. Hence, his mention of "sword" in Luke 22:36 must be taken in a symbolic sense of preparing his disciples to face persecution as kingdom-preachers.

Clearly, Jesus chose to overcome evil with the highest quality of goodness. His choice was an "in your face" confrontation with evil; his love absorbed evil even to his death. This offers what has been called a dynamistic understanding of the atonement. The British theologian P. T. Forsythe once said of the cross, "He took the sting and pulled out the stinger." Ellul says that love is

> in no sense authoritarian. The Lord is he who constantly stands
> at the door and knocks, waiting until the door is opened, not be-

cause he could not force his way in, but because, being love, he does not want to exercise his authority without the assent of the one upon whom he exercises it. Because the only face of this lordship is one of love, its only authority is that which is based on reciprocal love. The love with which God loves humanity can be rejected or flouted by humanity. If it is rejected, no authority or lordship is exercised. Everything depends on reciprocity. (1976:83-84)

• Third, recognizing that the Father and the Son act to overcome evil with good, we must ask how we expect the Holy Spirit to act. Of course, the Spirit would do no other than to function in the way we have seen expressed in the Father and the Son. He comes to fill our lives and work through us in a pattern qualitatively different from that of the world.

Paul urges believers, "Don't let the world squeeze you into its mold, but be transformed by the renewing of your minds, that you may demonstrate what is the good and perfect will of God" (Rom. 12:1-2, free trans.). After Paul has described the life of love in social conduct, he says, "Do not be overcome by evil, but overcome evil with good" (Rom. 12:21).

The Spirit empowers us to live in the spirit of love, and he does so by giving us the fruit of righteousness in love. "The kingdom of God is . . . righteousness and peace and joy in the Holy Spirit" (Rom. 14:17). As interpreted earlier, joy is the celebration of love, peace is the practice of love, patience is the preservation of love, kindness is the expression of love, goodness is the action of love, faithfulness is the loyalty of love, gentleness is the attitude of love, and self-control is the restraint of love (Gal. 5:22-23).

Love gives character to faith. Faith in a personal God is a faith that reconciles us to him. Hope goes with faith and love, for hope is the confidence of faith and the security of love. Thinking of our ethical responsibility in life, in the freedom of Christ, we come to each situation with the resources of Christ as our strength. We never come into a situation empty. We come with the love of Christ at work in us and through us.

In Christ we have the freedom to be interpreters of his will, and we have the power to "bind and loose," exercising moral discernment in disapproving or approving the behavior of other church members (Matt. 18:15-20). We have the privilege of serving as a "priest at our neighbor's elbow." We involve the community of faith in ministries of reconciliation that even reach those outside the church (2 Cor. 5:19-20).

As to a lifestyle of reconciliation, we need to seek the good as we face the evil. We need to find an alternative rather than to let evil determine our counterattack at its own level. Our alternative is to seek the greater good for the people involved in each case.

For example, answers to the problems of abortion are not so simple. Abortion is sinful violence, but it is not right for us to respond with violence at abortion clinics. The answer includes placing a better and a positive emphasis on sex education, building loving families, and finding more accessible ways of negotiating adoption as an alternative where there is an unwanted pregnancy.

Answers to sinful homosexual practices are not to be found in patterns of denial and rejection of those so inclined. We need to lovingly accept people suffering the perversion, including them in loving families and in heterosexual communities of loving relationships. By so doing, we can help them recognize the mistake of their "retreat into sameness" and help them move beyond their psychological fear of "otherness" into wholesome relationships. Appropriate friendships (without sex) can lead them from their obsession into a larger, enriching dimension of personhood. The same call to purity and integrity must stop heterosexual activity outside of marriage.

We cannot effectively deal with criminal violence by building more prisons and using capital punishment more. We need to seek better ways for helping nonviolent criminals work at restitution, and then provide for violent criminals a better redemptive context of life imprisonment. This approach is more redemptive than execution. Justice calls for accountability. The punishment must be in proportion to the offense, but it is punishment for the crime and not revenge on the part of society or those offended.

Above all, overcoming evil with good means that we give ourselves to create a better and more righteous social environment. This quality stands over against a social order that by its low level of morality keeps feeding sinful minds with unneeded stimuli.

It is difficult to answer questions on how we should carry out nonresistance and nonviolence in the face of violence. Of one thing we are sure: violence begets violence. One cannot be "a little bit violent," since violence doesn't limit itself (cf. Gen. 4:23-24). As noted in an earlier chapter, *nonresistance* means not using violence to counter violent acts (Matt. 5:39), though we are called to resist the devil (James 4:7; cf. 5:6). Nonviolence is based on deep principle and is not just a pragmatic strategy. Jesus taught the way of love and nonviolence by his words and his life. Such nonviolence is first a matter of our spirit before it can determine our behavior.

In the Sermon on the Mount (Matt. 5–7) and the Sermon on the Plain (Luke 6:17-49), Jesus says, "Do not resist an evildoer. . . . If anyone strikes you on the right cheek, turn the other also; . . . and if anyone forces you to go one mile, go also the second mile" (Matt. 5:39-42; Luke 6:29-30). This pattern is the Christian's strategy of operation, based on love. It is the way to overcome evil with good.

When we turn the other cheek, we are saying "Your treatment of me doesn't determine my treatment of you. I'll decide what to do on the basis of a higher principle." Turning the other cheek sets us free; we are deciding how to respond. This is not the position of a "wimp," doing nothing. It is not weakness or a surrender to evil; it is a love-based strategy of confronting evil. Thereby we say that we do not do to others as has been done to us; we do to others as we would have them do to us (Luke 6:31; Matt. 7:12).

The way of love is not easy. Love needs to be constant, unconditional, always caring, creative in building bridges, willing to give oneself for the good of the other. Love, Paul writes, never keeps a record, is not petty, and is slow to lose patience. Love always looks for a way to be constructive, is not possessive, is not touchy, does not seek selfish advantage. Love knows no limit to its endurance. There is no end to its trust, no dashing of its hope; it can outlast anything. In fact, it is the one thing that still stands when all else has fallen (1 Cor. 13).

Nevertheless, this is not to say that in the short run we always win in living by love. Sometimes love experiences the cross.

In our inner-city church work, I was frequently asked what to do if someone is mugging spouse or a friend. My answer is that we should not just fold our hands and pray. We can do a variety of things, but we don't start by jerking out a gun and shooting the offender. Jesus taught us that violence begets violence (Matt. 26:52).

We respond with firmness, with the strength of the inner person that will be evident in our response to the evil one. We try to personalize the situation as much as possible, such as starting a conversation with the offender. Then as we resist the evil, we do so with a strength of personal power that can often disconcert the other and may enable us to avoid a catastrophe (cf. Yoder, *What Would You Do?*). Yet if we suffer, it can be with a clear and unsurrendered spirit; it can be a confrontation with evil in which we are still the spiritual victor. As in the death of Christ, they crushed his body but could not crush his spirit.

Let me suggest an outline of Jesus' teachings in the passage from Luke, the Sermon on the Plain. In the larger context, I am impressed that Jesus, when he speaks of loving our enemies and not just our friends, is saying three basic things about love:

• Love elevates others above our self-interest; hence, if someone insults me, strikes me on one cheek, I turn the other (Luke 6:28-29). This is our way of building bridges, our pattern of behavior toward those who may offend us. We try to establish a relation of I-thou, not I-it; love places value on persons, and in doing so does not pursue self-interests. Love affirms the other, respects the intrinsic worth of the other, and gives oneself in the support or enrichment of the other. Love acts to change the relationship from hostility and enmity to acceptance and friendship.

• Love elevates people above the material. If someone takes our coat, we do not even withhold our shirt but give it to the one who begs from us (Luke 6:29-30). This is the Christian philosophy of economics: we are to use money for the good of all rather than to hoard it as our security. To counter the unselfish use of money, we bridge between the haves and the have-nots. This calls for more than simply a handout. It calls for a helping hand up. In our inner-city work, we were often asked for a handout. So we arranged a program with a local bank to supply loans to the needy, with our commitment as security. In so doing, we helped needy people, who learned how to make payments and build up good credit records.

• Love elevates behavior above bargaining; we are not to do good only to those who do good to us, or be hospitable only to those who will return the favor (Luke 6:32-35). Love practices hospitality and thus builds a reconciling relationship. Kindness is never lost; it is an investment in the future.

A story from Russia illustrates this. Andrew Neustetter's Christian hospitality included having his peasant farmhands sit with his family at the table for their meals, says his grandson. As this Mennonite offered grace, he would pray for the farmhands as he did for each member of his family. During the Marxist revolution, Neustetter was arrested and taken before the commandant.

The officer had worked for Neustetter and recognized him. Yet in a brusque voice, he asked, "Your name sir?"

"Cornelius Andrew Neustetter."

The commandant responded by repeating the name in a way to make it more Russian: "Alexus Neustettski." He did this loudly so that the guards standing around could hear him. Then he said, "Mr. Neustettski, you are very thirsty."

"No, I am not thirsty."

"Yes," he said, loudly, "You are very thirsty, and what you need is at the end of the hall."

"I'll show him," offered a guard.

"No," the commandant said, "you're needed here." He motioned Neustetter down the hall.

When the Mennonite reached the fountain at the end of the hall, he saw the unlocked door leading outside and understood what was happening. He slipped out the door and left. His life was spared by the commandant in a gracious response to his earlier kindness.

What Jesus tells his disciples in Luke 6 outlines for us the pattern of love in action, presenting the way of love in the face of evil. This dynamic changes relationships for the better. It is the disciples' working order of life. Thus the golden rule is found at the heart of the passage: "Do to others as you would have them do to you" (Luke 6:31). We can find similar statements in other systems of religious thought; yet they have the negative rule of not doing what you don't want done to you, rather than in the positive approach of Jesus' words.

Immanuel Kant makes a philosophical attempt to formulate a morality based on pure reason, using categorical imperatives. Several of his statements are similar to Jesus' golden rule: "Treat every person as an end and not as a means to an end." "Conduct yourself so that your behavior could be a universal law."

During a faculty conference at Moscow State University in 1992, I spoke on the matter of a "Christian Ethic for the Free Market System." I emphasized guidelines for the new freedoms that the Russian society was discovering. After the lecture, several faculty members told me that they were Christians.

Yet one woman said, "I am not a believer like some of my colleagues. But even so, isn't there a way for me to build a strong ethic for business?"

I assured her that she could build a strong ethic by using such principles as Kant's categorical imperatives.

She responded affirmatively. Then I added, "While you are working on those, you should also look at Jesus' words, 'Do unto others as you would that others do to you.'"

"That sounds great," she replied. "And where do I find that?"

Thus I was able to introduce her to the Scriptures.

Evil is a parasite, living on the good around it; evil self-destructs and cannot sustain itself. Some of the most awful extremes of evil—such as slavery, genocide, wholesale destruction from war, and apartheid—show that evil oversteps its own bounds and becomes self-destructive. Good exposes the inadequacy of evil, even while suffering from the parasitic behavior of evil. Evil may appear to win by crushing the good, but that is not the whole story:

> Truth is immortal/unkillable. (Balthasar Hubmaier)

> Truth crushed to earth, shall rise again,
> Th' eternal years of God are hers. (Wm. Cullen Bryant)

In the long view of history, the good is what lives on, not the evil. Our challenge is always to overcome evil with good.

The cross, the divine act of love in our redemption, teaches us that good will triumph, even in suffering; the quality of mercy and love continues to enrich humanity. It challenges the church and individual believers to live in the love of Christ. As we live this in-Christ life, we are in the world as a presence of the kingdom, working like yeast to permeate the whole (Matt. 13:33). We exude "a fragrance from life to life" (2 Cor. 2:14-17).

God has been patient through the centuries, operating by this principle of overcoming evil with good. In the course of exercising his love, God needed to expose evil in the life of his chosen people Israel; yet he continued to discipline his gathered ones and to show his love. In the long view, God has kept coming into the human arena in love and grace.

In Luke (10:25-37), an expert in the law asks Jesus, "What must I do to inherit eternal life?"

Jesus meets the man at his area of expertise, the law: "What do you read there?"

"Love the Lord your God with all your heart, and with all your soul, and with all your strength, and with all your mind; and [love] your neighbor as yourself."

Jesus affirms his answer and adds, "Do this, and you will live."

But he wants to justify himself: "And who is my neighbor?"

We all tend to use similar self-justifications, extending death by definition: "To define is to exclude and negate" (José Ortega y Gasset). With such a question, we say we want to be selective, deciding who we will count as worthy to be our neighbor.

Jesus then tells the story of the Good Samaritan and the example of costly love. At the end of the story, he turns the lawyer's question upside down. It is not for us to ask, "Who is my neighbor?" Instead, we need to ask, "Are we willing to be a neighbor?"

This passage calls us to social action, to see our responsibility to help those in need. Jesus also gives a clear call for justice, for us to set things right for those who suffer at the hands of others. People of privilege, the power brokers in society, have a responsibility to seek justice for the oppressed, to help the powerless.

In the NT the same Greek word (*dikaiosunē*) can be translated as "righteousness" or "justice." To act justly toward others means that we cannot walk past someone in trouble; instead, we are to be a presence for Christ in that person's need. Micah's words ring out to us across the centuries: "He has told you . . . what is good; and what does the Lord require of you but to do justice, and to love kindness, and to walk humbly with your God?" (Mic. 6:8).

Love seeks the best for others. Love calls us to share the most important thing in life with those about us: the gospel of Jesus Christ.

We cannot live in love without being involved in the mission of sharing Jesus Christ with others. While the great commandment to love God comes first, it leads us to the great commission. When we love people, we want them also to know the realities of life with God. Love keeps us from separating the social and the evangelistic aspects of the gospel; it focuses on the well-being of those we love, and this well-being is physical and spiritual. As Archbishop William Temple said, "We enjoy our life with Christ so much that we can't stand for others to miss out on knowing him."

In summary, I highlight three things:

• First, love personalizes relationships rather than institutionalizing them. We are to look at people as ends in themselves and never as a means to some other end.

• Second, love energizes relationships rather than legalizing them. Jesus moves us beyond codes to compassion. As we care for people, we regard the law only as a means for treating others with justice and mercy.

• Third, love immortalizes relationships rather than temporalizing them. We have been called to always look beyond the need of the immediate, to share the quality and the extension of the eternal. We are not to make our decisions solely on the basis of the needs of the moment. With eternity in view, we share to invest in a life. Paul says, "Now faith, hope, and love abide, these three; and the greatest of these is love" (1 Cor. 13:13).

Reconciliation is a present reality. We are children of God now, members of God's family (1 John 3:1-3). Our hope is the full restoration of all that God has created us to be, and this he will fulfill. We live in this hope; Paul even says, "In hope we were saved" (Rom. 8:24). Let us celebrate our reconciliation with God in Jesus Christ, knowing that nothing "will be able to separate us from the love of God in Christ Jesus our Lord" (Rom. 8:39).

12

Being More Itinerant in Mission

From now on, therefore, we regard no one from a human point of view; even though we once knew Christ from a human point of view, we know him no longer in that way. So if anyone is in Christ, there is a new creation: everything old has passed away; see, everything has become new! All this is from God, who reconciled us to himself through Christ, and has given us the ministry of reconciliation; that is, in Christ, God was reconciling the world to himself, not counting their trespasses against them, and entrusting the message of reconciliation to us. So we are ambassadors for Christ, since God is making his appeal through us; we entreat you on behalf of Christ, be reconciled to God. For our sake he made him to be sin who knew no sin, so that in him we might become the righteousness of God. (2 Cor. 5:16-21)

P ASTOR PARKER, a prominent preacher of England in the last century, demonstrated his commitment to the mission of Christ in an unusual way through his schedule and his charges. His fee for filling the pulpit of some poor pastor was nothing. His fee to speak at a public social gathering was five volumes of good literature. His fee to serve a bazaar was 50 guineas (= 52.5 pounds). And his fee to serve on a committee was 200 pounds!

This last charge reminds me of a time my wife and I traveled out from Oxford and visited a tiny parish church in the Cotswold. The walk leading to the front entrance led right through the cemetery. On one tombstone we noticed a startling inscription: "He died in committee."

We are not all so clear as Parker on priorities for our various ministries. But we have good news to share with the world. God is a missionary God, the great Reconciler! He has acted in Christ "to reconcile to himself all things, whether on earth or in heaven, by making peace through the blood of his cross" (Col. 1:20). This wonderful statement presents God's redeeming work of reconciliation, bringing all peoples into the fellowship of grace. We who are reconciled in Christ are in turn called to be agents of reconciliation (2 Cor. 5:18). To use a contemporary term, we are to be "missional" in our discipleship.

Already in Genesis, God makes a promise to Abraham that in his seed "all the families of the earth shall be blessed" (12:3). Later, God gives Israel special directions for including the "resident aliens" who join them. The unusual book of Jonah is a powerful story calling the prophet to cross cultural and racial lines to take God's message to Nineveh. Jonah recognizes that God's grace is to be extended to the Gentiles. But this missional character comes to full recognition in the words of our resurrected Lord; he commissions the disciples to make disciples of all peoples (Matt. 28:19-20).

Nevertheless, the church has tended to relegate mission or evangelism to the sidelines and to concentrate on refurbishing itself. Much of our focus in worship and theology is on ministries to the Christian community itself. Missiology is usually presented as an appendage to theology. Missions becomes a program involving only a few believers, the so-called missionaries.

A theology of reconciliation, however, places the mission of Christ—both in his earthly ministry and in the great commission—upon each of us as his followers. This mission is an essential aspect of our faith relation with him. The Christian's one vocation is to be a disciple of Jesus Christ, and the first step of discipleship is witnessing to our Lord.

James Denney has said that the witness

> who has himself been reconciled to God through Christ and who can make the NT witness to the reconciling power of Jesus his own, is a far more powerful minister of reconciliation than any institution or atmosphere can be. . . . A reconciled man, preach-

ing Christ as the way of reconciliation and preaching him in the temper and spirit which the experience of reconciliation creates, is the most effective mediator of Christ's reconciling power. (8)

This fact is essential to understanding the Anabaptist movement, the major evangelistic expression of Christianity in the sixteenth-century Reformation. Anabaptists were "set on fire" by several things: their new sense of assurance of salvation in their relation with Christ, their experience of regeneration and of the indwelling of the Holy Spirit, and their understanding that the Christian life means walking with the risen Christ as disciples. They were not satisfied simply to attend sacramental worship services in cathedrals or theological discussions at universities; instead, they felt called to share their faith with the populace.

The Anabaptists heard the commission of our Lord as a call to go and make disciples, and they became itinerant witnesses. They were misunderstood and vilified by the state-church authorities and persecuted to death. Even in their martyrdom, they shared a witness that led many others to come to faith in Christ.

In 1989, while I was president of the Coalition of Christian Colleges and Universities in Washington, D.C., we convened a think tank in Zurich, Switzerland. We focused on "Education and Global Mission as Christians." People gathered from ten countries, and we wrestled with the calling and character of our mission as Christians in education from a global perspective. Many of the participants from Europe, Africa, Latin America, and the United States emphasized the relational and the developmental aspects of mission; this is important if we are to give credibility to the gospel.

At an interlude, I led a walking tour of Zurich, the birthplace of the Swiss Brethren or free-church Anabaptists. We stood by the cold blue-green waters of the Limmat River, where the Zurich Council, under Zwingli's direction, had Felix Manz executed by drowning on January 5, 1527. His sentence included the charge that he converted and baptized adult believers and was evangelizing and calling others to this new way.

The authorities tied his hands together, pulled his arms down over his knees, and put a stick through under his knees so that he couldn't get free. They dunked Manz under the water until he drowned. His mother and brother stood on the bank, encouraging him and calling out that he should not deny Jesus. He died—but this did not silence the message. It lives on.

We need to rediscover that the primary task of the church is sharing our common experience in grace. As D. T. Niles has said, "Evangelism is one beggar telling another beggar where to find bread." We need to deliberately change the image of the church from institutions of religion to a people who share in reconciling grace. The dynamic sense that the church is a people in reconciling dialogue will better enable us to touch our larger world for Christ.

The Anabaptists were working at evangelism in a world that did not have one billion people until three hundred years later. Now we witness in a world of six billion people. How much greater is the challenge for us!

We need to rediscover the gospel as good news, remarkable news, that one can be reconciled to God in Christ, welcomed by the Father, and wrapped in his "robe of righteousness," right relation with God (see chap. 1, above; Luke 15:22; Isa. 61:10). In that relationship, we can work at our imperfections rather than thinking that we need the resolution of our problems before we can claim such a saving relationship.

With our psychological understandings, we know that as we provide therapy for people addicted to problems or perversions, we foster process toward full correction. Some scholars criticize the evangelist as being too simplistic in calling people into relationship with Christ. But the critics overlook the simple difference between our sin and our sins. Our basic sin is rebellion against God; our sins are the perversions of life.

The good news is that we can deal with the basic sin of rebellion through a deliberate decision of response to God's grace—a crisis experience, if you please, of surrendering oneself to God. Evangelists call for such a step. In turn, this new relationship with God will supply resources of grace for release from or correction of the perversion of our sins. This is the Christian counselor's role and the pastor's ministry. Therapists with a high level of maturity can provide the best counseling.

An evangelist invites people to respond to God's gracious call of reconciliation; that response can happen in a moment. The psychological counselor is God's agent in helping a person move toward the wholeness and healing that comes from an in-depth understanding of oneself, accompanied by an understanding of God's grace. There is no good reason for opposition to evangelistic appeals that call people to a decision in relation to Christ; in this decision, each person's life is focused or unified.

An evangelist draws people to the basic change of relationship with God; the psychological counselor then helps a person to further integrate the spiritual meanings for life with the total of one's personality. This is a therapy of wholeness.

The revival emphasis and the pastoral emphasis overlap the field of clinical psychology. In confession, the confessor breaks the tyranny of sin. Even so, we should not trade the mourner's bench for the psychiatrist's couch. We need to take seriously the therapy of genuine repentance, its release from sin's tyranny, and its consequent freedom. As Bonhoeffer emphasizes, whether a confession is made to one or to many, it is the act of confessing that breaks the tyranny of sin (1978).

The Christian church is in danger of becoming institutionalized and acculturated, often rendering it rigid in face of the challenge of mission to the larger world. One of the greater means of fulfilling the mission of Christ is simply to be present in society as people who walk with Jesus. We need a new vision as to how we can witness through professional and business ventures in areas other than in our comfort zone.

The people of God need to be more itinerant, a more mobile social force in society. We send a few missionaries to other people groups; beyond that, we ought to seek roles of helpfulness by making business and professional contributions in all countries. Such roles can give us place in the minds of the people since, as guests, we have a valid reason for being in their country. We need to lay aside our own nationalistic interests and seek the good of the people with whom we share. "Seek the welfare of the city where I have sent you," says the Lord (Jer. 29:7).

The Christian church, as members of the global kingdom of God, need to be far more itinerant and far less nationalistic if we are actually to spread the good news of the kingdom. The ministry of reconciliation, like the Incarnation, means to take the initiative, to move to people in faith, identifying with them so that they in turn can understand our message.

One of the exciting things about missions is the privilege of announcing the good news to those who have not known God as we know him in Christ. For people who think of many gods, it is good news to learn that the sovereign God has made himself known in Christ and offers us the way to reconciliation with him. The gospel also provides an answer for many who already believe that there is a God beyond all of the gods they have contemplated and worshiped. A delightful part of the good news is to discover it is possible for us to know this God, the God and Father of our Lord Jesus Christ.

Paul spoke about this same opportunity in Athens: "I found . . . an altar with the inscription, 'To an unknown god.' What therefore you worship as unknown, this I proclaim to you" (Acts 17:23). We share this good news with the assurance that some among our hearers are seeking eternal life. Thus Acts gives a descriptive report of the ministry of Paul and Barnabas to the Gentiles: "All who were appointed for eternal life believed" (13:48, NIV).

The new paradigm today is to think in terms of global community. In the pluralism of our own multicultural society, the world has come to us. Christ's Incarnation and the gospel call us to "think small" and show love and "hospitality to strangers" at our doorstep (Rom. 12:13; see Bonk). We can demonstrate the unity of the body of Christ with the diversity of its parts, racially and culturally. God has also given us new opportunities in religious pluralism for witness through dialogue. In dialogue, we must hear another until we can repeat satisfactorily to the other what we have heard; we must similarly be heard. This is the best style of witness.

We wonder, however, if the Christian community is clear enough on the essential elements of our faith to have meaningful dialogue with others. We do members of other religions little good in conversation unless we first hear them authentically, then share clearly with them the essence of our own faith. The good news is that God has fulfilled his covenant promise in Christ and in a people. God has done this in Jesus Christ, the Incarnation of God, and in the church, with Christ as the head. This is good news when understood as God's action in grace; we do not present this gospel as our religion or to belittle other religions.

In our pluralistic society, we deal with challenges similar to those the early Christians faced when they shared their faith in the pre-Christian world. They composed no majority movement; the Caesar of Rome was a powerful emperor. Yet their mission and conversation with others set forth clearly the person of Christ, his life, his death, his resurrection, and his lordship at God's right hand. Our message with theirs is that God's love, known in Jesus, is the good news, the gospel.

When Karl Barth visited Chicago, students asked him to name the greatest theological thought that ever crossed his mind. He responded, "Jesus loves me, this I know, for the Bible tells me so!"

The early church not only had pastors and teachers; they first had the apostles, who were more itinerant. They were traveling around the known world, preaching, planting churches, and appointing leaders. Their ministry was one of witness to the lordship of the resurrected Savior. Theirs was a special ministry beyond the local pastorate or educational work. They took the great commission as their mandate for mission.

God continues to give the church members who are called and gifted for various roles: "apostles, prophets, evangelists, pastors, and teachers, to equip the saints for the work of ministry" (Eph. 4:11-13, abridged). The church needs to put all these gifts to work.

Our institutionalism has often hindered us from calling more leaders than the local church can use, and then sending them out to obey Christ's commission. Thus we have seen parachurch programs emerging; they run the risk of individualistic patterns built around a personality, rather than around a community of the Spirit in the mission of Christ. Our failure to call, commission, and extend the community of accountability often leaves people to take an individualistic path.

Even when it comes to believers choosing to go to a seminary, we tend to leave the matter to an individual's own sense of leading. It would be better for the congregation to process a sense of calling and to send selected members to seminary. If we are to gain some of the stronger believers and sharper minds for the ministry, to impact the world, we need to revive the role of the congregation in calling and discerning together the will of God for members in leading ministries.

In the free-church movement of the sixteenth-century, radical believers were forced to take another path than that of the institutional state church; they developed a more mobile ministry. In turn, they were criticized for being "itinerants" and "hedge preachers" because they carried the gospel to the peasants rather than staying with cathedrals and universities. They did not feel that national boundaries had any direct bearing on their calling to share the message of Christ. This does not mean that they opposed pastoral roles; the documents show that they were semi-congregational in their polity. But congregations were working in relationship with other congregations.

In the earliest Reformation-era synod, Anabaptists met at Schleitheim, Switzerland, on February 24, 1527. They spelled out the role of the pastor, including financial support by the congregation. If the pastor was martyred, the congregation was to assemble and appoint another pastor "in the same hour"! (Yoder, *The Schleitheim Confession*, art. 5).

We need to become less institutionalized and more itinerant in the world of today. We especially need to free the Christian message from Western culture, from Americanisms, and even from identity with any particular political party. I salute the Korean church for actively sending missionaries on their own; this helps to change the face of missions for the good. The younger churches (in the East and South) are now sending out more evangelists than are sent from Europe and North America (see, e.g., Robert).

It nevertheless is imperative for us in the West to become, once again, a people who are faithful to Christ's mandate, "Go therefore and make disciples of all nations" (Matt. 28:19). In doing so, itinerants need to make certain to present the gospel, not their own culture. There is no Christian culture as such, though culture is ubiquitous and we must live in a culture. We need to represent the kingdom of God in a way that can be directly related to the culture in which we are moving and contextualized there.

My friend J. Lawrence Burkholder writes of this mobility among the Radical Reformers:

A general characteristic of Anabaptism is its preoccupation with
the purely redemptive processes. The orders of creation (Schop-
fungs-ordnungen) are acknowledged but they are left to Providence while the Christian devotes his energies to preaching the
Word. No necessary moral dualism between redemption and creation is implied, and certainly the Anabaptists were not ascetics.
Marriage was considered sacred, and honest work was sometimes
exalted. Nevertheless, between the socially unsettling mobility of
the itinerant and the stability of the "station," the Anabaptists in-
stinctively chose the former. They saw themselves in the line of
Abraham, who "went out not knowing whither he went." They
accepted as normative the "insecurity" of faith with Jesus who
had no place to lay his head and with the disciples who were
called upon to "take no thought for the morrow." Their first
command was to "go." The natural demands of home and occu-
pation were frequently regarded as "worldly concerns." Seldom
in history has the issue of security been so heroically faced. (in
Hershberger: 139)

We face a crucial question as we launch into the twenty-first century, called by some a post-Christian era, and float in a sea of six billion people. How shall we witness for Christ to the peoples of the
world? We cannot fulfill our mission by simply building big programs, megachurches, and media ministries that shuffle people from
one church to another, competing by offering benefits like a religious
shopping mall. We need more Christian people living among the peoples of the world as a presence for Christ.

If we are to be understood by our Muslim, Jewish, and Hindu
friends, and if we are to make faith in Christ an option for them, we
need to live among them and show the love and grace of God in life.
We preach the gospel by our presence, using words when we have
earned the right to be heard. By socializing, we win the understanding of others and can then share the gospel of Christ. Reconciliation
does not happen at a distance!

Positions taken by the Christian church amid pluralism are usually described as being either exclusive, inclusive, or pluralistic.

• Those with an *exclusive* position stress the singularity of the
gospel: Jesus is the only Savior, the full and final revelation of God.

• Those who hold to an *inclusive* gospel count Jesus as the center of the message of salvation. Yet they acknowledge other ways in which people may come to God and experience his grace without knowing the gospel of Christ, thereby becoming so-called anonymous Christians.

• The *pluralistic* view is that Jesus is not central or normative among the religions of the world. Some theologians, such as John Hick, have moved from a Christocentric faith to a Theocentric faith, which means that all God-talk is acceptable. Others have moved to salvation-centeredness, recognizing the similarity of religious quests in all religions. Still others see the Spirit as a free and moving God-consciousness in all religions. In short, pluralism holds that there are many paths to God; hence, religious consciousness is the norm.

Nevertheless, the early church and the NT message focus on the uniqueness of Jesus. There is "no other name" whereby we must be saved (Acts 4:12). Jesus is God's Word (John 1; Rev. 19:13). This is good news as the answer to human problems and conflict. God calls us to discipleship of Jesus Christ more than to religion. *God calls us into reconciliation.* We carry this conviction about God's purposes as we share the good news of the gospel of Christ.

We need to examine a number of issues raised in confronting pluralism while we engage in witness-dialogue:

• First, we need to recognize value in other religions, and find in them bridges of conversation. These points of contact will help us in explaining the uniqueness of Jesus Christ in a manner fair to them and their claims.

• Second, we need to recognize how the gospel relates to general revelation, a component of world religions and helpful as far as it goes. We can then focus on special revelation as the self-disclosure of a personal God who has come to us in Jesus Christ.

• Third, we need to have a clear message about the grace of God in its unique redemptive expression in Christ; God's grace in Christ brings reconciling forgiveness.

• Fourth, we need to seek a friendly relationship with adherents of other religions, not being judgmental, and often seeing the gospel of Christ as the complement to their faith. The disclosure of God known ultimately in Christ can function as filling out elements and aspirations of their faith (cf. Acts 17:22-31). We want our dialogue with them on these matters to help them come to a full faith.

This is like the approach of Paul in Athens, as he moved from religious practices and perceptions of his hearers to the message of the resurrection of Christ. We need to find the bases in Judaism, in Islam, in other religions that open the door for them to see Jesus as the Mediator of God.

The pluralism of our society offers us a new and remarkable opportunity to involve people of other faiths in conversation. Our approach must be full of understanding as we relate to peoples of different traditions. We must share in conversation with a genuine appreciation for their faith. Only as we understand and respect the values of their faith can we show them how Jesus came to reconcile us with God and each other, and not primarily to found a religion.

As we speak with those oriented to the biblical faith, in Christianity and Judaism, we need to explain God's purpose of creating a people beyond any one ethnic or cultural group; God is doing this in Christ. We want to help our Jewish friends to understand that God has taken their heritage the next step in the creation of a church for all peoples.

When we dialogue with people who have a religion of the biblical God—meaning those in Judaism, Christianity, and Islam—we have a challenge to move beyond the religion of a book, of a perfect law, to a relationship with God in his grace. This is the crux of the issue. God's love and mercy are expressed supremely, not in a perfect law, but in the person of Christ. Jesus came in suffering and redemptive love to reconcile us to God and each other.

The death and resurrection of Jesus are not peripheral issues. Instead, they are essential both to understand the difference between our faith positions and in completing the faith of any of the three religions. Badru D. Kateregga and David W. Shenk effectively state this in their unique book: *A Muslim and a Christian in Dialogue*. They supply a jointly written conclusion on the Incarnation and cross as the essential difference (205-7).

Finally, when we turn to the gospel and nonbiblical missionary religions, Hinduism and Buddhism, we face a polytheism of gods. In this dialogue situation, we need to be clear in our presentation of the trinitarian faith. Lesslie Newbigin says we must share the trinitarian faith lest polytheists think of Jesus as another god in the plurality of gods they worship (1964, esp. chap. 4, "Relevance of Trinitarian Doctrine").

As we discuss common values, there still are essential differences. For example, this will be found in our interchange with Buddhism and its emphasis on values, faith, the compassion of courage, and universal love as the basis for social responsibility and progress. As Edmund Perry writes,

> Christians speak of love as a relationship which unites what is separated and carried to its ultimate; this means that love is the power which unites the many selves even into eternity. But Buddhists know that not only are there no such selves to be preserved but also that relationships are also subject to change. Buddhist love is not the power which unites but the power that serves. (206)

The Buddhist disputes the resurrection of Jesus basically because he believes there is no helper for man except man himself (Perry: 224). But we as Christians have a conviction that in our sinfulness, the life of faith is impossible without the grace of God extended to us in Jesus our Lord.

Pluralism calls us to find the way to contextualize reconciliation in our social and professional relationships. Through our social and economic interchanges, we need to dialogue with people of different religions. This is in the worship-walk of our occupational life. Social friendships will help us to be understanding, caring, and considerate as Jesus was in his approach to people of a different class, race, or culture. We need to converse with people as we would like others to speak with us.

There is no place for bigotry or judgmental attitudes in the ministry of reconciliation. We may reject practices and positions, but we may not reject people if we witness in the spirit of Jesus. Further, as evidence of our commitment to be a reconciled people, a community of the Spirit, we can create small-group fellowships. Even where a congregation is scarcely developed, a small group can be our accountability fellowship in any culture.

In the past, we valued career missionaries more than short-term missionaries. For the future, we will need more career missionaries who are itinerants. Some will be earning their living as professionals, and at the same time they will be contributing to their host community. In addition to their work, even serendipitously, they will share the message of Christ. We can paraphrase the great commission to capture this point: "While going about in your personal world, make disciples. While going about in your professional world, make disciples."

Our challenge is to contextualize reconciliation in social and professional roles. It is also our most immediate context of sharing faith. In our professional world, we are sharing with peers, speaking the same language, pursuing common interests, and following a similar philosophy of living.

Dennis Bakke of our congregation in Washington, D.C., is president of Applied Energy Service, a company he helped to found in the 1980s. Today the business has energy plants in over two dozen countries of the world—a multibillion enterprise. Bakke has become a multimillionaire. Yet he is a Christian in business, operating by Christian principles of relationships, integrity, efficiency, and stewardship. He asked me as pastor to commission him and Eileen to be missionaries in business, just as others from the congregation were commissioned to traditional mission roles.

Dennis and his wife are just that, missionaries in witness, hospitality, and support roles. Each year, their various scholarship programs provide around a million dollars of gifts, and their Mustard Seed Foundation gives well over two hundred grants of about five thousand dollars each. His business makes him itinerant in crossing cultures and touching lives for Christ. He deals with many people in many countries and is their partner in business and often in faith.

In the history of Western missions, our early ventures were conditioned by colonialism; we were in charge. Then we shifted the emphasis to the indigenous church; yet we were still in charge as we orchestrated the local structure. The next emphasis has been on contextualization: finding meanings in other cultures by which the gospel can be expressed in that setting.

In my experience through numerous speaking engagements and seminars in overseas mission settings, I believe we have to take a further step. We need to learn to be *situational* within a basic cultural context. Each congregational fellowship must meet the needs in its own setting or situation with empathetic understanding. This identity with each people-group will be our guide in service, in word and in deeds.

My brother-in-law, Paul Kniss with his wife, Esther, have spent forty-three years in mission in Bihar, India. They became thoroughly acculturated to the Indian lifestyle and ways of thinking. They were sharing with their Indian colleagues without being controlling, serving as enablers of others, and following directions from others. During retirement back in America, they have continued to share in the mission in India. Each year the church in India has invited them to return for several winter months, to serve and witness as directed by the Indian church community.

The focus for the new century must be on partnership, sharing across national, cultural, and racial lines in mutuality. The term *mutuality* may offer a new perspective; it is the language and spirit of reconciliation. We have a special opportunity and challenge to enable others. In our approach, especially from the West, we have often been too controlling in our work with others. Contemporary mission calls for a new spirit of the itinerant as an enabler, one who can connect with others in mutuality.

In 1957 I was in Israel for the first time. During my visit, a Jewish immigration officer became a friend and asked to travel with me. I hired the taxi for trips to Nazareth, the Sea of Galilee, Sychar, Jerusalem, and more; the two of us enjoyed a meaningful excursion. We visited in both Arab and Jewish homes and discussed historic sites of Israel's history and from the time of Christ.

Near the end of our time together, we were at Joppa, swimming in the Mediterranean Sea. While resting on a reef off shore, Abraham Hariza commented pointedly about Christian missions in his country: "Why don't you American Christians wise up and quit trying to send missionaries as such? Why don't you recruit young professionals to come to Israel, get jobs with oil companies or other firms, live here as Christians, and let people understand their faith? Then when some of our people become Christians, they could baptize each other and conduct the worship services. Your people could be in support rather than in charge."

I looked at him with amazement: "You could become a modern

apostle Paul. That philosophy of mission is prophetic, far beyond where we are."

Some weeks later I received a letter from him, telling how he helped a widow and her children from Europe get settled. Then he added, "But they will be refugees of soul until they have found him who is known as the Messiah!"

While rejoicing in this communication of Hariza's dawning faith, I have never forgotten his challenge for missions. I am convinced that the Christian community needs to become more flexible and mobile in its mission patterns. We need to be more itinerant in missions, serving in some professional role that is needed in the host community. Today we stress education in business, computer science, food production and distribution, clean water, and sewage disposal: these all are needed areas of expertise in many countries of the world. We need engineers, agriculturalists, economists, and teachers of English whose interest is service in the name of Christ more than moving up the socioeconomic ladder.

To rejoin the mission of Christ in this way, we need to affirm that one's purpose is more important than one's position. We Westerns tend to find our security in our position rather than in God's purpose and providence. We often measure an individual's worth by what one does more than by who one is as a servant of God. In education, for example, we could discover universities all around the world to which we might apply as professors. We could bring them needed expertise as fully accepted colleagues and do so in the spirit and love of Christ. The same may be said for many other vocations, some of which were previously suggested.

Disciples are commissioned to make disciples—not to win an argument or call people to a merely intellectual confession of Christian doctrine. To be a "discipler" in this sense, we begin by being good disciples of Jesus ourselves. We must remember that we are always his disciples. Jesus doesn't graduate us but continues to walk with us in life. Many secular people and those of other religions would recognize a spirituality for the road as more appealing than a spirituality that is merely conceptual and carried primarily in a liturgy of worship.

With all our studies on mission and our theological motivation for sharing the unique message of Jesus, we are still left with the major problem of how to get Christian people in conversation with non-Christians. We need to discover the dynamic of relational evangelism; without it, we commit a sin of omission greater than some other evils we deplore. For this century, we need a church that is more cosmopolitan, informed, versatile, mobile, itinerant, and willing to actualize what we affirm about the global nature of the church and the kingdom of God. Our focus should not be on size so much as on presence, not on structure so much as on flexibility, not on denominationalism but on the risen Lord.

Projections into the future involve many issues. We need to consider the global village, interdependence, urbanization, population increases, technological developments, economic development, food distribution, ethnic defensiveness, religious pluralism, political alliances, the widening gap between the haves and the have-nots, terrorism, global media coverage, outer-space networking, global economy, and more. Such changes call for Christian leaders to be well grounded in the essentials of faith and more flexible in relating to other groups and changing situations.

I have met far too many pastors who are overly controlling and quite inflexible, often on issues that have little significance to a needy world. To be God's people in a changing future, we need to learn from history as to how God has been coping with a changing world through the centuries.

Flexibility is not easy but it is effective; it puts the value on the person in relationship rather than on protocol. Blanche Sell, a family friend, gave many years of her life to India in mission. She shares a meaningful story of having two young women from America as guests. They were being hosted for dinner by Aunti Dorcas, known as Doca Bai.

Blanche had forgotten to tell the young women that in eating with their fingers, the locals never use the left hand; in this culture, the left hand is used for toilet habits and is considered unclean. One of the young women was left-handed and began to eat with that hand. Blanche was nervous as she observed this and saw some Indian guests reacting. Then Doca Bai did something an Indian woman never does. She began to eat with her left hand and thereby avoided embarrassing the visitors.

Change also happens in a given culture over time and in the changing social order, and we must adjust with flexibility. Futurists say we have experienced more changes since 1935 than happened in the whole history of the human race up to that time. My generation has lived in a period of major change, shaping our expectations and leading us to feel that nothing is permanent. But God is giving us a kingdom in which the things that cannot be shaken will stand amid the things that are being shaken (Heb. 12:27).

While Esther and I were ministering in Asia, I came to the conviction that we have a great challenge of translating the gospel into the culture and language of other settings. Other peoples need not come to Christ through our Western route. They can come to Christ through Paul and Peter and John, and not necessarily through Augustine, Luther, Calvin, or Menno. For Westerners nurtured in the Western traditions of the faith, this is difficult for us to recognize and to accept. It calls for us to put the message of Christ and the Scripture at the forefront, especially in a day of pluralistic communication.

Pluralism challenges us to engage our society in witness dialogue and evangelistic conversation. In so doing, we must be clear on the core of the gospel. There will be boundaries; yet it is important for us to focus on the core and spend less time on marking boundaries (cf. King, 1990: chap. 5). If we are clear that the heart of our faith is Jesus Christ, we can extend the meaning of that core out as far as possible in every field or professional endeavor. In one sense, the boundaries will tend to establish themselves in our dialogue. Our witness is not to place one system of life and thought against another so much as it is to call people to a radically new life of joining the Jesus community and living as disciples of Christ.

The structures of the church, as we have known it, will keep changing; but the essential nature of the church, as the people of God, will continue till the end of the age. We are not primarily building structures, as much as they may be needed. Rather, we are inviting people in and through Christ to experience reconciliation with God and fellow humans, and thereby to become part of the kingdom of God. The form of the church may be in small groups or in large congregations; church happens when two or three gather in the name of Christ and worship with the awareness that he is present with us.

A church grows when what is put at the forefront is not denomination but Christ. The presence of our Lord, moving among us by his Spirit, provides the essential life and dynamic of the church.

Sharing the good news of Jesus Christ is exciting, a positive and loving thing to do. Krister Stendahl calls dialogue "love language." Similarily, Jürgen Moltmann says that "God Is Unselfish Love" (in Cobb, 121). Far too often the urge to do evangelism makes it into a task or even a burden. We should recognize that it is a privilege for us to introduce people to the most important Person in life! Ours is the privilege of sharing with others the source of our own security and joy. We are children of God, members of his family, and heirs of eternal life!

Our calling, as a community of the reconciled, is to live in hope. We already know the meaning of a living relationship with God; through hope, we see that reality extending into the future. We focus on God's intention, and in doing so we participate in God's action. The Lord, who has redeemed us, has set us free in relationship with him and with one another. In this redemption, he "fills us with all joy and peace in believing" (Rom. 15:13, adapted).

As a people of hope, we look for the personal return of our Lord to consummate the gathering of a people, the completion of his kingdom. When this is done, he will turn this reign over to his Father, in the ultimate victory of his redemption (1 Cor. 15:24). The return of Christ, spoken of more than three hundred times in the NT, is the *telos*, the goal and culmination of our Lord's redemptive work, the full expression of his victory over sin, Satan, and death. The triumph is that he ushers us into the glory of God's presence. Heaven is awaiting the believer, the wonderful and unimaginable privilege of being with God for eternity. Fifty billion years from now, I expect to be living on with God. Hallelujah!

Bibliography

Althaus, Paul, et al. *Jesus of Nazareth, Savior and Lord*. Ed. Carl. F. H. Henry. Eerdmans, 1966.

Augsburger, David. *Pastoral Counseling Across Cultures*. Westminster, 1986.

_____. *The New Freedom of Forgiveness*. 3d ed. Moody Pr., 2000.

Augsburger, Myron, *The Peacemaker*. Abingdon, 1987.

_____. *Principles of Biblical Interpretation*. Herald Pr., 1967.

_____. *Quench Not the Spirit*. Herald Pr., 1961.

_____. *Practicing the Presence of the Spirit*. Herald Pr., 1982.

Augustine of Hippo. *The City of God*. Cambridge Univ. Pr., 1998.

_____. *The Confessions*. Vintage Bks., 1998.

_____. *Enchiridion*. Regnery Gateway, 1961.

Aulén, Gustav. *Christus Victor*. SPCK, 1950.

Bainton, Roland. *Here I Stand*. Abingdon-Cokesbury, 1950.

Bakke, Ray. *The Urban Christian*. InterVarsity, 1987.

Banks, Robert, ed. *Reconciliation and Hope: New Testament Essays . . . Presented to L. L. Morris*. Eerdmans, 1975.

Barth, Markus. *Justification*. Eerdmans, 1971.

_____ and Verne H. Fletcher. *Acquittal by Resurrection*. Holt, Rinehart and Winston, 1964.

Bauman, Clarence. *On the Meaning of Life: An Anthology of Theological Reflection*. Evangel Pr., 1993.

Bender, Harold S. "Discipline, Concept, Idea, and Practice of." In *The Mennonite Encyclopedia*, 2:69-70. Herald Pr., 1956.

Benton, Wilson Jr. In *Tabletalk*, Ligonier Ministries, Sept.-Dec. 1994, 10.

Bonhoeffer, Dietrich. *The Cost of Discipleship*. Macmillan, 1951.

_____. *Letters and Papers from Prison*. Ed. Eberhard Bethge. Rev. ed. New York: Macmillan, 1967.

_____. *Life Together.* Harper S.F., 1978.

Bonk, Jonathan J. "Thinking Small: Global Missions and American Churches." *Missiology* 28 (Apr. 2000): 149-161.

Bosch, David. *A Spirituality for the Road.* Herald Pr., 1979.

Bracht, Thieleman J. van. *Martyrs Mirror.* 3d English ed. Trans. J. F. Sohm from Dutch original, 1660. Herald Pr., 1938. Includes early Anabaptist confessions such as "Dordrecht," 1632.

Brunner, Emil. *The Divine Imperative.* Westminster, 1947.

Buber, Martin. *I and Thou.* Trans. W. Kaufman. Macmillan, 1974.

Bullinger, Heinrich. *Wiedertöufferen Ursprung.* Zurich, 1560.

Burkholder, J. Lawrence. *The Problem of Social Responsibility.* Elkhart, Ind.: Inst. of Mennonite Studies, 1989.

_____. In "Readers Say." *Gospel Herald,* 9/6/1994:4-5.

Burkholder, J. R., and C. Redekop. *Kingdom, Cross, and Community.* Herald Pr., 1976.

Buswell, James Oliver. *A Systematic Theology of the Christian Religion.* 2 vols. Zondervan, 1962-63.

Calvin, John/Jean. *Institutes of the Christian Christian Religion.* Trans. H. Beveridge. Eerdmans, 1989.

Childs, Brevard S. *The New Testament as Canon.* Trinity Pr. Intl., 1994.

Cobb, John B., and Christopher Ives, eds. *The Emptying God: A Buddhist-Jewish-Christian Conversation.* Orbis Bks., 1990.

Confession of Faith in a Mennonite Perspective. Herald Pr., 1995.

Coward, Harold. *Pluralism: Challenge to World Religions.* Orbis Bks., 1985.

Denney, James. *The Christian Doctrine of Reconciliation.* London, 1917.

Dosker, Henry E. *The Dutch Anabaptists.* Judson Pr., 1921. AMS Pr., 1988. The Stone Lectures at Princeton Theol. Sem., 1918-19.

Driver, John. *Community and Commitment.* Herald Pr., 1976.

_____. *Understanding the Atonement for the Mission of the Church.* Herald Pr., 1986.

Ellul, Jacques. *The Ethics of Freedom.* Trans. G. W. Bromiley. Eerdmans, 1976.

_____. *The Subversion of Christianity.* Trans. G. W. Bromiley. Eerdmans, 1986.

Erickson, Millard J. *Christian Theology.* Baker Bks., 1983.

Escobar, Samuel, and John Driver. *Christian Mission and Social Justice.* Herald Pr., 1978.

Fee, Gordon D. *The First Epistle to the Corinthians.* Eerdmans, 1987.

Finger, Thomas. *Christian Theology.* 2 vols. Herald Pr., 1987-89.

Foster, Richard. *Celebration of Discipline.* Rev. ed. Harper S.F., 1988.

Friedmann, Robert. *The Theology of Anabaptism.* Herald Pr., 1973.

George, Timothy. *Theology of the Reformers.* Broadman, 1988.

Gerard, René. *Violence and the Sacred.* Tr. P. Gregory. Johns Hopkins Univ. Pr., 1977.

Gollwitzer, Helmut. *The Way to Life: Sermons in a Time of World Crisis.* English trans., David Cairns. Edinburgh: Clark, 1981.

Grenz, Stanley. *Theology for the Community of God.* Eerdmans, 2000.

Gunton, Colin E. *The One, the Three and the Many.* Cambridge Univ. Pr., 1993.

Hall, Douglas John. *Thinking the Faith.* Augsburg Fortress, 1991.

_____. *Professing the Faith.* Augsburg Fortress, 1993.

Harder, Leland, ed. *The Sources of Swiss Anabaptism.* Herald Pr., 1985.

Hauerwas, Stanley. *The Peaceable Kingdom.* Univ. of Notre Dame Pr., 1983.

_____ and Wm. Willimon. *Resident Aliens.* Abingdon, 1989.

Hershberger, Guy F., ed. *The Recovery of the Anabaptist Vision.* Herald Pr., 1957.

Heschel, Abraham J. *Man's Quest for God.* Scribner, 1954.

Hodge, Charles. *Systematic Theology.* 3 vols. Eerdmans, 1952.

Hughes, T. H. *The Atonement.* London, 1949.

Huntington, Samuel P. "The Clash of Civilizations?" *Foreign Affairs,* Summer 1993.

Janowsky, Philip. *The Evangelical Essential.* Gresham, Ore.: Mission House, 1994.

Jeschke, Marlin, *Discipling in the Church: Recovering a Ministry of the Gospel.* Herald Pr., 1988.

Jones, E. Stanley. *Mastery.* Abingdon, 1955, 1992.

Kant, Immanuel. *Critique of Practical Reason.* Trans. T. K. Abbott, from the 1788 German original. Prometheus Bks., 1996.

Kateregga, Bandru D., and David W. Shenk. *A Muslim and a Christian in Dialogue.* Herald Pr., 1997.

Kaufman, Gordon. *Systematic Theology.* Scribner's, 1968.

Kempis. *See* Thomas.

King, Martin Luther. *Stride Toward Freedom.* Harper, 1958.

King, Michael. *Trackless Wastes and Stars to Steer By.* Herald Pr., 1990.

Kivengere, Festo. *I Love Idi Amin.* Revell, 1977.

Klaassen, Walter, ed. *Anabaptism in Outline.* Herald Pr., 1981.

Kniss, Lloy. *Why I Couldn't Fight.* Herald Pr., 1971.

Kraybill, Donald B. *The Upside-Down Kingdom.* Rev. ed. Herald Pr., 1990.

Kraus, C. Norman. *The Community of the Spirit.* Herald Pr., 1993.

_____. *Jesus Christ Our Lord.* Herald Pr., 1987. Rev. ed., 1990.

_____. *God Our Savior,* Herald Pr., 1991.

Law, William. *A Serious Call to a Devout and Holy Life* (1729). Westminster John Knox, 1968.

Lederach, Paul. *A Third Way.* Herald Pr., 1980.
Leith, John, H. *Basic Christian Doctrine.* Westminster John Knox, 1993.
Lewis, C. S. *Christian Reflections.* Eerdmans, 1994.
Lints, Richard. *The Fabric of Theology.* Eerdmans, 1993.
Littell, Franklin. *The Anabaptist View of the Church.* 2d ed. Boston: Star King Pr., 1958.
MacIntyre, Alister. *Three Rival Versions of Moral Enquiry.* Univ. of Notre Dame Pr., 1991, 1997.
Martin, Faith. *Call Me Blessed.* Eerdmans, 1988.
Martin, Ralph P. *Reconciliation: A Study of Paul's Theology.* Rev. ed. Academie Bks., 1989.
McClendon, James William Jr. *Systematic Theology: Ethics,* 1986; *Doctrine,* 1994. Abingdon.
Menno Simons. *The Complete Writings of Menno Simons.* Trans. L. Verduin. Ed. J. C. Wenger. Herald Pr., 1956.
Metzger, Bruce, M. *The New Testament: Its Background, Growth, and Content.* Enlarged ed. Abingdon, 1983.
Migliore, Daniel. *Called to Freedom.* Westminster, 1980.
Moltmann, Jürgen, *The Crucified God,* Harper & Row, 1974; Fortress, 1993.
_____. *The Spirit of Life.* Augsburg Fortress, 1992.
Morris, Leon. *The Apostolic Preaching of the Cross.* Eerdmans, 1955.
_____. *The Epistle to the Romans.* Eerdmans, 1988.
Morse, Christopher. *Not Every Spirit: A Dogmatics of Christian Disbelief.* Trinity Pr. Intl., 1994.
Murray, John. In *Tabletalk,* Ligonier Ministries, Sept.-Dec. 1994, 10.
Newbigin, Lesslie. *Christ Our Eternal Contemporary.* Madras: Christian Literature Society, 1968.
_____. *Foolishness to the Greeks.* Eerdmans, 1986.
_____. *The Gospel in a Pluralist Society.* Eerdmans, 1989.
_____. *Proper Confidence.* Eerdmans, 1995.
_____. *Trinitarian Faith and Today's Mission.* John Knox Pr., 1964.
Niebuhr, H. Richard. *Christ and Culture.* Harper, 1951.
Nygren, Anders. *Agapē and Erōs.* Westminster, 1953.
O'Donovan, Oliver. *Resurrection and Moral Order.* Rev. ed. Eerdmans, 1994.
Palmer, Earl. *1, 2, 3 John, Revelation.* Communicator's Commentary, 12. Word Bks., 1982.
Paton, Alan. *Cry, the Beloved Country.* Scribner, 1961.
Perkins, John M. *Beyond Charity.* Baker Bks., 1993.
Perry, Edmund. *The Gospel in Dispute.* Doubleday, 1958.
Phenix, Philip Henry. *Realms of Meaning.* McGraw-Hill, 1964.
Pinnock, Clark H., ed. *The Openness of God.* InterVarsity, 1994.

Rempel, John D. *The Lord's Supper in Anabaptism.* Herald Pr., 1993.
Ritschl, Albrecht. *The Christian Doctrine of Justification and Reconciliation.* English trans., ed. H. R. Mackintosh and A. B. Macaulay. Reference Bk. Pubs., 1966.
Robert, Dana L. "Shifting Southward: Global Christianity Since 1945." *International Bulletin of Missionary Research* 24 (Apr. 2000): 50-58.
Schaeffer, Francis A. *The God Who Is There.* InterVarsity, 1998.
Schleitheim Confession, The. See Yoder, 1973, 1977.
Schmidt, Henry, ed. *Witnesses of the Third Way.* Brethren Pr., 1986.
Schweizer, Eduard. *The Church as the Body of Christ.* John Knox, 1964.
Shenk, Calvin E. *Who Do You Say That I Am?* Herald Pr., 1997.
Shenk, David W. *Global Gods.* Herald Pr., 1996.
Shenk, Wilbert R., ed. *Mission Focus: Current Issues.* Herald Pr., 1980.
Shideler, Mary McDermott. *A Creed for a Christian Sceptic.* London: Marshall, Morgan & Scott, 1968.
Shriver, Donald W. Jr. *An Ethic for Enemies: Forgiveness in Politics.* Repr. Oxford Univ. Press, 1998.
Simons. *See* Menno.
Snyder, C. Arnold. *Anabaptist History and Theology: An Introduction.* Pandora Press, 1995. Rev. student ed., PP/Herald Pr., 1997.
Stott, John R. W. *The Cross of Christ.* InterVarsity, 1986.
_____. *The Message of the Sermon on the Mount: Christian Counter Culture.* InterVarsity, 1988.
_____. *Romans: God's Good News for the World.* InterVarsity, 1995.
Sugden, Chris. *See* Vinay.
Swartley, Willard. *Slavery, Sabbath, War, and Women.* Herald Pr., 1983.
Taylor, Vincent. *The Atonement in New Testament Teaching.* London, 1946.
Thielicke, Helmut. *Theological Ethics.* Vol. 1: *Foundations.* Fortress, 1966.
Thomas à Kempis. *The Imitation of Christ* (ca. 1427). Image Bks., 1955.
Tozer, A. W. *The Knowledge of the Holy.* Harper, 1961.
_____. *The Pursuit of God.* Christian Pubns., 1948.
Trueblood, Elton. *The Incendiary Fellowship.* Harper & Row, 1978.
Turner, H. E. W. *The Meaning of the Cross.* London: A. R. Mowbray, 1959.
Vinay, Samuel, and Chris Sugden, eds. *Sharing Jesus in the "Two Thirds" World.* Eerdmans, 1984.
Volf, Miroslav. "The Social Meaning of Reconciliation." *Interpretation* 54 (Apr. 2000): 158-172.
Weaver, J. Denny. *Becoming Anabaptist.* Herald Pr., 1987.
_____. *Keeping Salvation Ethical.* Herald Pr., 1997.
Wells, David F. *No Place for Truth.* Eerdmans, 1993.
Wenger, J. C. *An Introduction to Theology.* Herald Pr., 1954.
Willard, Dallas. *The Spirit of the Disciplines.* Harper & Row, 1988.
Williams, George H. *The Radical Reformation.* 3d ed. Truman State Univ. Pr., 1992.

Wink, Walter. *Engaging the Powers*. The Powers Series, 3. Fortress, 1992.
_____. *Naming the Powers*. The Powers Series, 2. Fortress, 1984.
www.thirdway.com (a Mennonite ministry and information Website).
Yancey, Philip. *What's So Amazing About Grace?* Zondervan, 1997.
Yoder, John Howard. *As You Go: The Old Mission in a New Day*. Herald Pr., 1961.
_____. *Body Politics: Five Practices of the Christian Community Before the Watching World*. Discipleship Resources, 1992.
_____. *The Legacy of Michael Sattler*. Herald Pr., 1973. Includes "The Schleitheim Confession" and its setting.
_____. *The Politics of Jesus*. Eerdmans, 1972. 2d. ed., 1994.
_____. *The Priestly Kingdom*. Univ. of Notre Dame Pr., 1984.
_____. *The Royal Priesthood: Essays Ecclesiological and Ecumenical*. Herald Pr., 1998.
_____, trans., ed. *The Schleitheim Confession*. Herald Pr., 1973, 1977.
_____. *What Would You Do?* Expanded ed. Herald Pr., 1992.
_____. *When War Is Unjust*. Orbis Bks., 1996.

Index for Scripture
and the Early Church

Index of Persons

(Outside the Bible and the Bibliography)

The Author

MYRON S. AUGSBURGER is widely known for his academic career and for his preaching missions across North America and in many countries abroad. Born in Ohio, he has lived most of his life in Virginia, with his wife, Esther, and their three children.

Augsburger was educated at Eastern Mennonite College and Seminary, Harrisonburg, Virginia; at Goshen (Ind.) Biblical Seminary (now AMBS); and at Union Theological Seminary, Richmond, where he earned a Th.D.

Following twenty-two years on the faculty of Eastern Mennonite, fifteen as president of the college and seminary, Myron and Esther moved to Washington, D.C., and planted a thriving church on Capitol Hill. This innovative congregation was a testing ground for much of the content of this book. Myron pastored there for fourteen years, overlapping with six years as president of the Coalition of Christian Colleges and Universities.

In 1994 the Augsburgers returned to Harrisonburg, where Myron is an adjunct Professor of Theology at Eastern Mennonite Seminary and part-time Minister of the Word at Zion Mennonite Church. They are members at Park View Mennonite Church.

Myron Augsburger has written twenty published books. Several are historical novels, and one was produced in film. Two of his books are biblical commentaries. He coauthored several books and contributed chapters to a dozen others.

Augsburger is known more widely in ecumenical circles for his many years of evangelism, especially in citywide interchurch meetings. He has ministered through overseas speaking and teaching appointments in several dozen settings, from 1964 to the present. Augsburger is a communicator of the gospel, a discipling evangelist. He calls people to commit themselves to walk with Jesus in daily life and with fellow members in the church. His emphasis on a spirituality of discipleship permeates this book.